ALTERNATE ENDING

"*Alternate Ending* is a truly inspiring story that captures the voices of those who so often go unheard. I spent 11 out of 18 years in the foster care system. It's tough on everyone and leaves a permanent scar only the person affected can see and feel. I thank Jean Féinics for not giving up on herself. I thank her for choosing life. And, for all the foster youth who feel alone, I thank her for telling her story. Jean Féinics is a hero!"

—*Raven Jones, BA Psychology, Fostering STARS at Lansing Community College & Former Foster Youth*

"Haunting, profound…Jean Féinics tells a story that will resonate with anyone who has lived through the muck of abuse, neglect, foster care, mental health challenges, and/or emotional deprivation. Her story speaks to the soul and embraces all the ugliness with a truth that needs to be heard and understood as not dysfunctional for those with experience in care, rather, such reactions are quite normal for thousands of children and youth. Dr. Féinics beautifully describes what it means to feel love for those who hurt us, to feel invisible, to want to give up, yet to live another day to create a new tomorrow."

—*Shannon Turner, LCSW, Regional Research Institute at Portland State University*

"An intensely personal account of the impenetrable bond between a mother and her daughter."

—*Mary Jo Sekelsky, Ed.D., University of Michigan-Flint*

"L. Jean Féinics shares a lifetime of trauma with stunning, haunting detail. In doing so, she gives clarity to chaos and hope to those born into hopeless circumstances. That Dr. Féinics survived her childhood is remarkable. That she did so with the courage and compassion necessary to use her story to help others is a gift to us all."

—*Jeff Hobbs, Author of the New York Times Bestseller,*
The Short and Tragic Life of Robert Peace

"I couldn't put down this memoir. Jean Féinics' writing is immediately accessible, subtly layered, and thoroughly engaging. In *Alternate Ending*, Féinics lays out the fragile, the broken, and the cruel aspects of humanity in bright sunlight, but she does so with an astonishing lack of contempt and bitterness. As a result, the reader is left to feel whatever it is he or she might feel without interference. It is a humble account of a horrible childhood and the writer's emergence from that childhood. It is a book written from the point of view of one who has walked through fire, was burned, felt all that burning does, found healing, and who now looks back with clear eyes. It is a must-read for anyone who wants to understand the ripples and waves that emanate from mental illness, and a must-read for anyone interested in exploring the tenacity of compassion."

—*Anne Dohrenwend, PhD*

"Féinics paints a vivid and gritty portrait of a life lived in and after foster care, while providing a rare, yet accurate, look at the struggle of a mother-daughter relationship wracked with both love and resentment. While exploring the trauma of generational poverty, abuse, and mental illness, Feinics shares a message of hope, resilience, and ultimately self-love. This message will undoubtedly impact others like her who deal with the pervasive outcomes of living as an adult with experience in foster care."

—*Jamie L. Bennett, MSW, Center for Fostering Success*
at Western Michigan University & Former Foster Youth

"*Alternate Ending* disrupts the common narrative of foster care. By weaving stories of intergenerational trauma throughout the book, Féinics deftly examines her conflicting emotions surrounding her relationships with her family, while also remaining candid about the difficulties she encountered both in foster care and after emancipation. I highly recommend this book for anyone interested in learning more about the emotional lives of young people who have experienced foster care. In particular, clinicians and educators working with alumni of care would greatly benefit from reading this book.

—*Melissa Raap, MSW, University of Washington Champions Program*

ALTERNATE ENDING

AN INSPIRATIONAL TRUE STORY ABOUT BEATING THE ODDS

L. Jean Féinics, PhD

Copyright © 2016 by Lisa Jean Féinics

All rights reserved. This book or any portion thereof may not be reproduced or used in any manner whatsoever without the express written permission of the author.

For enquires about booking the author for an event or for ordering information, please email: info@jeanfeinics.com or visit jeanfeinics.com

ISBN: 978-0-692-66666-1

Printed in the United States of America

Cover Design by Lisa Jean Féinics
Cover Photograph by Angeleta
Back Cover Photograph by Benjamin Weatherston

20 19 18 17 16   1 2 3 4 5

First Paperback Edition

Dedicated to my mother, my daughter, and all the current and former foster youth who want to do more than just survive.

For years I didn't really understand there was something wrong; everything that happened just seemed normal.

–L. Jean Féinics

Author's Note

In these pages, I have told the truth to the best human memory allows any of us. The stories from my very early childhood are a blend of memories that come to me as static images so profound they could not be forgotten. From these images, I have tried to construct stories for the reader that capture my feelings during those early years of my life—the fear, the helplessness, the need to protect and be protected. The static images, however, do not allow me to form a clear timeline for events and I suspect my memory jumbled some events together. After age six, the memories become clearer and run like movie reels in my head. Those stories were much easier to write down as they unfolded. The reader may find some of these stories hard to believe because they describe such shocking behavior on the part of the people involved. All I can say is, "Some folks do in fact behave that way. And yes, it is the truth."

Many of those in my world as I was growing up were deeply flawed. I have empathy for those individuals because no human being is perfect. Yet, I needed to tell the truth as I experienced it, which meant writing about people in honest, and sometimes, unflattering ways. I did not do this to create hardship for anyone, which is why names and identifying characteristics have been changed. I also delayed publication of this book until after some of the more tormented souls from my youth had passed on. At times the reader may wish I had given more, but I hope the omissions will be forgiven once the nature of the stories has been fully understood.

L. Jean Féinics
March, 2015

PART ONE

Family Versus Strangers

Chapter 1: Behind Blue Eyes

On June 16, 1976, I was removed abruptly from my mother's care after she was hospitalized. Through a process I did not understand, I was permanently designated as a *Dependent of the Court* and all decisions regarding my care were left to the authority of a judge. I was eight years old going on nine. Over the next eight years I would be referred to during hearings as the "minor" referenced in case number: J-73355.

A number of strange events occurred leading up to the moment when I stopped being just a kid and became a case number. I say "strange" now, but at the time, I could only experience those events as "normal" because I had never known anything different. By 1976, my mother had been hospitalized many times. The first time I remember visiting her during one of her "sicknesses" was sometime in the early months of 1974. I was six years old. The visit is tied in my memory to the period in which we were Mormons. Later we would become Baptists, then Catholics, followed by a dizzying array of other religious affiliations—some perhaps cults.

At the time of my first visit to the hospital we weren't really going to church anymore. Still, folks from the church continued to stop by and I think it was a woman from the congregation who took me to the hospital that first time. When Mom's hospitalization went on beyond a single day, the same woman took me into her home until my mother was released. I can't recall the woman's name. What I do remember is that the woman and her husband had several children close to my age. I remember the woman most vividly, not only because she took me to the hospital, but because of a bad day involving a stain on my dress. In my mind that stain and my visit to the hospital are strangely intertwined. I'm pretty sure the stain came first and the hospital visit second, but it could have been the other way around. All I know is that both the stain and the visit left me feeling like I had failed the people in my life. It was a feeling that would plague me into adulthood.

During that period we were living in an old house located in a small mountain town about 90 miles east of Los Angeles, California. The rental was painted a dingy white and became known to everyone as "The White House." I don't think my dad found the same joy in that house as the more remote forested rental we had previously; still, he paid the rent on it until he split. That was sometime around my 5th birthday. After my dad left, Mom couldn't pay the rent herself and she quickly took up with other men who could. I have few positive memories of that house, and the few I do have never seem to block out the rest I'd like to forget.

It was during this same period that people began to whisper that my mother had had a nervous breakdown. I was too young to know what that meant. All I remember is how worried I was that she was in the hospital. When I was taken to visit her, I imagined the whole way there that she was going to die and I would be left alone like Bambi. That's why when the woman from church opened the door to Mom's hospital room a huge sense of relief washed over me.

Mom was reclining on a partially raised hospital bed. She was in a white hospital gown with faint blue diamonds printed on it. Sun from the window near her bed flickered across the sheet covering her legs. She smiled when she saw me. Her face looked strange without her usual perfect makeup and her blonde hair was dirty, but other than that she seemed all right. I was hugely relieved that she wasn't attached to any of the strange Frankenstein-like equipment I had seen when we had walked down the hall to her room. The only thing that seemed unusual was the white gauze wrapped around Mom's wrists like fuzzy bracelets. I released the hand of the woman who had brought me and ran over to hug her. She leaned over the side of the bed to hug me back. Her arms felt wonderful around me.

"Oh, Jean Baby, it's so good to see you," she said, squeezing me.

"Mom, when will you be coming home?" I asked.

"I don't know, Honey. We have to wait until the doctors say I'm well enough."

"Why? What's wrong with you?"

"Nothing, Baby. I'm just tired," she said, turning her face away from me toward the window.

I looked up from my place in her arms. I could see tears on the side of her cheek. Her big blue eyes seemed so sad. Frightened that I had hurt her, I stopped hugging and gently moved my arms to my side. Feeling bad, I said, "I'm sorry. Did I hug you too hard?" She cried harder and put her hands over her face. "Don't worry, Mom. I won't hug you anymore," I said, hoping that I could make her stop crying. It didn't help.

The woman who had brought me moved closer to the bed and said, "Jean, maybe right now isn't a good time to visit." Taking my hand, she led me toward the door and kindly said to my mother, "I'll bring her back another time."

"No, no, not yet! Please don't take her yet," Mom pleaded, as she roughly wiped away her tears and tried to compose herself. When she reached out for me again I saw a small stain of dried blood on the gauze covering her wrist.

Blood! Why is there blood? I wondered in surprise. It was the first sign I had that she was injured in some way. An image from two nights before when I was woken by a loud commotion downstairs popped into my mind. By the time I was brave enough to go downstairs, I heard a car leaving and my mother was gone. I wandered into the bathroom where my sister was running the sink. It was covered in blood. Before I could ask what happened she pushed me from the bathroom and ordered me to go back to bed. After that, when I tried to ask about what happened she told me, "It's nothing you need to know about."

I wanted to ask Mom if the blood on the sink had anything to do with the blood on the gauze, but Mom spoke before I could get the question out.

"Jean Honey, go get my purse on the chair over there and bring it here," she said, pointing with a hand that shook as if she were very old.

Not sure what to do, I looked up at the woman holding my hand for guidance. She nodded and let go of my hand. I walked over to my mom's old tan leather purse and picked it up. Slowly I handed it to her; trying to make sure I didn't hurt her again. She dug through it until she found a piece of hard candy. The wrapper was dirty and small bits of loose tobacco were stuck to the seam where the paper had come open slightly. "Here Baby, this is for you," she said, holding it toward me. I reached up and took it from her while staring at the spot of blood that had seeped through the gauze. She smiled and said, "Go ahead! Eat it, Baby."

The bloody gauze was hidden again as she hugged her purse to her body in a childlike manner. Wanting to make her happy, I ignored my queasy stomach and tore off the wrapper. I wiped off the bits of tobacco that had gotten inside and popped it into my mouth. It tasted like black licorice. *Yuck,* I thought with annoyance.

"It's good, Mom. Thank you," I lied, trying not to suck on the candy. My mother's face lit up—but only briefly. Like a kabuki dancer rapidly changing her face to express emotions, Mom's features took on a weary sadness and her smile went away, leaving behind a woman in personal agony. We chatted for a few more minutes beneath the concerned gaze of the woman from the church. Mom was having a hard time keeping herself from crying. After a short while the woman walked over and took my hand.

"Jean, I think we should go. Your mother still needs her rest," she said.

I swallowed the candy whole and turned toward Mom with my mouth wide open. I wanted to show her I had finished her gift. She smiled at me, but the smile did not reach her eyes.

The lady began leading me from the room one more time. Mom waved goodbye with silent tears running down her face.

"Bye Baby, remember I love you," she said.

Returning her wave, I noticed that the gauze from one of her fuzzy bracelets had shifted lower, perhaps pushed down from hugging her purse. On the exposed skin of her wrist I could see a large cut stitched with ugly black thread. I started to ask her what had happened, but the woman gently pushed me out of the room. The door closed between us and my mother slipped from view. I looked at the woman, hoping she would explain. She looked away.

* * *

The woman from the church handed me the dress from the bed and told me to go get changed. I put it on. It was a bit too big and very white. Most clothes were big on me. I was a skinny kid, all knobby knees and pointy elbows covered in very pale freckled skin. My siblings always complained about my skinniness when I had to sit on someone's lap during car rides. They'd whine that the bones of my pelvis dug into their laps. This led to one of my least favorite childhood nicknames: "Boney Butt." The only nicknames I hated more were "Hairy Ape" and "Little Monkey." I got these because of the fine blonde hair that thickly covered my arms and legs. It was a painful reminder that I was my father's child no matter how much at times I longed not to be. Like him, I was agonizingly hairy. Later in life, I would realize that I also inherited his Irish temper, but during that period of my childhood I was still too scared to show anyone how angry I really felt.

When I heard the woman calling my name a short while later, I obediently went downstairs into the living room. The other children and the woman's husband were also assembled there.

The husband scared me. The brutal nature of my own father left me particularly uncomfortable around men.

"All you kids go outside and play in the yard until it's time to go," he said. He didn't say it harshly, but I immediately moved toward the door.

As we walked out, I heard the woman yell behind us, "And don't get dirty." I looked down at the white dress and felt a flutter of panic in my stomach.

I exited the house into the yard and stood stiffly while the other kids played around me. My own mother was very hung-up on my staying clean whenever we went someplace. If my siblings and I didn't stay clean when told, Mom would get furious. The focus on cleanliness at home left me overly concerned about not being dirty. Mom could clean for hours but somehow the dirt was never gone. If she found stains on my clothes, I immediately had to go change. Even worse, my father would hit us if we spilled things in the house or made a mess. The woman from church seemed nice, but I was worried that she too might get mad if I got dirty.

With the other kids screaming and chasing each other around I somehow managed to keep the white dress spotless. Then the front door opened and the women stepped out with a box of frozen Otter Pops and a pair of scissors.

"Who wants a popsicle?" she asked. The other kids ran forward and put out their hands. I wanted one too but I was worried about getting spots on the white material.

"Stupid dress," I muttered very quietly. I turned my head and stared at the pine tree in the middle of the yard instead of at the other kids getting a treat.

"Jean, come get your popsicle," yelled the woman's oldest son.

I shook my head. The woman interpreted my reluctance as shyness and walked toward me with the box of popsicles and scissors. She snipped the top off an electric-blue frozen treat.

"Here Jean, have this one, but be careful not to get it on your dress," she said, handing it to me. Then she walked back inside. Not sure what to do, I held the Otter Pop away from my body while it slowly melted.

"Jean, you better eat that because it's starting to leak over the edges," warned one of the other kids. Startled, I raised the tube to my mouth, trying to get rid of the liquid. The other kids began to point and hoot. I looked down and noticed a bright blue stain spreading across the front of my white dress.

"No, no, no. Please no," I cried, dropping the plastic wrapper with the rest of the popsicle onto the ground. I stood paralyzed with shame as I looked down at the bright blue spot on the ruined dress. One of the other children ran inside to tell on me. The woman came out of the house. Before she even had a chance to cross the yard to scold me I began to feel sick.

"Jean, what have you done? Didn't I tell you not to get your dress dirty?" she asked. Her husband came out on the porch after her.

"Time to go! Everyone in the car," he shouted.

"Please, can't I change my dress before we go to church?" I asked the woman as she approached me.

"Sorry Jean, there's no time. You're just going to have to wear it. Maybe next time you'll be more careful," she said.

A hot flush spread across my face. Numbly, I walked across the yard with my head down. With the other kids snickering as I climbed into the backseat of the couple's station wagon, we headed off to church.

Once we arrived, I tried to hide behind the woman so that no one would see the blue blot on my dress. In my mind the stain stood out like a flashing neon sign, and I was sure that everyone one knew I had failed to be the good girl my mother wanted me to be. The woman shooed me out from behind her to go with the other children for Sunday school. I walked, head down, toward the classroom while other kids whispered and laughed. In their whispers I heard the disappointment of my mother, and shame burned my cheeks. *Why can't I be good?* I wondered.

* * *

I looked around the dilapidated house I had been living in for more than a year. My daughter was asleep on a cot standing where the kitchen table used to be because the roof was leaking heavily in her bedroom. The roof was also leaking in the living room. The small kitchen nook was one of the few dry places left in the ramshackle rental. The wood stove, the only heat in the house, had already burned out. There was no more wood and the house was quickly growing cold from lack of insulation. I gritted my teeth and thought, *I hate this fucking place,* but I couldn't afford to live anywhere else. With a growing sense of desperation, I went into my tiny bedroom and sat down on the thrift-store bed. The walls I had painted a calming sea foam green did little to lift the hopelessness I felt. It was like a black shadow had invaded my being and blocked out any hope and light.

For the last three years, I had been killing myself to give my daughter a better life. I was 21 years old and a junior at the state college, closing in on a 3.7 GPA. I was the first person in my family to attend college, which I was doing even though I had dropped out of high school and had learning disabilities. From the outside, my accomplishments seemed amazing—but from the inside it felt completely different. We were desperately poor and living off welfare; we had no car; there was no family to help us out; and my landlord had stopped making any repairs to the house after I had rebuffed his sexual advances. We were utterly and completely on our own. Looking around at what I had achieved for my daughter, I felt nothing but a sense of failure.

On the shelf next to me sat the bottle of antidepressants I had been prescribed by a doctor at the campus student health center. They hadn't helped. Tears streamed down my face as I picked up the bottle and opened the cap. Then, I swallowed the pills in groups of three until the bottle was empty. I followed the antidepressants up with an entire bottle of over-the-counter painkillers. Slowly I lay down on the bed. "I'm so sorry baby," I whispered to my daughter who was sleeping unaware in the kitchen. Using the phone by my bed, I called a guy I had started dating the previous month. I asked him to come very early in the morning to take my daughter to preschool. I said it was an unexpected emergency and I didn't have anyone else to help me. "I'll just leave the door unlocked for you. Please just come right in. 6:30 a.m., okay? I don't want her to be late," I told him. He seemed confused but agreed. Then I closed my eyes and waited for death.

I lay there hoping my exit from the world would come quickly. As the minutes ticked on I could not keep thoughts of my daughter from my mind. *Who's going to take her? Mom can't. Who else can? Do you want her to go into foster care? Do you really want her to see you like this? Remember Mom? Do you want to do that to your daughter? Are you that selfish? If you are going to do this, you better find a way to take her with you. You ready to do that?* The condemning questions ran nonstop, and I hated myself for my cowardice.

* * *

"Can you please send an ambulance to 1690 Bay Road? I've taken a large number of pills. I tried to throw up but nothing came out. Now I'm feeling very dizzy," I said to the 911 operator. Next, I called the same guy I had asked to come first thing in the morning. "I know you don't know me very well, and I am so sorry to do this to you, but I need to go to the hospital. Could you please come stay with my daughter until I get back? Also, whatever happens, you have to promise me you won't bring her to see me at the hospital," I said, just as the ambulance's siren echoed down the street leading to my house.

The next 24 hours were filled with Ipecac, vomit, charcoal smoothies, IV bags, a psychological evaluation, and regret.

Chapter 2: Strange Magic

I became a *Dependent of the Court* shortly after my mother got her first pair of fuzzy bracelets. The designation is basically the same as *Ward of the Court* in other states, except in California being a "dependent" means you ended up under the Court's jurisdiction through no fault of your own. I guess the designation is sort of a way to separate the good kids from the juvenile delinquents who are referred to as "wards." Whatever the designation of my status, I had no awareness of it at the time. My fate was in the realm of adults, and I only knew what they told me. All the details I didn't understand were put into a court file—a file I hated so much that I had it destroyed when I turned 18. I did so without reading a single word. Its destruction was a symbolic act. I just wanted to put my childhood behind me.

Around my 7th birthday, I held the vague knowledge that my mother had been sick in some way and that my dad was never coming back. I also knew that my two oldest half-siblings, Joni and Jerry, had gone back to live with their father and we were no longer able to communicate. This left only my two other half-siblings, Joanne and Jimmy (Mom named all us kids with the same initial) home with me and Mom. Jimmy was just one year older than Joanne, and Joanne was four and-a-half years older than me. Perhaps their biological father had legal custody of them at the time, but let them stay with Mom. I can't really say because I don't know much about their particular custody status. All I know is that they were still at home when my mother got out of the hospital.

Following Mom's hospital discharge, I had the sense that other adults came to check on us more often, but they never told me anything about her illness or about the change in my custody status—if they even knew. It was only when I reached adulthood and found a letter outlining my court case that I realized the Court took official control of my person during those dark and confusing days from April 30, 1974 to May 15, 1975. This meant that though I continued to live with my mom during that period, she did not have legal custody. Instead, a judge was my legal parent, and he or she had granted my mother physical custody over that year. Likely, my mother had to go to court and meet with people bearing important titles, but whatever the process, no one bothered to explain things to me.

After Mom's first trip to the hospital, we lived the best we could as a normal family, but I often found myself awash in my mother's odd moods, sorrow, and erratic behavior. I did my best to take care of her and make her happy, but it never seemed to have a lasting effect. She had a sickness I didn't understand—and though I loved her more than anything in the world, I couldn't make her well. Like the stain on the pretty white dress, I was helpless to change what happened to her—helpless to change what happened to us.

* * *

After Mom got out of the hospital that first time, we moved to a small oddly built house a few miles closer to town. Surrounded by a thick pine forest, the house was dark inside even on the sunniest days. Three stories tall but built with very small rooms in weird places, it had a spooky feeling. The top floor contained the small attic bedroom with dark wooden rafters. This floor stuck out from the main roof of the house sort of like a chimney. If you crawled out the attic window you found yourself on the main roof. At various times this room housed up to four people: me, Jimmy and Joanne, and the occasional friend of the family in need of a place to stay. When four people stayed in the room, it was very cramped, so someone would have to sleep in the room's small walk-in closet on a cot. My twin bed sat precariously close to the edge of the stairway that wound its way into the attic from the living room. To get out of the bed, I had to crawl out the top or I risked falling down into the stairwell.

Squeezed in the middle floor of the house below the attic were a small living room, bathroom, bedroom and kitchen. The miniature kitchen was weirdly placed in what felt like a hallway wide enough to accommodate just one person at a time. By walking through this tiny space with a stove and refrigerator on one side and a sink on the other, you entered Mom's bedroom. It was literally a "bed" room because it fit only her queen-size bed closed in on three sides by walls. Off the living room was a closet-size bathroom with a toilet and sink but no tub or shower. The main entry to the house was on this floor. To get to the front door from the outside, you had to walk across a porch that hung over a steep incline. There were lots of windows in the living room but because of the woods surrounding our house the windows did little to lighten the interior. Even so, this floor was where we spent most of our time when Mom was home. When she wasn't, we tended to hide in the attic.

The middle floor was the nicest because Mom had made an effort to give it warm touches. One of these was a bowl of plastic fruit that sat on the coffee table. Grapes, an apple, an orange, a pear, and a banana collected dust but never rotted. When clean, the fruit looked very real. Mom said the fruit made her safe because she had gone hungry as a child, especially when she was in the orphanage. Besides the fruit, the room also contained a fish tank, a bird cage, a vinyl couch, a large heavy oak desk, and a black-and-white TV.

The bottom floor of the house was the scariest. It was just a large empty room with uncovered windows that looked out upon the forest behind the house. I was sure that demonic monsters peered in through those windows each time I ventured down there. They were fleeting shadows that would simply disappear when I turned my head to see them. My siblings told me I was making it up, but I knew the monsters were there. They were just waiting to catch me off guard. I was sure that if they did, they would drag me out into the dark forest behind the house. In that same room, a bathtub was set off in an alcove, which meant that I couldn't avoid the room altogether.

The staircase leading down to the bottom floor had a low roof and closed-in walls that created the feeling of being in a steep, dark tunnel. As soon as you opened the door to go down, it was like you had stepped into a horror movie just before the killing starts. I was terrified to go down that staircase. It didn't help that I was afraid of the dark, and that at the bottom of the stairs was a flimsy door that led outside to the woods and that would pop open when the wind blew hard. To make matters worse, the light switch for the basement was outside the door on the living room wall. My siblings found it hilarious to lock me in the staircase with the lights turned off whenever they caught me going down to take a bath. They would laugh hard as I screamed and begged to be let out. They usually only opened the door right away if Mom was around to catch them. If she wasn't, I could expect my horrifying agony to last a long time. It really made me hate being the youngest.

For the first few months after we moved into the house, we were pretty happy. Mom, relieved to be out of the hospital and back with her kids, doted on us. We went for hikes, swam in the lake, and ate popcorn and candy while lying together on blankets in front of the TV. We also went to the movies at our little theater in town whenever a new show came out. Though we did most of these things together as a family, it was pretty clear that Mom preferred my company to that of my half-siblings. She was exceptionally warm and loving toward me. We went everywhere together, and if I got scared, she even let me sleep with her in her bed. It was painfully clear to my siblings that I was spoiled in ways they were not, which made them hate me, and perhaps explained why they took such joy in locking me in the staircase with the lights off.

I was too young to understand the harm that being the favorite kid was doing to Jimmy and Joanne. In ignorant bliss, I took all Mom gave to me and then some. She indulged my love of animals and let me bring home pretty much any one I found. All I had to do was whine, "Mom, it doesn't have anywhere to live," and she would let whatever animal it was stay at our house—at least for a while. As the months went by, we collected a menagerie of five dogs (two adults and three puppies), a guinea pig, a tortoise, a horny-toad, two cats, four rats that kept having babies (which sadly, they ate), two birds, a tank full of fish, and one baby goat. I loved the baby goat the best because it made me laugh when it chased the puppies around the yard. The goat didn't have a single name because we couldn't decide on one as a family. I had been calling him Billy the Kid, but my siblings didn't like the name Billy. No matter what you called him, he liked to follow you around and suck your fingers if you let him. He was my favorite pet.

* * *

One day, we came home from a long day trip to a large lake in another town and were met with a terrible sight. The sun was setting, but the listless kid was easy to see lying on the ground in the gathering darkness. His stomach was hugely swollen.

"What's wrong with Billy, Mom? Is he going to die?" I asked.

"No Baby, he'll be all right. We'll call Rosa, the breeder, and get her to tell us what to do," Mom said.

I followed Jimmy as he carried the baby goat up the hill from its pen in the backyard to the front of the house. Jimmy laid Billy down gently on the porch. Mom went inside to make the phone call. While she was inside, Jimmy told me the goat was dying. I started to cry, and ran inside to ask Mom if it was true.

As I stood in front of her, filled with worry, she reached for her pack of cigarettes and tapped it on the palm of her hand until a single Benson and Hedges cigarette slid out. I looked at her impatiently, and asked again if Billy was dying. She looked away. With a practiced motion she quickly lit the cigarette and inhaled smoke deep into her lungs. Her exhale was a long, slow sigh. The smell of menthol filled the living room. After placing the lit cigarette on the lip of a colored glass ashtray, she looked at me and spoke.

"Jean, the goat's just sick. Rosa said it sounds like maybe he ate too much and now his stomach is filled with gas," Mom said. "If we can get the gas out, he'll get better. Can you run to the closet and get me an old sheet?"

Her answer sounded very weird. *Gas inside a goat, a bed sheet?* I wondered about the strangeness of it. None of it made any sense. Still, I desperately wanted the goat to survive, so I ran to do as I was told without asking any more questions. Mom went back out onto the porch, and I followed her with the sheet in my hand. Mom and Jimmy worked together to hang Billy from the porch rafters with the sheet passing under his stomach the way Rosa told Mom to do. The kid's legs hung loosely from the sling, making it look like a marionette that had swallowed a very large pumpkin. Pressure from the sheet on the goat's bloated belly was supposed to force out the gas; if it didn't, the goat would die. Mom told Jimmy to run to town and buy a baby bottle and some 7-UP.

While we waited for Jimmy to return, Mom paced around nervously while puffing on a cigarette. "Is he gonna live, Mom?" I asked several times.

"Yes, Jean! Now stop asking me that."

Billy would occasionally bleat plaintively, but then he grew more listless and made no sounds at all. When I asked Mom again if he would live, she got angry at me and went inside the house. I stayed on the porch talking to Billy and asking God to save him. The height at which he was dangling placed his head at eye level with me, and I was able to look directly into his golden eyes. Prior to getting sick, Billy's eyes were bright and full of mischief, but they didn't look that way then—instead they were listless and vacant.

Jimmy came back from the store, and we all took turns feeding the baby goat with the bottle of 7-Up. At first he drank a little, but it didn't seem to make any difference. Then he stopped taking the bottle at all. As the night wore on, I stayed out under the dim porch bulb watching my pet closely. Mom's agitation increased once Billy stopped taking the bottle and his stomach remained hugely distended. "I'm going inside for a cigarette," she said. She didn't come out again. Long into the night we rubbed the baby goat's stomach in an attempt to make it burp up the trapped gas that was slowly killing it. I was petting his head, begging him to burp, when his eyes clouded over. I had never seen anything die before, but somehow I knew his life had slipped away. I ran back into the house sobbing.

"Mom, I think he's dead! You said he would live, but the goat died," I screamed, as I pulled Mom back out to the porch.

She looked at the goat and put her hand on its chest and her ear to its nose. After a few moments she said, "Oh Baby, I'm so sorry. He's dead and there's nothing more we can do."

I cried harder.

"I'm sorry, Baby. We did what we could. Jimmy, take the goat down and put him in the backyard. We'll need to bury him in the morning."

Mom reached out to hug me. I wanted to be comforted, but I was also angry at her. I didn't understand why things I loved kept going away, and why the adults in my life didn't seem able to protect me from so much hurt.

As my brother worked the goat out of the sling, Mom said, "I can't watch this," and went back inside.

Once Jimmy laid the goat back on the porch and wrapped it tightly in the sheet as if it was a death shroud, I went up to the attic and sobbed on my bed. The image of the goat's eyes clouded over in death followed me into fitful dreams.

The next day, Mom tried to explain that Billy's death was an accident, and I shouldn't be mad at anyone. She had left the duty of Billy's care to one of the men who frequently rotated in and out of our lives. They, however, were usually worse than my mother at caring for things. The man of the month that spring was some guy Mom met while sunbathing nude at a local swimming hole. He lived in a nudist camp, but spent many nights at our house. The day before the goat died, Mr. Lazy Nudist had left an enormous bucket of grain for Billy so that he wouldn't have to feed him again the next day while we were at the lake. I guess he didn't know that goats will eat themselves to death on grain. Mr. Nudist was well-intentioned. But, as was the case with many of the well-intentioned things my mother did too, the end result was bad.

The death of the goat taught me that some things you love never return no matter how badly you want them to. I didn't know this at the time, but the goat's death was an omen for the suffering that was about to come. Lessons of loss were soon to be repeated, and sadly, more times than anyone could have imagined. Time lessened the hurt of Billy's loss, but the image of his dead eyes stayed with me for the rest of my life.

* * *

After the goat died, life seemed normal for a little while. Sporadically, we attended different churches like Assembly of God, Kingdom Hall of the Jehovah's Witnesses, Foursquare, and the Catholic Church where Mom sometimes went for Alcoholics Anonymous meetings. We spent a lot of time watching TV together. Like government food subsidies for the poor, TV was a staple in our house. Though we lived in the mountains where it snowed every winter and ski resorts were in abundance, none of us learned to ski because it cost money. During the summer, boats sailed on the bigger lakes, but we couldn't do that either, because it cost money. Plain and simple, if it cost money we couldn't do it. TV in the 1970s, however, was free. That we could do at no cost, so we did it all the time.

We had an old black-and-white TV long after most households had bought color TVs, but we didn't care. It was on all the time just the same. Errol Flynn, Clark Gable, Abbott and Costello, Laurel and Hardy, Lauren Bacall, and Rita Hayworth were all bygones of another era, but we didn't know that. If they were on TV, they were new to us. TV made us a family.

"Jean Baby, go get the blankets ready. Okay?" I'll make us some popcorn with lots of butter," Mom would say shortly before the primetime hour. I was almost always allowed to pick the TV program we were going to watch. My favorites were *Mutual of Omaha's Animal Kingdom* and *Jacques Cousteau's Undersea World*. My siblings, however, did not share my deep fascination with animals.

"Ugh! Please Mom, can't we watch a movie? We always watch that stupid animal show," one of them would usually complain.

"No! I already told Jean we could watch *Animal Kingdom*, and that's what we're watching," Mom would reply. Her tendency to always take my side clearly irritated my siblings.

With gloating satisfaction, I would smooth the blankets on the floor and fluff the pillows while glancing smugly at Jimmy and Joanne. Once everything was set up with our blankets and pillows down; popcorn within arm's reach; TV tuned to the correct station, it was time to enter the gates of Heaven.

"Jean Honey, come lie next to me," Mom would say. Gleefully, I would plop down right next to her, ready to snuggle.

"Mom, that's not fair! How come Jean always gets to lie next to you?" Joanne, and sometimes Jimmy, would ask indignantly.

"Don't whine! You're old enough to lie by yourself," Mom would snap in response.

On the rare occasion, I would offer to move over so Mom could lie in the middle between Joanne and me. Unfortunately, this arrangement rarely worked out. Mom's mental state was hard to predict, and she suffered from severe claustrophobia.

When she was in the middle, she would almost always get up a short while later saying, "Let me out. I need a cigarette." Then she would extricate herself from the blankets and head off to find an ashtray. Rarely did she come back.

I would usually fall asleep before the show was over, especially if I was lying next to Mom. Then Mom would tell Jimmy to carry me up to bed. If I woke up during these trips, I wouldn't let on, preferring instead to be carried all the way. If Jimmy caught me opening my eyes, he would drop me to the floor roughly. "Walk," he would command with disgust.

When Mom stayed at home, rather than prowling the local bars, we would repeat our family TV ritual on a nightly basis. On those nights, we were just a normal family, mostly. On the other nights when Mom wasn't home, we also watched TV, but there was a veneer of apprehension that kept it from feeling as good, and I almost never got to pick the program. That usually meant we watched a horror movie, and my terror of the house with its monsters lurking in corners only grew worse.

* * *

It would be a lie if I said I didn't enjoy being my mother's favorite, or that I felt guilty about it. During that period of our lives, I was too young to feel real guilt. I loved all the attention Mom lavished on me, especially when she wasn't behaving strangely. Being the favorite had many advantages, but it did little to improve my relationship with my half-siblings. Jimmy always accused me of being spoiled, and he did a lot of cruel things to show me how much he hated that I got all the attention. In most families, this might have been just normal sibling rivalry, but little in our family was normal.

The truth is, Jimmy hated me from the moment I was born. According to Mom—and verified by others—a few weeks after I was brought home from the hospital he lit my crib on fire. Mom never said whether I was in it or not. He was five years old at the time. The instability that drove that act of pyromania actually showed up before I was born. When Mom described Jimmy as a baby, his good looks always came up first. She would talk about how beautiful he was with piercing aqua-blue eyes, blond hair, and incredible dimples. But she also described him as an overly clingy and emotional infant. By the time he was a toddler his behavior had become noticeably odd. Mom described how, after eating huge quantities of baby food, he would scream until he was fed more, only to throw it all back up again. The cycle would then repeat, because if he wasn't fed he would scream and scream. He would also bang his head against the wall and throw himself off furniture without any fear. Mom once told me that when Jimmy was two years old, she took him to a psychiatric hospital to be evaluated. He stayed for several days. At the end of the evaluation period, a psychiatrist told Mom that he believed Jimmy was suicidal. Mom was assured that he would grow out of it, but she would have to watch him very closely to make sure he didn't hurt himself. Mom said that by the time Jimmy was three, he was obsessed with fire. By age four, he was lighting them.

When Jimmy entered school, others also noticed that there was something odd about him. One year his elementary school teacher asked Mom to come in to speak with the school counselor. They were worried about a story Jimmy had related when he was asked to tell the class about something he did over summer vacation. According to his teacher, Jimmy told a very graphic story about killing a lizard and cutting it into pieces. The elaborate details he gave were frightening, not just to the other kids, but also to his teacher. The school suggested my parents get him some psychological help to deal with such violent fantasies.

Mom came home and told my father, Jimmy's new stepdad. According to my mother, my father was offended, and went to yell at the teacher and counselor. He told them that Jimmy did not have violent fantasies; that in fact, his stepson had actually killed the lizard and cut it up. He knew this because he had been with Jimmy at the time, and didn't see anything wrong with Jimmy's behavior—boys will be boys, after all. The school's recommendation was soundly ignored and no psychological help was sought.

Jimmy's behavior only became more challenging as he grew older, especially when Mom was single. Then Jimmy took on the status of being the "man around the house," and Mom forgave him very quickly for the violent things he did. This happened even if she got very angry in the moment and did things like smash Jimmy's new BB gun to pieces after he shot me with it.

* * *

As the long days of summer 1976 approached, Mom began to behave strangely again, only this time more so than ever before. We quit going to *any* church, and Mom replaced her Christian faith and sobriety with an interest in the dark arts and excessive drinking. She got occult books, filled the house with various items thought to have supernatural powers, and began engaging in strange activities. She often included me in these activities in one way or another. Torn between my devotion and my fear, I would do whatever she asked of me because, unlike my siblings, I loved being with Mom—even at her worst.

In one particularly bizarre instance, Mom decided I should join her on a nocturnal adventure. It was around midnight when Mom shook me and said, "Jean, wake up!"

"What's wrong, Mom?" I asked, rubbing my eyes to clear the grogginess.

"Jean, just get up! The time is right now. We need to go right now!"

"But where are we going?" I asked apprehensively.

"Jean, you're wasting time! This is critical. I've seen the signs. I'm the vessel because I've been chosen. I am the goddess, the wife, the saint. If we don't move now, I can't control the results.

We have to talk to the spirits tonight if I am going to stay in control."

The pace of Mom's voice was so frantic and fast that it was hard to understand the individual sentences. I quickly climbed out of bed. Mom grabbed the blanket I had just thrown from my body. I followed her in my bare feet. As we neared the front door I slowed and hesitantly asked, "What about Joanne and Jimmy, should we wake them too?"

"No Jean, there's no fucking time. Do you think the messengers want every fucking person to hear what they say? I am a princess born when the King of Moors raped the Irish. I'm the chosen one. Only the chosen can do this. We have to do this now, alone!"

I knew from Mom's tone that the best thing to do was to say nothing more. As I followed her outside, I wondered if she really was a princess. Having a princess for a mother seemed cool to me. I didn't know anything about spirits except that they sometimes were evil, and that scared me a bit, but not enough to keep me from following her. When we were out on the street, Mom began describing how she felt the presence of both evil and good spirits. These spirits came to her in the bodies of owls, bats, coyotes, and even domestic animals like black cats or light-eyed dogs that resembled wolves. "I need to get wild animals close to us so that the spirits can communicate through them with me," Mom said, standing in the middle of the dark road. She began howling like a wolf and told me to do the same. After a while similar howls came back to us, probably coyotes or dogs since there weren't any wolves where we lived. "Good Jean, keep it up so they'll come closer," Mom encouraged.

I kept howling until my throat was sore. Mom paced up and down in the dark, talking to spirits I could not see or hear. Abruptly she stopped and said, "Jean, we have to catch a bat. I need a dark spirit, one that can hold my power." I looked up into the sky for the bats that were almost always swooping low in the summer to catch mosquitos that hatched in the lake nearby. I saw several bats dipping up and down in the moonlight and pointed them out to my mother. "I need them to get closer Jean, so I can catch them," Mom said. Then she picked up the blanket she had left near the porch when we first came outside. My desire to make her happy kept me from saying that I was scared of catching bats. Instead, I picked up very small stones from the ground and tossed them up under the bats flying by. It was a trick I had seen my brother perform before. Confusing the stones for insects, the bats raced after them until they were almost to the ground. Mom tossed the blanket several times before she managed to snag one. I could hear the poor bat thumping on the ground as it tried to lift itself free. Fear and pity gripped me as Mom scrunched up the blanket and picked it back up. Then she slowly began opening it, ready to grab the bat trapped inside. The panic-stricken animal just barely escaped before Mom could grab it. I thought she was going be mad and make me try again, but as it turned out, it didn't matter. In her wildly energetic mental space, Mom somehow got her power to the dark spirits, and I was free to go back into the house and climb back into my bed.

* * *

When things went well, I enjoyed our night outings and believed whatever Mom told me. I got to do things that other kids didn't, and I found that exciting. Sometimes though, things would get too weird. Mom would talk about demons trying to get us; or, sometimes she would become very angry and unpredictable, even verbally abusing any neighbor who dared to come out to see what was going on. On those nights, the hair would stand up on the back of my neck, and I would be afraid of being outside in the dark, but going back into the house often didn't seem like a good idea either. In my mind, the house was a magnet for anything evil, especially monsters. Plus, it didn't help that the house contained the most terrifying picture I had ever seen: a picture of Jesus.

The picture was hung in the living room above the old wooden desk. Mom had placed it there before she began dabbling in the dark arts. Some might have found the picture of our Lord and Savior comforting, but I didn't. It was one of those pictures where the eyes of Jesus followed you around the room, courtesy of the same 3-D technology that made scenes move inside of children's picture books. It was eerie the way Jesus seemed to look at me no matter where I went. Having eyes follow me around the room left me very unsettled. When Mom had first hung the picture, I examined it endlessly. I would take it carefully down off the dark wood paneling and turn the cheap golden frame over and over again in my hands. My mission was to understand the trick that made the eyes move. But no matter how much I looked at it, I couldn't figure it out. I wasn't the only one who felt troubled by that picture. Mom, Joanne, and even Jimmy came to find it menacing. Eventually, we all avoided the corner of the room with "Creepy Jesus."

As Mom's interest in witchcraft intensified, the eerie picture of Jesus became even more ominous and threating. Eventually, it stopped being Jesus at all and became something much darker. Everyone in the house hated it. Having been forced to go to a number of very fanatical Christian churches, I had become sure that the picture had been inhabited by Satan in some attempt to trick us. Mom started to think that too. One night, in a frenzy to cleanse the house of evil, Mom decided to burn the picture. I was asleep when it happened, but her blood-curdling screams echoed up the attic stairs and woke me up. Joanne also shot up in her bed, startled and confused. "What's going on?" she asked.

"I don't know. Mom just started screaming," I said, as I pulled the blankets tightly over my head for protection. Once my head was covered, I felt safer. The screams from downstairs continued.

"Shit!" Joanne said, before climbing out of her bed. She usually managed to be a lot braver than I was. She headed down the attic stairs to find out what was going on. Reluctantly, I slid from my covers and crept to the bottom of the attic steps after her. When I reached the door, she had already exited through into the living room. I crouched down and listened quietly. I could hear Jimmy talking to Mom in the living room.

"Mom, just go to bed. It's fine now," Jimmy said.

"Satan was in that picture. He was in it! His face came right at me. I lit it on fire, and the face came out. Satan is in this house!" Mom said. I could hear her panicked voice move from place to place as she paced frantically around the living room.

"Okay Mom, but it's over now. So let's go back to bed," Jimmy said reassuringly.

"No Jimmy, we have to protect the house from Satan and his demons!" Mom yelled.

I could tell by the tone in her voice that she was close to hysteria. Pushing her to do anything while in that state of mind usually only made matters worse. Though I was scared, I knew it was time for me to help Mom. Protecting the house from Satan seemed like a great idea, and I was ready to volunteer my services. Mom had confirmed that the spooky Jesus picture was evil, just as I had suspected all along. Preventing further evil from entering our house was simply prudent at that point. I stepped through the door into the living room.

"Mom, I'll help get rid of Satan," I said.

"This is crazy! I'm going back to bed," Jimmy replied in frustration. He stomped back downstairs to where he had moved his cot a month or so before. Joanne looked at his retreat from the living room and walked toward the kitchen out of Mom's line of sight. She quietly stood there without saying anything.

I walked over to the desk where Mom stood talking with intensity about the face coming out of the picture of Jesus as she set it on fire. On the desk's surface sat a large ashtray overflowing with ashes, the remnants of the demonic Jesus. I stared at it as Mom retold her terrifying story. I believed her. Satan had come out of the picture and was lurking somewhere—I felt it. I looked around the room to make sure he wasn't hiding close by. "Mom, what should we do?" I asked.

In one of her occult books on witchcraft, Mom had read that demons wouldn't pass over salt. She sent me to get all the salt I could find in the house. She began pouring it around the desk where she had burned the picture of Jesus. Then she sent me outside with the rest of the salt. In what was now the gloom of early dawn, I poured the salt on the ground to make an unbroken circle around the house like the one Mom had made around the desk. Joanne joined me and started pouring salt on the other side of the house until we connected the lines. The sun had begun to turn the sky orange, and in the early daylight, the horror of Mom's story began to fade. I became curious about why salt held such power against demons. Questions raced through my head as I completed my job. *Do they hate it because it's white like the color of the good angels? Or do demons not like the taste? Do demons prefer sweet things? Does the salt somehow burn them? Can it melt them, like the way water melted the Wicked Witch in the Wizard of Oz?* I didn't know the answers to any of those questions, and I didn't think it was a good idea to ask Mom right then. Instead, I tried to focus on the fact that the salt would protect us from Satan, and we would be safe.

* * *

Mom's strange behavior continued to escalate after the burning of the Jesus picture. She drank heavily. She would be gone for days at a time. When she did come home, it was often with strange new men. Our lives were disrupted in lots of ways, which began to take a toll on everyone. My childish fears grew, as did my fear that we weren't safe as a family anymore. In response, I took to sleeping in Mom's bed whenever I could. Her bedroom was very small and the bed barely fit, which meant there was only one side to enter into and exit from. The sense of enclosure made me feel safe, like when I used to hide in the closet at our old house. It was absolutely the best when Mom was home too and we could snuggle. Even when she wasn't home, I liked her bed better than my own, and I rarely had nightmares when I slept there. It turned out that my sense of safety was an illusion.

One night in Mom's bed, I woke to the smell of hot beer breath on my face and the pressure of something heavy across my throat and upper chest. At first I didn't know what was happening; I only knew it was hard to breathe. Panicked, I opened my eyes and tried to sit up. I couldn't, something was pinning me down. As I struggled, the motion disturbed the person next to me. I glanced to where my mother usually slept and saw the outline of someone whose arm was thrown like a dead animal across me. As I tried to move my head to get a clearer view, rough whiskers scratched against my cheek, telling me it was a man next to me and not my mom. I had no idea who he was. The arm across my neck and upper chest bent at the elbow, and a hand grasped the back of my head to pull it closer to the whiskered face. The man's mouth opened slightly and he mumbled, "Umm Baby" into my ear as he pushed his groin toward my hip. Then he took a deep breath and started snoring.

Terrified that he might wake up again, I laid very still. I stopped breathing for as long as I could, and then, when I couldn't hold my breath any longer, I took just tiny inhalations of air to keep my chest from moving. Minutes passed and then the man rubbed his groin against my hip in a circular motion for a few seconds. I held as still as I could, and again he fell back into a drunken sleep. Frightened that he might keep touching me, I waited until he was snoring soundly and very carefully pushed his arm straight up from my throat and slid my head out from underneath, lowering his arm slowly once my head was out. He grunted and shifted toward me. I lay frozen like a rabbit frightened by dogs. I didn't move again for a long time to make sure he had fallen back into a deep sleep.

The longer I stayed in the bed the greater my desperation grew, but getting out meant climbing over the strange man. I thought about how to do it for a long time before I made my move. Since the bed was enclosed on three sides and I was on the inside, I scrunched to the bottom corner of the bed. Once there I spread my arms out until I was wedged into the corner where the two walls met. I stood up slowly, using the walls for support. My head was just a foot below the low ceiling once I was fully upright. Using my hands to keep myself balanced, I pressed them one at a time to the ceiling above me. Then I gently stepped over the snoring drunk to the edge of the bed. Carefully, I squatted and slowly lifted one leg down the floor, then the other. I stood like a statue for several minutes to make sure he did not wake up again. Then I fled the room back to the attic.

"Joanne, wake up. Please wake up," I begged. Joanne responded with a heavy snore. "Please Joanne, wake up. There's a strange man in Mom's bed and he rubbed himself on me," I moaned, grabbing her shoulder and shaking it.

She just moved farther away, turned her back to me and grunted, "Leave me alone," before falling once again into a heavy sleep. I climbed under the covers beside her in the twin bed and began to cry silently. I felt sick. The smell of the man's hot breath on my cheek and his groin pressing against me wouldn't leave my mind.

The next morning, I heard a man talking to Jimmy downstairs. A little while later I heard a car leave. Only then did I go down into the basement to wash the smell of beer and the dirty feeling I had from my body. When I came back upstairs, I asked Jimmy why a strange man was sleeping in Mom's bed. "He's just some boyfriend of Mom's. He was drunk when he came by last night looking for her. He didn't seem like he should be driving, so I told him he could go sleep it off in her bed. The dude's alright. What do you care who sleeps in Mom's bed?" Jimmy asked nonchalantly. I was too ashamed to tell him what had happened.

* * *

I went to my first foster placement not long after the baby goat died. Jimmy had already left to go live with his father a few weeks before, following a terrible fight with Mom. That left Joanne and me to manage alone the best we could. Each day that passed, Mom's mind unraveled further. She rarely came home, and when she did, she was usually drunk, mad, and often violent. We had learned to be self-sufficient and not draw attention to ourselves, so we kept getting up and going to school, even when Mom wasn't there to wake us up. If there was food in the house we made meals and cleaned up after ourselves. We washed our clothes in the sink and put them out to dry. When Mom came home alone or with some man, we did our best to avoid her, but mostly she just didn't come home. I missed her, but I also felt uncomfortable when she was there.

Joanne said Mom was an alcoholic, and sometimes it seemed as though Joanne hated her. I felt sad about that because I still loved Mom with all my heart. As May turned to June, school let out, and Joanne and I lived like invisible spirits inhabiting an empty house. We stayed as silent as we could so as not to draw our neighbor's attention to the fact that we were two children living pretty much on our own. Most days we hung out on the roof just outside the attic window, in the sun. Joanne would read or do word puzzles. I would pick at the scabs on my bony knees or bite my nails, wondering if Mom was okay. That's where we were when finally someone came to tell us that in fact, Mom wasn't okay.

I jumped when the unexpected knock echoed up the attic stairs. Joanne and I looked at each other, both automatically deciding the best thing to do was remain silent. I tried to ignore the knocking, but the person doing it wasn't giving up easily. I sat frozen on my bed, my heart pounding. In the pauses between the knocks I could hear a man calling our names. "Jean? Joanne? Are you here? Please open up, this is the police," a deep voice said. We carefully pulled back the curtain on the small round attic window and looked outside. A police cruiser was parked in front of the house. Realizing we had little choice, Joanne and I argued about who was going to open the door. I lost.

With a feeling of dread, I went down the attic stairs. Once I unbolted the door and opened it, I felt even worse. There on the porch stood a very tall police officer. My heart raced and I wanted to run back to the safety of the attic. My mom hadn't been home in several days, and I had a profound sense that the cop was not there to give us good news.

Although I probably felt less hatred for the police than the rest of my family, most of my experience with cops up to that moment had been negative. My oldest half-sister Joni had run away countless times when she still lived with Mom. The last time had been just before my dad took off and left us. That was what led to her being sent back to live with her own father. Shortly after that, my other half-brother Jerry, Joni's full-sibling, also left to live with their father. Joni's escapades, along with the petty crimes of my half-brothers, made the back of police cars and visits to juvenile hall as common in our house as trips to the food bank for surplus government cheese and potted meat. Plus, my parents fought violently in the years prior to their divorce. They destroyed the house and beat each other bloody, though my mother always got the worst of it. When their fights went on too long, some neighbor would finally become disturbed enough to call the cops in to break up the fight. When the cops got there, things sometimes just got uglier. Even when I covered my head with my pillow or hid in the closet, I could hear my family screaming at the cops, and often the cops shouting orders at my family. After my dad left and my mom began disappearing for days, she also gave us direct orders to avoid the police because they would take us away. Those experiences, along with my family referring to them as "dirty pigs," left me very uneasy when police came around.

So when I opened the door that day after coming down from the attic, it's not surprising that I did it with a horrible feeling in my stomach.

"Hi, are you"—the tall officer standing on the porch looked down at a small pad with names written on it—"Jean?" he asked in a kind voice full of concern.

I nodded reluctantly, fighting the urge to bolt past him and make a run for the woods. I remained quiet and looked down at my feet.

"Hey Jean, I'm not here to hurt you. Something has happened to your mom, and I'm here to make sure you're safe. Tell me Honey, are you here alone?" he asked, squatting down to be closer to my height. I nodded again. I thought that if I kept quiet he might not find out about my sister upstairs and she'd be safe. What I didn't know was that by then, she had stepped into the living room. The cop looked beyond me and said, "You must be Joanne." I turned to see Joanne glaring at him. She didn't reply, and the cop went on as if she had answered, "So hey girls, why don't you both step outside a minute. I need to talk to you."

The officer stepped to the side, beckoning us to come and stand beside him. We moved to the porch. "I'm sorry girls, but your mother is sick and in the hospital. She'll likely be home in a few days, but you guys can't stay here alone. Is there anyone you can stay with? Any relative or friend's parents?" he asked.

I knew there were no relatives in our small mountain town to take us. My mother's sister Ginny lived not that far from us, but Auntie never let us stay the night there. I didn't even mention her name. I stared at the ground, mute, and tried to think of someone who would take me. The police officer prodded us gently and explained that it would likely be just for a night, because he was sure my mom would be home soon. Joanne told him in a very angry tone that she had a friend who would take us. We weren't given time to pack anything. This only made Joanne madder, and by the time we sat in the police car, she was fuming. When we got to her friend's house the officer explained the situation to the parents, but they said they would only be able to take Joanne for the night. It was an awkward moment for my sister. I told her I understood, and gave the cop the name and address of my friend Angie, who I sometimes played with. Joanne hugged me quickly and stomped off up the stairs and into her friend's house. The cop gently grasped my shoulder and guided me back to his car.

The drive to my friend Angie's was short. Once I saw the large white house on the hill, I began to feel a lot better. It was a place I knew and where I felt safe. The officer said I'd be home in a day or two, so that meant I didn't have to worry much about my mom. I didn't think that she could be very sick if she was going to be home so soon, which made it easier to put my worries aside. It also helped that my playmate, the daughter of a doctor, had toys I had only fantasized about. Unlike my family, her parents were wealthy and still married. Never did anyone call them "white trash," and I had never heard Angie say that cops had come to their house. Maybe that's why Angie's mom freaked out a little when we showed up. The cop took her out of earshot to have a private conversation. I watched them through the living room window as they talked out on the front porch. Angie's Mom stood rigidly with her arms crossed over her chest. The officer asked her something and her head moved back and forth as if saying, "no." The officer kept talking, and finally, I saw Angie's mom nod her head. They returned to the living room where Angie and I had been told to wait. In spite of her feelings toward me, or maybe more likely my family, Angie's mom informed me that I could stay over. I was relieved. The officer said he would be back in a day or two to get me once my mom was out of the hospital.

Angie and I went upstairs to play. Angie was overjoyed that I was finally going to be able stay overnight. Her mother had never let me do that before. She asked me lots of questions about my mom, questions I had too little knowledge to answer like, "Is your mom gonna die?" I could sense that Angie felt sorry for me, and I used her sympathy to my advantage to get something I had always wanted.

Angie's room contained the largest Raggedy Ann doll I had ever seen, and not only a Raggedy Ann, but a Raggedy Andy too. I had secretly coveted those dolls since the first time I had laid my eyes on them. Never had I wanted a doll as much as I wanted Angie's life-size Raggedy Ann. *What little girl wouldn't want it?* It was almost as big as me and made of colorful soft fabric with bright red hair made of yarn. I saw it as a personal playmate that would never hurt your feelings like real people did. Plus, if you were scared at night and had to sleep alone, it would be like having a real person in bed to protect you. After seeing the doll for the first time, I tried to make my own by tracing a similar size outline on two pieces of butcher paper. I drew a face on one side and colored in clothes on both sides; she had a cute blue skirt, a white top, a pearl necklace, and black shoes. After using gobs of staples, I got the two sides put together, forming a large paper doll that I stuffed with newspaper to give it a more lifelike feel. It was a crappy imitation but it was better than having no doll at all. For weeks I slept with my counterfeit Raggedy Ann, up until she tore and spilled paper guts onto my sheets. When that happened, my paper friend had to go into the trash. For weeks I missed her companionship and thought all the time about how lucky Angie was.

So with the assistance of my mother's absence and the police drop-off, I found myself with my friend's sympathy— maybe even her mother's sympathy. I figured it was my chance to use the bad circumstances to my advantage. As we played tea party with the two dolls up in her room, I began my desperate plea.

"Angie, please let me have your Raggedy Ann. I like her soooooo much," I begged.

"No Jean, I don't think my mom would like that," she said, but it looked to me like she was feeling bad about it.

"Please, Angie. You already have the matching Raggedy Andy. You know my mom's in the hospital. Pleeeeease give me your doll so I won't be so sad."

"I don't know. I like my doll."

"Pleeeeease, Angie! You have a mom and a dad. I don't have either right now. If you didn't have parents to take care of you, I would give you my doll! I'm not sure you're really my friend," I said, feeling a little guilty.

Angie looked down at Raggedy Andy, which she was holding, and touched his hair. She seemed uncertain but after a few moments said, "Okay, you can have her, but you have to ask my mom if it's all right."

I swore in my head. Asking her mom was not something I wanted to do. I knew I wouldn't be able to face her mother no matter how much I wanted the doll. Any bravery I felt was quickly lost whenever I had to face an adult. I wanted the doll so badly though, I knew I couldn't just give up, either. After making lots of excuses about why I shouldn't go, I was able to convince poor Angie that she should go without my help to ask on my behalf. After Angie went back downstairs I sat there waiting, hoping, and praying that her mother would let me have Raggedy Ann. The minutes crept by at an agonizing pace. After about 10 minutes, I heard Angie's feet on the stairs. Before she could enter the room I jumped up, ran to the door, and asked her over and over again, "What'd your mom say?"

Sounding a little defeated, Angie replied, "You can have her."

I started jumping around the room, swinging the doll by its arms. After a few minutes of ecstasy I said, "Thank you Angie! You'll be my friend forever!"

Due to her simple act of giving, I decided I would never be mean to Angie again, even if other kids wanted me to. I would never leave her behind to go with friends that were more fun because their parents let them run around completely unsupervised (even into town). I couldn't do those things anymore, though I might have been guilty of doing them a few times in the past, because Angie had given me the best doll in the world. "Angie, you're my hero," I told her.

That night I went to bed with my body pressed tightly to Raggedy Ann, feeling both guilty and grateful. When I woke up, I had a nagging fear about my mother. I tried to reassure myself. *The police officer said she would be fine, so she's fine, right? Yeah, she's fine. Just a day or two and she'll come home.* When the same police officer showed up later that day my gut told me something was wrong, really wrong.

The cop said I needed to come with him and his tone wasn't reassuring. He was all business. I got ready to leave, feeling a bit sad that I couldn't play with Angie for longer, but my mind was on my mother. I hugged my friend and thanked her mom before picking up my new Raggedy Ann from the chair and heading toward the police car. Before I got far, the cop gently stopped me. "You'll have to leave the doll here," he said. When I protested, he assured me that I would be able to come back to get it from my friend another time. I got a real bad feeling then. *If I'm going home, why can't I bring the doll?* I wondered.

When I got to the car, my sister Joanne was already in the back with her arms crossed tightly over her chest. The look on her face told me things weren't good. The officer told me I could sit up front with him. I really wanted to but both fear and loyalty toward my sister made me decline his offer. I climbed into the back, which felt like being in a cage. Once I sat down I asked, "Are we going home?"

The cop turned around in his seat to face me just as my sister spat out an angry—"No, we're not!"—and then flipped him off.

The cop ignored her and said in a gentle voice, "I'm sorry, but your mother is sicker than everyone thought. She won't be able to come home right now and take care of you. We're going to the police station so I can make some calls and hopefully find somewhere else for you to stay temporarily." He didn't explain where that somewhere else might be. I was so scared, but I didn't want to tell anyone. My dad had always punished me for being a crybaby. I tried to look brave even though I didn't feel it. During the drive to the police station, I retreated into the silence of shyness and fear that I had so often felt around my father.

When we arrived at the station, the officer offered us snacks from the vending machines that lined the back wall of the small room. I picked out a pack of powdered donuts and a grape soda. My sister refused the snacks and sat as far from the cop as she could. He asked me to sit down too, while he figured out where he had to take us next. He assured us that it was going to be okay, but I wasn't feeling sure about that at all. Leaving me in a chair, he went to his desk and began making phone calls. The first was to Joanne's father. That call was short, but the next was longer. The station was small—just a couple of desks and a few chairs for visitors—so I could hear everything he said. "Are you sure there isn't anything for her? Her sister's father already said he won't take her. Plus, there may be legal issues there. Okay, give me that number," he said to the person on the other end. I watched him hang up and dial several more times. Seeing that I was listening, he dropped his voice. I still caught his end of the conversation. "I feel terrible about this, but I guess there isn't any alternative. I'll drive them down now," he said, before slowly hanging up the phone.

The tone of his voice told me something bad was about to happen. I picked at the powdered donut in front of me but didn't feel like eating it. He came over and squatted down. "Don't like powdered donuts, huh?" he asked. I shrugged my shoulders. "Well, you don't have to eat them if you don't want to, Sweetie," he said. I stopped picking at the donut and began chewing my nails nervously. He glanced at my sister and took a deep breath. "Girls, I'm sorry, but there doesn't seem to be anyone who can take you right this minute," he said. "I'm going to have to take you to the Juvenile Detention Center down the mountain. Joanne, your father has been contacted. It's my understanding that he's coming for you soon, but that will all be sorted out at the center. Jean, you'll only have to be there until they find another placement for you. That shouldn't take too long."

I looked at him, shocked. I knew right then things were not going to be okay like he said when he had first come to pick us up. *Juvy! I'm going to Juvy!* I thought. I couldn't believe it. My older siblings had been carted off to the County Juvenile Detention Center on occasion, but they were older than me and went because they had done something bad. They had told me all about "Juvy." I was pretty sure it was someplace I didn't want to go. I couldn't understand why the officer had to take me there. *I'm only 8!* I cried in my head. Maybe I had tricked Angie a bit, but I had given Raggedy Ann back, and it had been a long time since I had taken something from the candy counter without paying. *How could I be going to Juvy?* I wondered, still in shock. It was unbelievable.

Stunned, I bit my lip as hard as I could to keep myself from crying. When my dad was around, whenever I got hurt emotionally or physically and cried, he would say, "Stop that crying or I'll give you something to cry about." If I didn't stop crying, he'd hit me. To keep from getting smacked by him, I learned that if I physically hurt myself somehow, I could keep the tears inside and avoid the worse fate of him making me cry. The metallic taste of blood filled my mouth as I ground my teeth into the flesh of my lip. The pain distracted me from what was happening.

The officer asked if I wanted to keep the donuts for the ride. I shook my head. He picked them up with my soda and put them in the trash. We went out to his car. Once again, I climbed into the back with my sister. She was whispering obscenities at the cop under her breath. I knew I should sit up front because it helped me not get car sick on the curvy roads down the mountain, but I just couldn't bring myself to do it. I felt so betrayed by him, first my doll and now Juvy. *Guess my family was right about cops. They are pigs, no matter how nice they seem,* I thought.

* * *

After a long and silent drive down the mountain, the County Juvenile Detention Center came into view. It loomed in front of us just like a prison. Buildings were surrounded by chain-link fencing topped with razor wire. The officer parked in front of the main entrance. We left the car, and the cop guided us into the building through a series of locked doors. A stern woman met us and led us through corridors into the processing area for new arrivals. Before he left, the cop tried to assure us that we would only be staying a little while. By then though, I didn't trust anything he said. I was sure I would be in Juvy for a long time.

Just before my 7th birthday, my mother had told me that my father was dead. It was hard for me to even remember what he looked like, since Mom had cut his face out of all our family photos. His face was just a hole in the pictures—and my mind. Since he was dead, I didn't hold out much hope that I would be rescued like my sister. Even if Aunt Ginny knew where I was, she wouldn't come get me either. She and Mom had stopped talking in the months prior, and besides, my aunt had never really gone too far out of her way for us kids. It might have been because of my uncle Eugene being sick all the time, but she had always seemed a bit selfish to me whenever it came to helping anyone but herself. My last hope might have been my oldest half-sister and brother, but they had not been in contact with us for years, so I knew they weren't coming for me either. I was on my own.

The stern woman took us from the cop and explained to my sister that she would not be staying long. Her father would be arriving soon to pick her up. We were ushered into a small processing area lined with chairs and told to wait. A short while later Joanne's father arrived. Fearful of being left alone, I started to sob and begged her not to leave me. "Please, can't I take Jean with me? I promise I'll take care of her," my sister asked the woman, her voice thick with emotion.

In response, the woman calmly explained the regulations. "No, I'm sorry, your sister will have to stay. She can only be released to someone approved by the court. Since your mother is too sick to care for her and her father can't be located, the only option we have is to keep her here until a foster home can be found."

"No, please,"—I grabbed Joanne's hand—"I can't stay here." My sister pried my fingers from hers and hugged me goodbye while trying hard not to cry. I began to sob uncontrollably. In vain, I tried to follow her as she was taken to the main entrance where her father waited. "Please, let me go. Please. I don't want to stay here. Joanne, wait! Don't go!" I begged, as she slipped from view.

Still sobbing, I was taken to a small room near the showers and placed in front of another woman sitting at a desk. She told me to remove all my jewelry and my belt, if I had one. I didn't have a belt, but I was wearing gold stud earrings that were used to pierce my ears just a week before.

"I can't take my earrings out. I just got them pierced," I told the woman.

"You have no choice. They need to come out and go into this envelope," she replied.

"But the holes will close if I do that. The lady at the shop said I had to leave them in for at least a month. It was a birthday gift from my mom, please don't make me," I said.

"Earrings, along with all other jewelry, are a safety risk. Remove them now, or I will have you restrained and remove them myself," she responded sternly.

I had stopped swallowing small objects long ago, so I was having difficulty understanding how my earrings could be a safety risk. I didn't want to take them out, not just because my ears might close, but because they were the only connection I had right then to my mother. Getting our ears pierced was the last special thing we had done together. Reluctantly, I removed them while thinking of that strange day.

* * *

Mom decided we would get our ears pierced to celebrate our birthdays, which were still a couple of weeks away. We did have a car then, but like many other times in my childhood, it was broken down. So we walked into town together, holding hands and feeling very excited. Since we lived in such a small community, walking really wasn't so bad. I only minded it when we had to carry groceries or laundry home up the steep roads. Walking also wasn't as fun in the winter when it snowed too heavily. Then you had to be careful of ice or you'd end up with bruises, or worse, a broken bone. On that day though, we trekked down warm sun-dappled roads surrounded by sweet-smelling pine. My excitement grew greater when we hit the main street through town. The main street was about two miles long, stretching from the lake on one edge to the Post Office on the other. I felt warm and happy as we walked past the grocery store, the movie theater, the small arcade, and our favorite A&W hamburger stand.

We also walked past several of my mother's favorite local bars, which the town had more of than any other type of business. They had names such as the "Stagecoach" and "Last

Stand." Over the years, she had taken me into many of the local bars while she drank. Those days were boring and weird. Creepy drunk friends of my mom, as well as strangers, touched me and talked to me while I drank Shirley Temples and ate chips. The best days were when Mom took all us kids to the Stage Coach, which had an air hockey table. Then we could at least play with each other, and then, the drunks were more likely to leave us alone.

Our walk to get our ears pierced ended near the lake where I had spent countless days learning to fish and swim. Up from the lake was a small brick building containing the only jewelry shop in town where you could get your ears pierced. As we climbed the stairs to the building, I felt both excited and scared. Mom was excited too, and talked about how beautiful we were going to look. We held hands as we entered. The woman running the shop greeted us warmly as we came in. Mom greeted her back, but something in her tone made me feel uneasy. Her voice had a kind of agitated and fast pace to it that I knew wasn't a good sign.

Once we began selecting earrings, my worries were quickly overcome by excitement. The nice woman running the shop gave me a choice between gold and silver surgical steel studs. The gold studs were, of course, much more expensive. I wanted the gold, but I selected the silver knowing we never had much money. After I picked them, I was surprised to hear Mom say to the woman, "Give her the gold. She's my daughter and she deserves to wear gold. We're not just anybody, we're special and people need to know it!" The comment wasn't really strange for a mother and daughter out on a special occasion, but the way my mother said it made it seem so.

The woman pierced my mother's ears first, also with a pair of gold studs. Then she loaded the gold earrings into the piercing gun and rubbed alcohol on my ear lobes. When she squeezed the trigger I felt a burning sensation, but I didn't cry. When she finished, she handed me a mirror and I looked happily at my new earrings. My happiness, though, was short-lived. My mother began arguing with the shopkeeper about wanting to put in a different pair of earrings. I hopped out of the piercing chair and stood near the door, holding the little mirror I had been gazing into. Mom's voice was angry. I froze and silently prayed that she would remain calm. Up until that moment, our outing had been so special and fun, I didn't want it to be ruined.

"Look Honey, I don't want studs. I want those earrings right there," Mom said, as she held up a pair of large silver cowboy-boot earrings covered in multicolored stones. The earrings looked huge, even to my inexperienced eyes.

"I'm sorry, but if I put those heavy earrings in they will rip your earlobes. You need to leave the studs in at least eight weeks before you put in any large earrings. And truthfully, you should wait even longer for a pair that heavy," the shopkeeper said, clearly upset.

"You don't tell me what to do! I paid for these earrings, and I want them in my ears," Mom insisted, while jabbing the air near the woman's face with the earrings cupped in her fingers.

"I'm sorry, but I will not be responsible for harming anyone. I think you and your daughter need to leave the store," the shopkeeper replied coolly.

The woman's words only antagonized my mother further. She leaned forward just inches from the woman's face. I set the mirror down on the counter and prepared myself for whatever was about to come.

"Don't you know who I am? I have every cop in this town ready to kill for me. You think you can treat me like this? One phone call Baby, and you, and this shop, will cease to exist. Bam! Just like that! Don't you dare tell me what I can and can't do!" my mother hissed. The woman's eyes widened.

Mom often made these kinds of threatening statements when she got upset. I suspected they were exaggerations. I wanted to tell the woman that Mom didn't mean it, but I wasn't 100 percent sure. Plus, I knew that if I said anything against Mom, she would turn her anger on me. Feeling concerned for the woman and afraid that things were going to get worse, I pulled my mother out of the shop, saying over and over again, "Mom, it's fine! Let's go, I'll help you put them in."

Outside on the street, I helped Mom put in the larger earrings. After I took out her brand new studs, blood ran down her earlobes—a lot of blood. It scared me, but I knew there was no stopping Mom from putting in the other earrings. She handed me the heavy silver boots. My hands were shaking as I tried to put them in, and the blood made them slippery. As I worked, Mom ranted on and on about having the power to order the killing of the shop lady. I tried to ignore what she was saying and kept quiet. I couldn't get the earrings into the holes easily, and as I forced them in, the bleeding got worse. I felt sick seeing the damage I was doing to my mom's earlobes. When I finally finished the task, Mom appeared satisfied and returned to her earlier happy mood. Little by little the tension went away and the joy of the special day returned. We walked up the street to get an ice cream float at the A&W. We laughed and smiled, telling each other every few minutes how beautiful the other one looked. I soaked up my mother's attention and pride over our enhanced beauty. I still felt tense, but I tried really hard to make the best of it. After the root beer float, we walked home hand-in-hand, feeling like princess and queen.

* * *

Though I desperately tried to convey the importance of the earrings to the woman behind the desk at Juvy, my efforts were fruitless. Defeated and afraid, I handed over my precious earrings. She catalogued them with the rest of my meager belongings and put them into the manila envelope. I stared sadly as she walked the envelope over to a cabinet and locked them inside. Once I was stripped of any personal identity, I was led to the showers and told to take off all my clothes. There the woman liberally covered me with a fine white powder, apparently to kill any lice I might have. My mom had always kept us kids immaculate so the insinuation stung. I whispered, "I don't have lice." I felt so vulnerable standing there naked in front of a total stranger.

"Hold your breath and close your mouth and eyes!" the woman barked, as she applied the dust. My hair, my armpits, and even my hairless pubic area were covered with the powder. Embarrassed, I tried to cover myself with my hands but the woman ordered me to keep them at my sides. After being deloused I was allowed to shower in the communal shower area. There, all the emotions I had been trying to keep at bay flooded in. I was afraid, sad, and empty.

Once I was dressed in regulation clothing, I was given a quick tour of the facilities. My block had a game room with a pool table, a guard/counselor station, and a corridor with dorm rooms lining each side. The block was only a fraction of the facility. I would learn there was also a cafeteria, a school, and other housing blocks for the more delinquent kids spread out across the large parcel of land. Following the tour, I was led to my dorm. It was a small room enclosed in painted cement block walls. There was single gray metal door to the room with a thick Plexiglas window. The door could be locked only from the outside, which didn't make me feel any better about being in there.

Inside the room there were two twin beds, one of which belonged to my roommate, a surly teenage girl with bad teeth, stringy hair, and an unfortunate collection of zits. She looked around 14 years old. I was left in the care of my new roommate. She asked me if I understood the rules and how to get extra privileges or have them taken away. While I had been given a brief overview during my tour of the facilities, I was too upset to really listen. I shook my head, so she explained to me in detail the information I had missed.

"You have to follow all the rules. If you do what they say, then you get points. If you don't, you'll lose them. The points get you privileges, losing points gets you on another block. Understand?"

I nodded.

"Also,"—the girl looked at me with a wicked gleam in her eyes—"you have to do everything I say."

"What? Why do I have to do what *you* say?" I asked.

"Because, if you don't, I'll tell them that you're breaking the rules. Then you'll lose points. If you lose enough points, you won't have any privileges. You won't be able to play pool or leave the room. You might even be moved to another block, one where they keep really bad kids. So, if you're smart you'll do what I say. Got it?"

I nodded, but from that moment on I didn't like the girl. I sensed that she was just a bully, but what could I do? She was much older, not to mention, twice my size. Feeling hopeless, I retreated by lying down on my bunk with my back to her. I pressed my face pressed against the wall and tried to make her disappear.

"So what'd you do to get here? Did you run away?" she asked, clearly unconcerned about my giving her the cold shoulder.

"Please leave me alone," I begged.

She persisted in asking me about why I was there. She was baffled that someone so young would be in enough trouble to warrant time in Juvy, and she wanted all the details. I think she expected me to tell her some dark tale involving drugs or murder or hurting other kids, but my story was drab compared to those of most Juvy residents. As the girl grilled me, once again I found myself faced with questions I had too little information to answer.

I knew something was wrong with my mother but I wasn't exactly sure what. Whatever it was, she was my mom and I still loved her. She took me on outings to the movie theater with homemade popcorn and store-bought candy hidden in her purse. She would eat with us kids as a family in front of our small black-and-white television, usually 10-cent pot pies and TV dinners, but it was wonderful. We went together on trips to the lake to fish and swim. We laughed and joked. We had lots of fun. It would all be so good, but then something would change. All of a sudden we'd stop being good Mormons, Catholics, or Baptists, and I would be expected to practice witchcraft, go to nudist camps, or leave the house in the middle of the night on some weird adventure. Mom's behavior would become hostile, sometimes even brutal. Things I did that were once accepted as normal kid stuff suddenly evoked violence. Mom might throw glasses of water, cups full of coffee, plates, or anything else close by. She would hit, kick, or pull us to bed by the hair for something as innocuous as falling asleep on the couch. Since I was the baby in the family, I avoided a lot of the brutality my siblings experienced. But, that didn't mean I wasn't afraid. The thing that was so hard for me to understand was that Mom was often the kindest and most loving person I had ever known—and then— she wasn't. I just didn't know how to put all her contradictions together to explain to the mean girl I shared my Juvy room with, as to "why" I was there.

Years would pass before the medical community gave my mom a diagnosis, and it would be years after that before I was old enough to understand what the diagnosis really meant. All I knew on the day I arrived at the juvenile detention center, and that I could clearly understand, was that my mom sometimes drank—a lot! So that's what I told my Juvy roommate: my mom drank. I thought after I told her, she might feel bad for me that I got stuck in Juvy for something I couldn't help, but she didn't. I received no hug, no words of encouragement, no sympathy. Rather, my explanation led her to tell me that "alcoholics never change." Her words stabbed me in the heart, and I felt so helpless to protect myself. "Get used to it here. You're going to be here a long time!" were her final words as she got up and left our cell. I didn't want to believe her, but part of me knew she was right—my mom might never change.

Mom had been going to Alcoholics Anonymous meetings on and off for years; I knew this because she could never afford a babysitter, so I went with her. People chain-smoking, drinking excessive amounts of coffee, telling countless tales of terrible addictions and destroyed lives—that was AA. By the time I arrived at Juvy, I had heard so many ugly tales about the darkness people lived with it was hard to believe there were people who actually lived happy lives. In meeting after meeting, I listened while my mom and other lost souls confessed to self-destruction and abuse of loved ones. I watched as they all held hands and prayed for strength and forgiveness, each hoping that God would somehow make it better. I wanted badly to believe there was hope for my mom. "God grant me the serenity to accept the things I cannot change, the courage to change the things I can, and the wisdom to know the difference," I chanted along with her and all the other broken people. But, no matter how many times people said those words, they seemed to come back week after week to talk about "falling off" the wagon. Mom prayed. I prayed. Other people prayed for her. *God is going to help her change. Just 12 steps and she'll be okay. She's trying. She'll get better,* I thought to myself. At least that's what I wanted to believe, but in my heart, I knew it wasn't that easy.

My days in Juvy had a surreal rhythm, where points for good behavior were given and then just as quickly taken away. The days went something like this:

Day 1: Admission; Cry; Refuse to eat dinner (− points); Sleep.

Day 2: Wake up; Cry; Eat breakfast (+ points); Attend Juvenile Hall's idea of school (+ points); Refuse to eat all my lunch (− points); Return to my room in order to avoid others and cry in privacy (− points); Refuse to eat dinner in order to continue avoiding others (− points); Cry; Sleep. Day 3: See Day 2. And so on…

* * *

It is unclear to me exactly how long I was left in Juvy; maybe it was a few days, maybe it was a month. I just don't know. And unfortunately, shortly after my 18th birthday I had all my juvenile court records destroyed. I never even looked at them. It was a past I wanted to leave behind, but by doing so, I lost documented details that might have helped fill in where my memories got lost or confused. The only paperwork I still have documenting my time in care was hidden in my mother's folder of self-authored poems. The letter is a notice of an emancipation hearing instigated by my social worker shortly after I ran away. The letter broadly outlines my years under the Court's jurisdiction without going into all the horrible details. From reading it, I know that I became a *Dependent of the Court* for a second time on June 16, 1976, and went into my first long-term foster home on August 18, 1976. In the period between those two dates, I was sent to Juvy and later placed in my first short-term shelter home. The length of time I spent in either of those I'm not really sure about, but it was the start of a journey no child wants to experience. Starting from those first placements, I would bounce in and out of foster care until 1983, when I finally decided I had had enough of judges and courts being my parents.

Chapter 3: Delta Dawn

What I know of my mother's life before I was born or old enough to remember came from the stories my mother and her sister Ginny told me. It's hard to judge the accuracy of the information, since my mother sometimes said one thing and my aunt another. I suspect that in many cases the stories were tainted by my mother's sickness and my aunt's drinking, as well as later the dementia that stole my aunt's mind in the years prior to her death. Perhaps some of the details became distorted with time and blended with other memories. Regardless of the accuracy of each detail, what I do know is that my mother's life before and after my birth was full of misery.

Christened Joy Angeleta Adams at birth, my mother lived the early years of her life in a remote town in the Upper Peninsula of Michigan. Mom always described the town and surrounding woods as so full of chiggers and mosquitoes that people didn't really stop running from them until the snow came. Then folks spent the winter trying to survive the cold. Those long, cold winters were made colder by the poverty my mother lived in as a child. Heat and food weren't always easy to come by. Though historically a mining town that brought English, Scottish, and Irish miners, by the time my mother was born mining jobs were scarce. Mom's hard life was made even harder due to her mother Millie, and her grandmother Florence, and their own history of "sickness" that sometimes required hospitalization.

I don't know when my maternal grandmother was born. I only met Millie once, just before her death. She looked old and withered, not a pretty woman at all, but my Aunt Ginny told me she had been very attractive as a teenager. According to Ginny, my grandmother Millie attracted her fair share of suitors—and one in particular—a black-haired, blue-eyed older man named Clay, was determined to have her whether she wanted him or not. According to the stories, Millie not only didn't want Clay, she detested him.

Unfortunately for Millie, her teen years came at a time when few people had jobs and many lived together to make ends meet. To ease overcrowding in the house during the summer, Florence made Millie sleep outside in a tent behind the house. During this period Clay came by and chatted up the family, hoping to get Millie's attention, but she remained uninterested in him. Her lack of interest upset Clay and he decided he wasn't going to take "no" for an answer. So, one night he entered the tent and raped her. According to both my aunt and my mother, Millie told her mother about the attack, but Florence was convinced Millie was lying. She thought that Millie had really wanted to have sex with Clay outside of marriage. This was a scandal Florence refused to tolerate. Since Clay came from a respected family, Florence decided that Millie would have to marry him—something Clay was happy to oblige. Against her will, Millie was forced into marriage with Clay—the man who had raped her.

According to my aunt, people who knew my grandmother at that time claimed it was shortly after the wedding that she began to show signs that something was amiss in her mind. Pregnancy and parenthood followed for Millie. First she had a couple of girls, including my Aunt Ginny, then some years later a son. My mother was born second-to-last, 13 years after Ginny. With the birth of each child, Millie became progressively more unstable, and by the time my mother was born, Millie was experiencing long periods of strange behavior that made her unable to take care of her own children.

The age difference between Mom and Ginny allowed my aunt to take on a parental role to my mother. That seemed to go okay for a while, but when my mom was around three years old Aunt Ginny got married and joined a traveling carnival with her new husband. They worked their way out West to California, leaving my mother behind with Millie and Clay.

Although she had abandoned her husband and children on many occasions, it was not long after Ginny joined the carnival that Millie fled Michigan and her detested husband for California. She never came back. That left my mother and her youngest brother in the care of Clay and her paternal grandfather. My mother was around four years old at the time. This left my mother alone in a house full of men who didn't think it was their job to take care of children. Even worse, Clay's father was a known child sex offender who was once arrested for molesting the local sheriff's 5-year-old daughter. It was an awful situation to abandon any child in, and sadly, that child was my mother.

After arriving in California, Millie's mind deteriorated further and she became increasingly out of touch with reality. Needing a place to stay, she moved in with her biological uncle, who had moved to California some years earlier. Not long after she moved in, they began to have a consensual sexual relationship. According to Auntie Ginny, they did little to hide the fact they were engaging in incest, which shamed my aunt until the end of her days.

Hounded by her grown children to stop the relationship, Millie moved out of her uncle's house and became a live-in housekeeper for a couple who offered to help her. There, she began having an affair with the husband. This led to an unwanted pregnancy, which Millie hid, apparently with great success, since my Aunt Ginny visited her often during that period and had no idea Millie was with child.

My mother told me the baby was Millie's uncle's child, but Aunt Ginny said the baby was that of Millie's employer. Whoever the father was, Millie hid the pregnancy under the extra weight she carried, and loose dresses, telling no one. She gave birth to the baby, and it wasn't until years later that anyone in the family knew she had put the baby girl up for adoption immediately.

Millie's mental health continued to deteriorate after the birth of her secret daughter, and not long after that she was committed permanently to an institution for the mentally ill. She spent the next 26 years in a psychiatric institution. Sometime in those long years, the institution became primarily a place for the "criminally" insane, so I can't imagine Millie lived a happy life there. She was not released until just before her death in the early 1970s.

My mother never talked of her mother, so it was a surprise when she brought her home to stay with us for a few days when I was four or five years old. I remember Mille as an old woman in a wheelchair who lit cigarettes but forgot to smoke them until they burned down to her fingers. It was such a shock to suddenly have a grandma, especially one who would sit in a catatonic state for hours, and then suddenly sit up very straight to say, "Oatfart! By god Clay, thank you Millie! The end, and that's the truth." Then she would sink back into her wheelchair and hours would pass where she was just a silent statue in the room. Then at some moment when you had forgotten she was there, she would abruptly sit up again and repeat the same phrase. She died not long after her visit to our house and was buried at the expense of the State in an unmarked mass pauper's grave. We tried to locate the grave once to leave flowers, but we never found it among the other mass graves marked only with numbers. It made me sad even though I only met her once.

When my mother was a grown woman she found the baby Millie had put up for adoption, after she too had grown into a young woman. Her name was Susan. She and my mother grew close. I never met her (or any of my other relatives besides Aunt Ginny) because she killed herself before I was born. It's likely that she just inherited the genes that made suicide so easy in our family, and like the other relatives on my mother's side who took their own lives, Susan was doomed from birth.

* * *

While Millie unraveled in California, my mother was back in Michigan being sexually abused by her presumed grandfather, Clay's father. I say presumed because my mother did not look anything like her siblings. Where they all had dark hair, my mother was blonde. They were all tall, but my mother was short. My mother's eyes were blue like everyone else's, but they were exceptionally large, another oddity. Many people suspected that Clay was not really Mom's father, and it's possible he wasn't, since Millie's feelings toward her rapist husband and worsening periods of special sickness made her prone to sleeping around. The circumstances, along with the way my mother looked, led to rumors that my mother was actually the child of someone else. My aunt denied these rumors vehemently, but in the back of my mother's mind there was this ongoing questioning of her paternity. Sadly, the possibility of illegitimacy would later play a central role in the themes of my mother's own special sickness when she would proclaim that her "real" father was a king, some other kind of powerful leader, or even a god.

The sexual abuse of my mother started not long after Millie split for California. My mother described the abuse as brutal and said that during the attacks her grandfather often choked her. The abuse went unnoticed, or at least ignored, until my mother entered kindergarten. When her kindergarten teacher asked about the bruises on her neck, my mother told her about the things her grandfather had done to her. The Department of Social Services was called in to assess the situation, and they decided to remove her from Clay's care. Since there was no other relative to take her in, she was eventually placed in an orphanage. I'm not sure what happened to her older brother.

This is where my aunt Ginny's version and my mother's version of events begin to differ in the telling. In my aunt's version, the question of my mother's paternity led her first to the home of a stranger, not the orphanage. According to my aunt, the mother of another man came forward saying that my mother was really her son's child, and was her de facto grandchild. Apparently, the woman's request was motivated by a lack of grandchildren of her own, and she told Clay she wanted my mother to come live with her. Clay, I'm sure all too happy to unburden himself, gave my mother up easily. The way Aunt Ginny told it, the woman decided my mother was too "odd" and decided she didn't want her after all. When the woman claimed that my mother was not her son's child as she had thought, Mom was placed into an orphanage, where she was officially put up for adoption. Aunt Ginny claimed she didn't know my mother was in the orphanage until after the adoption had occurred. She insisted if she had known, she would have returned to Michigan to take her to California. My mother never had any recollection, at least that she talked about, of living with the woman my aunt described. She only remembered the orphanage and the family that adopted her later.

My mother lingered in the orphanage for two years before she was adopted by a family of fanatical Christians. Her memories of her adopted home were not pleasant. It started with her adopted parents' decision to legally change her name; not just her last name as one might expect, but also her first and middle names. She went from being Joy Angeleta Adams to being Mary Lou Kutschef. My mother hated the name and her feelings weren't helped by the fact that kids at school started calling her "Mary Loose Cat Shit." She was never allowed to use her birth name during the two years she lived with the Kutschef family. Adjusting to being someone else was hard on her.

My mother said that her role in the family was to be a scapegoat for the Kutschef's biological daughter, who was a year younger than my mother. The girl was prone to telling lies whenever she did something she wasn't supposed to. She would then blame the things she did on my mother to avoid punishment and the family always believed her. The Kutschef's followed the "spare the rod spoil the child" principle of childrearing. My mother was beaten black and blue for all transgressions, even when they were not her own. In recalling the beatings, my mother could never forget how easily her adopted sister lied to get her in trouble. She never recovered from the unfairness of it.

Just after her 9th birthday, my mother became sick. Aunt Ginny claimed her symptoms were psychological, the first signs of my mother's unstable mind. But, according to my mother, she had been diagnosed with tuberculosis, which made her defective in the Kutschef's eyes. Whatever the cause, she was seen by the Kutschef's as defective and returned to the orphanage after living with them for two years. The adoption was basically annulled as if it had never happened. Either due to the legal process or by the Kutschef's direct request, my mother was given back her birth name. No longer was she Mary Lou Kutschef; she became once again Joy Angeleta Adams. The experience of having multiple names, questionable paternity, and being unwanted marked my mother in many ways. A central theme in her life revolved around the question, "Who am I?" She never seemed to find the answer and always struggled with who she really was.

* * *

My mother was around 10 years old when Aunt Ginny found out she was back in the orphanage and sent for her. For the next three years, she lived with my aunt and her husband Eugene in the small California mountain town where I would later be raised. My mother loved Eugene (who we all called Unkie) deeply, and remembered him as a gentle and kind man (I remember him the same way). Unlike gentle Eugene, my aunt Ginny was a mean drunk and for the majority of her life a very selfish person. It was not uncommon for Aunt Ginny to beat Eugene in her drunken rages, though my uncle never raised a finger to her in response. There was one particularly horrific night when Ginny got drunk and stabbed my uncle in the arm with a broken beer bottle. Then she stormed out of the trailer, leaving my 11-year-old mother to pull the beer bottle out of Eugene's arm. Mom didn't want to remove it, but Eugene begged her to because he didn't want to go to the doctor. He didn't want to explain to anyone how the bottle got there. Mom told me she had to pull really hard before the bottle came out with a rush of blood that splattered all over my mother's legs and shoes. Eugene vomited in the sink from the pain. Sobbing, Mom helped wrap a kitchen towel tightly around Eugene's forearm to stop the bleeding. She never recovered completely from that incident; years later, she would have odd reactions anytime she saw someone bleed or vomit. Usually she would start to laugh uncontrollably, while apologizing the whole time for doing so. She couldn't stop herself, it was like a reflex. Maybe it was a way of unconsciously deflecting her deeper feelings.

The memories from that period of my mother's childhood were full of other dark moments. One incident she vividly recalled to me was lying in her bed one night and hearing a feral female cat eating her litter of newborn kittens on the roof of the trailer where they lived. There was a small air vent above my mother's bed and the cat gave birth on the roof very close to it. Mom described to me with horror how she heard the mewing of the babies and then the crunching of their bones through the open vent. Mom didn't know how many kittens were eaten, but she said it took hours before it was silent again. As she told the story to me I could see her as a terrified girl lying wide-eyed, helpless to stop the horror happening above her.

* * *

When my mother turned 13, she ran away from Aunt Ginny, and also by default, Uncle Eugene. The only other place she could think to go was to Eugene's brother's house about 120 miles away. She never said how she got there. Uncle Eugene's brother and his wife took her in after she arrived, but they made it clear they could not keep her. In the short period she stayed with them, they took her to church often. It was there that she met Greta and her first husband. They were very devout members of the church, and when they heard my mother's story they took her in as their foster child.

Sometime during this same period, my mother began dating the boy she would marry. I'm not 100 percent sure, but I think the marriage might have been prompted by my mother's pregnancy with my oldest sister, Joni. Regardless of the reason for the marriage, I think my mother's first husband must have wanted to help her. Of all the husbands my mother had, I never heard her talk negatively about him. Not long after Joni was born, my mother found herself pregnant again. After having had a very difficult three-day labor with Joni, she didn't really want the experience of having another baby. Abortion was not an option then, so my mother told me she did everything she could to try and miscarry. She rode horses as hard as she could. Cleaned the house until she was so exhausted she could barely stand. She smoked heavily and drank. Nothing worked, and by the time she was 15 years old she was the mother of two—a girl and a boy.

Aunt Ginny told me it was around the time when my first two half-siblings were born that my mother began to show signs of sickness similar to Millie's. Mom told Ginny that she "saw supernatural things in the woods," and that at night, "something was trying to get in the house." Soon, Mom didn't want to be left alone while her new husband went to work and she began having an affair. The affair led to my mother's first divorce. Not long after Mom married again, she had my next two half-siblings, Jimmy and Joanne, in quick succession. I don't know much about my mother's second marriage, but from what little I was told by Aunt Ginny and my mother, it wasn't good. It came as no surprise to anyone when that marriage, too, ended in divorce.

* * *

My mother's looks brought an almost constant stream of men into her life. Getting men was easy for her because she was very beautiful—at least until life wore her down (after that, no one would have called her pretty). During her teens and 20s she might have been described as a somewhat curvy blonde version of a young Lucille Ball. I guess I thought of her that way because of her very large blue eyes, round face, and perfect nose. Barely 5'2", she had a voluptuous body with D-cup breasts. Though she often struggled with her weight, her well-proportioned curves made her look like a seductive pixie rather than an overweight woman. For better or worse, my mother learned early that her looks could get her things in life. This meant that she valued beauty more than any skill or talent. I remember vanity as her most dominant personality trait, which is sad, because her generosity and intelligence got lost behind it.

As her beauty faded away with her youth, she became devastated. The summer I went into foster care for the first time, she seemed to be overly focused on the fact that she was getting older and constantly worried she was losing her looks. It was painful to watch, and even at a young age, I vowed never to let myself be fixated on my physical appearance because it seemed like something that was lost so easily.

Mom spent several hours every morning observing herself in front of a large circular magnifying mirror. Cigarette in hand, she would sit in the living room or at the dining table with a large collection of beauty aids. There she would primp. Her morning makeover was by far the lengthiest, but she would also take other beauty breaks throughout the day to make sure she looked attractive. She always started her morning ritual with her hair. She would use curlers, a ratting comb, and stiff hair gel to achieve the perfect pixie bouffant. Gallons of Aqua Net hairspray cemented the whole thing down. She always smoked during the process. As a kid I worried that the hairspray she used might catch on fire, but luckily, it never did.

When her hair was done, it was time for her makeup. She did this with the precision and skill of a surgeon, leaving her face beautiful even after late nights of drinking or crying. She also devoted a lot of time to her nails. My mother's nails were long, and getting them into the correct shape, perfectly smooth, and expertly colored took time and commitment. Since she didn't have a job except for the occasional house cleaning gig, the care she took to look good often seemed to me like a waste of time. Hours of effort every morning—at least the mornings she wasn't too depressed to get up—just so she could sit around the house all day looking perfect.

My oldest sister Joni inherited most of our mother's attractiveness. It might be said that she even looked the most like her, but like the rest of us, she was much taller than Mom. Even after Joni ran away and went back to her father, Mom still talked about how beautiful she was. I suspect it was because they looked so similar, and it was a way Mom could feel good about herself, too. Joni, Jimmy and I inherited Mom's blonde hair, though mine was the darkest. Jerry had red hair, and Joanne, light brown hair. Everyone had blue or green eyes. All of us girls developed ample cleavage starting at around age 11 or 12. We weren't supermodels by any stretch, but attractive enough that my mother could take pride in how her children looked.

Unfortunately, in our family beauty came with a hefty price tag. While other kids were praised for doing a good job in school or behaving properly, we were praised for looking nice. The only thing I ever remember Mom telling us, or others for that matter, was how proud she was of our looks. Somehow, in my mother's mind, her looks were enhanced through the beauty of her children. I think looks mattered to my mother so much because she never even finished junior high school, and with little education she had few avenues to follow to get ahead. Beauty got her attention and help. I guess that's why she learned to value it.

When I was little, I enjoyed looking pretty for Mom. It made me feel nice that something I did made her happy. As I grew older I liked it less. I remember being forced to sit for hours at night on the floor in front of her while she wound my hair into tight pin curls that left my scalp raw. The next morning when the pins were taken out, I was left with a mass of Shirley Temple-like curls. Mom would then clothe me in a frilly dress and parade me around our small town as if I were some sort of celebrity. On these trips, one of my mother's favorite questions to friends or strangers was, "Isn't my daughter beautiful?" It made me uncomfortable, yet I still felt happy I got to go with her into town.

For Joanne, I think Mom's focus on beauty must have been brutally painful. Joanne liked school and books. She was a straight-A student who never got into trouble. She deserved praise. Unfortunately, she was also very shy and never seemed to like being paraded around. I think she should have been Mom's favorite; and in any other family she likely would have been, but strangely, she rarely registered on Mom's radar. Looks—it was all about looks.

In addition to enduring Mom's beauty rituals, it also helped if you wanted to be seen with her, which was something my siblings rarely enjoyed. I had the distinct advantage of being just cute enough, the baby in the family, the kid who wasn't embarrassed by my mother's behavior, and the child of the only man my mother ever claimed to love. This allowed me to spend a lot of time building our bond even when Mom was very sick. Sometimes I think my siblings never had a chance once I came along. I find that so sad to think about now.

* * *

My father Martin was one of the men drawn to my mother's good looks. He was a sanitation engineer, AKA the garbage man. She said she met him while taking out the trash one day. She liked that he was physically appealing, muscular, and well over six feet tall. I can imagine that in her eyes he was a big hardworking man ready to protect a tiny vulnerable woman. Because that's what she was at the time—vulnerable. Only in her mid-twenties, she was already twice divorced with four kids. A school dropout at age 13, she had few skills and no means by which she could support herself. To make matters worse, when she met my father she was living off the charity of Greta, the woman who had been Mom's foster mother when she ran away at age 13. In spite of the fact that Greta disapproved of my mother's sinful behavior and running off at age 14, she and Mom still maintained contact over the years. Marriages, divorces, kids, hospitalizations—Greta would have no contact for a while and then pop back into Mom's life to offer assistance, usually along with a big helping of condemnation.

Tensions were high in Greta's house after Mom moved in following her second divorce. A deeply religious and overly rigid woman, Greta placed many demands on my mother and siblings that were unrealistic, given the situation. There were just too many people in the house, and Mom was not managing things well. Mom became depressed after Joni's and Jerry's father took them for a visit and refused to return them. That left only Joni and Jimmy to care for, but Mom wasn't doing that to Greta's liking. The more pressure Greta put on Mom to do things differently, the more depressed she became and things just got worse.

Greta loved Joni for all the same reasons that Mom hardly noticed her—quiet, good in school, well-behaved; but Greta couldn't handle Jimmy. Jimmy was hard for anyone to handle. Then Jimmy lit a fire in Greta's laundry room and Mom was asked to move out—immediately. The situation left my mother desperate and overwhelmed. She needed a man.

That's where my father came in. He didn't seem to care that my mother already had four kids and not a penny to her name. Given how I came to know my father later, I would say that in fact, a helpless woman suited him just fine. Wanting to rescue Mom was probably the trait she found most attractive in him, but he had other things she liked too. He liked to dance and was a great ice skater. He was a man's man—he hunted, fished, camped, and could throw one hell of a punch when someone pissed him off. For a woman who felt so helpless in the world, his manliness provided a magnetic pull she had no desire to resist. However, like most of the men who entered my mother's life, he was a conglomeration of good and bad traits. In time, she would come to learn that the bad traits far outnumbered the good.

My parents had a whirlwind courtship due to the fire. Dad moved everyone into a motel and paid for whatever they needed until they found a suitable house. I'm not sure when he proposed, but somewhere along the way they were married and moved to the small mountain town where I grew up. Mom had insisted on the move because she wanted to be near her sister Ginny again. The marriage lasted seven years. My mother described the first two years of their marriage as wonderful, but what made them wonderful, I'm not sure. I only remember the period after their marriage had turned ugly and they were well on their way to a divorce. Those times were impossible to forget.

* * *

The first memories I have of my parent's relationship are of the period when we were living in an A-frame house with dangerously steep wooden steps. The house was painted a slate blue and was located not far from town. I must have been around three or four at the time. We had a beautiful German Shepherd named Smokey, and Joni and Jerry had returned from their father's house to live with us again. Mom was so relieved to have all her children finally living under one roof. If it hadn't been for my father's temper and my mother's moods it might have been a beautiful period of my childhood.

The A-frame was within walking distance to the lake, and my father frequently went fishing, often with us kids in tow. The strange thing about my father being a fisherman was that he didn't like to eat fish. We kids, however, had to eat whatever he caught whether we liked fish or not. For my father fishing was about the sport. He loved the challenge of fish that fought hard, which made catfish one of his favorite trophies. As an avid fisherman he made an effort to instill in us kids his passion for the sport. And, when I was very young, I did find excitement in watching him land a flopping fish onto the shore.

It was with Dad's help that I caught my first fish before I could ride a bike. Proudly, I brought it home from the lake and draped the stringer it was hanging from over the doorknob of our coat closet.

"Jean, take that fish off the doorknob and put it outside," Mom said.

"No, Mommy, it's mine! I caught it myself," I whined.

"Jean, you can't keep it"—Mom said, walking over to the closet and lifting the fish stringer from the doorknob—"because it will rot."

"No, Mommy! Give it back," I yelled. I ran over and held the fish stringer against the closet door.

"Let her keep it. It is her first fish, huh, Jean? You caught it all by yourself," Dad said with a chuckle.

Of course, I didn't really catch the fish all by myself. I just helped Dad reel it in on my pole. I was proud of the fish, but even more, I liked that my father was proud of me. We had gone fishing countless times at the lake near our house, but I had never caught a fish before that day. Normally, I would just go and play in the dirt while Dad fished. I would have preferred to play in the water, but if I did, Dad would yell at me for scaring the fish away.

Dad always kept a pole in the water on my behalf whether I was fishing or not. Kids didn't need a fishing license so he could increase his odds of catching something without any added expense. If the Game Warden came around, Dad would just point to me or my siblings and say the extra poles were ours. This was a lie because most the time Dad wouldn't even let us touch the poles. That day when I caught my first fish, instead of telling me to stay out of the way, Dad had let me hang out near him with an unusual show of warmth. Probably because the fish were biting like crazy and he was in a good mood. After catching his limit of trout and catfish, he called me over to reel in a fish he had snagged on my line. Daddy's little girl became, just for a moment, the little boy he had really wanted. When we landed the fish it turned out to be a small carp, nothing we could eat, but I didn't want Dad to throw it back. Instead, I carried it back home on the stringer, feeling proud.

Though Mom wanted the carp off the doorknob and back outside as soon as possible, she was not up to the fight it would take to change Dad's mind. Instead, she lined the floor under the fish with newspaper. The little carp hung lifeless on the doorknob all day in the summer heat. When the smell in the house worsened, Mom repeated her attempt to throw the fish out. I flailed my arms and stomped my feet, demanding that she put my fish back. Once again, Dad came to my rescue. He laughed, and told Mom, "Leave it hand there a bit longer. It won't harm noth'n." In that moment, I was filled with love and admiration for him. Later in the day, my mother was beside herself with disgust and my father realized he could no longer support my position.

"Half-Pint, let's take the fish outside so we can really look at it, okay?" Dad said.

"How come, Daddy? I want to keep it. You said I could keep it," I whined.

"Look Half-Pint, you can keep it, but we have to take it outside."

I knew better than to argue. Reluctantly, I removed the stringer from the door and followed my father. Dad took the fish from me and put it on the stump of an old cut tree. He manipulated the mouth and showed me the tongue and tiny teeth lining the fish's jaw. I found it fascinating. After he went back into the house, I stayed there to take the fish apart and look at its insides. I picked up a stick and began poking at its lifeless body. I was completely fascinated with its eyes. I tried to remove them with the stick but they just kept rotating around and around. No matter what I tried, I just couldn't get them out.

Engrossed with the fish, I didn't hear my parents' argument until my father slammed the door and got into his truck. My mother came out shortly after screaming at him, "Martin, you son of a bitch! You piece of shit! Fuck you!" Then she slumped down on the porch and began crying. My father drove off. I looked up, frightened, and saw blood running from my mother's mouth. Her lips were split, and I could see a red welt on the side of her face. I was frozen in place. My oldest brother came out and took her back inside. I stood in the yard holding the stick, not sure what to do. I wanted to go inside to check on her, but I couldn't make my feet move. The front door was still open and I could hear my mother repeating over and over again between sobs, "That son of a bitch! That worthless son of a bitch!"

In the chaos of the moment, I was forgotten. I stood in the yard staring down at the lifeless fish, suddenly feeling very bad for it. "I'm sorry, fish. I wish I hadn't hurt you," I whispered.

*　*　*

Such violent fights between my mother and father happened on at least a weekly basis. I'm not sure who started them or what caused them, but only threats of arrest could stop the brutality they inflicted on each other. Over the last year of my parents' marriage when we were still living in the place next to my aunt, almost every item in our house was damaged. Dishes, silverware, knick-knacks, and pieces of furniture were smashed during fits of anger, thrown out windows, or kicked to pieces. Some became projectiles meant to harm the other person. I remember the fights seemed to just come out of nowhere, often at night after I had gone to sleep. My parents' screaming, the first sign of the violence to come, would usually wake me up. While their fights raged on downstairs I would cower under my blankets hoping it would all be over soon, but rarely did their fights end quickly. My parents' fights were terrifying and usually only ended after my mother or one of us kids got physically hurt.

* * *

"Martin, you mother fucker, don't you touch my car! Martin, don't you dare, don't you fucking dare!" Mom shrieked one night, shortly before my parents' divorce. Upstairs, I heard the front door slam and my parents' angry voices moved outside. Their screaming was followed by the shattering of glass. "You fucking bastard, Martin. Here, you want to ruin my car? Well, two can play that game!" Mom shouted. Her words were punctuated by loud metallic thuds. Then there was the sound of my father's truck starting and tires spinning in the gravel. I could hear my mother sobbing in the yard until one of my brothers brought her back into the house.

The next day, I saw Mom's cuts and bruises. I listened to her relive the night in a conversation with Aunt Ginny over beers. "The asshole threw a log though the windshield of my car. Can you believe that? Bastard! But, I didn't take it lying down. I fucked up his truck with the shovel," Mom said. Aunt Ginny laughed and Mom joined in. Looking at Mom's black eye, I didn't understand how she could find it funny.

***

We did our best to live with the ongoing violence. Like poverty, it was something we didn't like but had no power to change. When we moved to the White House, the brutality my father inflicted only escalated, and we kids became targets just as often as Mom. I remember once when we were playing cards quietly in my brothers' room when Dad abruptly walked in. "Who got this peanut butter on the bedspread?" he demanded, pointing to Jimmy's bedspread. Everyone in the room tensed. We all had small plates with crackers and peanut butter beside us. Mine had fallen from my plate when I sat down on the bed. I looked at the spot Dad was pointing to and mumbled, "me." But, I had said it too quietly for him to hear.

"What did you say, Jean?" he asked harshly. I was suddenly frozen speechless. All I could do was stare at the small spot of peanut butter smeared into the fabric of my brother's bedspread. Everyone remained still and silent.

"Who got the peanut butter on the fucking bedspread? Did you do it, Jean? Tell me right now," Dad demanded. I could feel the anger emanating from his tense body. My mind wandered to the image of my brother Jimmy being beaten with a belt by Dad just a few days before. My heart raced. I continued to stare down at the bedspread in silence. *If Dad hits me like he hits Jimmy, I'm going to die*, I thought.

Patience gone, Dad grabbed my chin and pulled my face up to look at him. "Did you do this, Jean?" he asked again.

"I didn't do it," I blurted almost unconsciously.

"Who did it then?"

"It was Jimmy and Joanne," I lied.

"No we didn't, it was Jean," Jimmy protested.

"I'm going to ask this one time, and you better tell the truth. Who got peanut butter on the bedspread?"

"Jean did it, I swear," Jimmy cried. Joanne nodded her head in agreement.

"It wasn't me! I swear, Dad," I sobbed.

Dad advanced toward Jimmy and Joanne where they sat on the floor. "You liars! Don't you ever lie to me again!" he yelled, as he grabbed Joanne by her hair and threw her out of the bedroom door. She landed on the stairs that led to the living room. She couldn't stop the force of Dad's throw and tumbled the rest of the way down the staircase and into the wall at the bottom.

Jimmy tried to intervene to keep Joanne from being thrown, but once my father's hands were free, he lifted Jimmy up and threw him against the wall of the bedroom. He hit with such force that he just went limp and slid down into a heap. Stunned, I stood motionless and I stared at my brother slumped against the wall, unconscious. Everything felt weird and unreal. I was too startled to even cry. My daze was broken when my father yelled, "Jean, go to bed in your room right now!" As I passed the stairs leading from the landing, I could see my sister sobbing as she tried to stand. I started to cry soundlessly because I knew if my father heard me he would hit me.

Back in the room I shared with Joanne, I silently opened the door to our closet and crept inside. From the floor of the closet I picked up my ragged-eared stuffed mouse and began to rock him, an attempt to soothe us both. It was not very long before I heard my sister come into the room. The bed squeaked as she laid down. The door of the closet was not thick enough to muffle the sound of her sobs. I wanted to comfort her, but I was too ashamed to come out. I knew, and of course my sister knew, that I was the one who dropped the peanut butter on the bed. The lie would haunt me the rest of my life.

* * *

It was a public act of brutality against my mother that finally put my father in jail. I was not present for the event that led to his incarceration, but according to my Aunt Ginny who was drinking with my mother at the time, my father went into a jealous rage and yanked my mother from a barstool and dragged her out the door. Her clothes were ripped in the process. He then beat her badly and left her partially naked and bloody in the snow outside the bar. My mother was taken to the hospital, but as usual, she refused to press charges. Laws on the books in California at the time required the battered spouse press charges. If they didn't, the cops could not make an arrest. So Dad was never arrested in all the fights we kids had to witness. Usually, if the cops came at all, Dad would just be told to leave the house for a while to "cool off."

After the very public beating of my mother at the bar, it was the local judge and his wife who forced her to finally file charges. Judge Wolfe and his wife Sunny were friends with both my parents. When they weren't fighting or wasted, my parents were well-liked, especially my father. I remember that Judge Wolfe and Sunny would have us all over to dinner on occasion. I loved to go there because everything seemed so different than at our house. They were nice people, and they had children our ages. My parents would stay downstairs talking and laughing with the Wolfes after dinner while we kids played games or watched their pet chinchilla dust itself.

When Judge Wolfe heard about my mother's trip to the hospital for serious injuries, he told Mom she had to file charges because it was the only way to make Dad stop hitting her. She was reluctant, but under pressure, she eventually went to the police department to file. I'm not sure if it was Judge Wolfe who sentenced my father, but it was a very lenient sentence. Dad was given weekends in jail so that he could continue to work during the week and provide for the family. Every Friday evening we would drive down the mountain to the jail to drop him off. On Sunday afternoons we picked him up.

The trips to the jail were weird. As soon as she saw Dad pull in from work on Fridays, Mom would spring into action. "Jean, go get your coat and a plastic bag. We have to take Daddy down the hill," she would say, as she fixed her hair and makeup for the drive. I would get my coat from the closet and on the way through the kitchen stuff a couple of leftover plastic bread bags into my pockets. Then we would pile out of the house to the truck, still warm from Dad's trip home from work.

Mom would make me sit in the center of the front seat between her and my dad. My siblings would climb into the bed of the truck. With Dad driving, we'd start down the mountain. Cold wind often swept up through the steep mountain ravines that fell off from the main highway that led to the city below. Turning to look into the back of the truck, I would see my siblings hunched against the rear of the cab for protection against the wind. As the road left the crest of the mountain known as Top-Town, sharp turns began to appear in rapid succession and my Dad loved to take each corner at top speed. My siblings swayed against each other while they clung to the sides of the truck. But, rather than looking scared, they laughed. I wanted to be outside with them but Mom always said I was still too little.

About halfway down the mountain, I would start to feel queasy and say, "Mom, I feel sick. Can we pull over?"

"Just stare straight ahead at the center line, Baby. You'll be fine," she'd always reply. I'd look straight ahead but it didn't help.

"I'm going to throw up. Please, can we pull over?" I'd whine.

"No Jean, there isn't any time. Your dad has to be at the jail before 6:00 p.m. Just throw up in the bag," Mom would tell me, as she patted my back.

I'd hold off for as long as I could. Then I'd have to retch into the bag. The smell permeated the cab of the truck. I'd watch the vomit move about through the clear places in the plastic bread bag and I'd retch again. "Jean, quit that! You don't need to throw up. It's all in your head," Dad would say harshly. He was always annoyed by any show of weakness.

Sometimes if Dad was in a good mood he'd try to distract me from my queasiness.

"Hey Half-Pint, why don't you climb up on my lap and steer the truck," he would say.

"Really Daddy, I can?" I'd ask excitedly, just to be sure.

"Martin, these roads are too dangerous for that," Mom would interject with concern.

"It'll be fine. Come on Half-Pint, climb over on Daddy's lap," Dad would say with a grin.

Gleefully, I'd climb over onto my dad's lap, put my hands on the steering wheel, and instantaneously, I wouldn't feel sick anymore. Instead, I'd feel exhilarated. Dad would drop his hand down to the side of the steering wheel without touching it, ready to take control again when necessary. Gripping the steering wheel tightly, I'd move it in the direction of the curves, but I wasn't very good at it. The car would swerve toward the center line and sometimes toward the cliff edge.

"Martin, please put your hands on the wheel," Mom would beg. My father would just laugh and then quickly put the truck back in the right place. Then he'd take his hands off again.

"Stop it, Martin! Please, I can't take it! You're going to get us killed," Mom would cry, while my siblings stared wide-eyed through the rear window into the cab of the truck to see what was going on.

"Half-Pint, your mother doesn't want you to steer. How about you work the brakes?" Dad would say, giving me a wink.

"Okay, but I can't reach."

"Sure you can, just slide down a bit."

I'd slide down my father's lap so I was lying directly under the steering wheel while putting both of my feet over the brake pedal. Dad would lift his foot off the gas. "Go ahead Half- Pint, slow the car," he'd say while my mother gripped the dash in front of her. Using both feet, I'd push the brake pedal as directed by my father, usually all the way to the floor. The truck would jerk to a stop, and Mom would scream. In the back, my siblings laughed nervously with their faces pressed against the rear window. I'd take my feet off the brake pedal and the car would roll forward. Then I'd push it down again, bringing the truck once more to a jerking stop. Everyone would laugh except Mom. Then my parents would begin one of their all-too familiar escalating arguments.

"Martin this isn't funny. You're going to get us in an accident. Please stop," Mom would say.

"It's fine. We're barely moving. She can't do any harm."

"What about the cars coming around a corner behind us. They might hit us."

"You worry too much. It's fine."

"Martin, I can't handle this. Just take over. We need to get to the jail."

"You're not driving, are you? Don't tell me what to do! I'm at the wheel here."

Whenever I sensed a real fight might start, I would take my feet and hands off of the controls and sit very still. The truck would roll forward, gaining speed and Dad would have to take over to keep us on the road.

"Okay Half-Pint, why don't you climb back to the middle? I'll take over from here," he would say, his voice low and deep as he fought to control his anger.

Once we reached the jail, Dad would say his goodbyes and kiss my mother if he wasn't mad for some reason. Then he would walk inside to serve his time.

For the return trip, Mom would get behind the wheel of the truck and Joanne would usually take the seat next to me in the cab to get warm. Then we'd start back up the mountain. The trip back up was somber. Mom actually hated it when Dad left her alone, and she felt sad about his having to serve time. Halfway up the mountain, I'd get sick again and puke into the second empty bread bag, hating myself and car rides with equal loathing.

When Sunday rolled around we'd repeat the process in reverse: Mom would drive down and Dad would drive up. This went on for about eight weeks.

* * *

After Dad served his time in jail, my parent's marriage was never the same. Not long after, he left the house to get gas and pick up a pack of cigarettes. He didn't come back. Not long after that, he filed for divorce after meeting another woman he found slumped over, sick, at a bus stop. She needed him more than Mom, I guess. Mom fell apart. She began spending a lot more time in bars and bringing home men she'd picked up.

In Dad's absence, I felt lost and bewildered, even if I spent less time being afraid. It was the first time I remember us kids fending for ourselves by cooking meals and getting off to the bus stop in time for school without help. Strange men came and went. Mom's behavior, usually distorted by alcohol, became more and more unpredictable. My two oldest siblings, Joni and Jerry, left the mountain to live with their father after my mother married some guy she'd known just a few months. He fought with Mom just as much as my dad had, the only difference being he was much smaller so their fights were more likely to end in a draw. Our new stepdad's presence led Joni to run away again, though the cops brought her back to the house just a few days later. That's when Joni's and Jerry's father sent for them. Mom had the marriage annulled, so the problems did not last very long. But, by then the damage was done; my oldest siblings were already gone. I would not see them again until I was an adult.

Weeks passed, then months. Christmas was around the corner and we were broke. Mom applied for welfare when our refrigerator sat empty for days and there was no man to fill it. We also stood in line at the food bank for blocks of Government cheese, surplus canned juice, and potted meat, which all tasted terrible. My siblings and I tried hard to ignore the desperation that seemed to seep into every family activity. Just before

Christmas, someone from the church we used to attend dropped off a bag of wrapped unmarked toys. We were super excited and randomly marked them with our names without knowing the sex and age level the gifts were meant for.

On Christmas morning, we woke early and ran downstairs to open our gifts. Mom remained in bed, depressed. Once the gifts were torn from their wrapping paper there was a lot of confusion and disappointment. I got a wooden glider while my brother got a doll. Other gifts were also mismatched to the recipient. Without adult guidance to solve our dilemma we decided to deal with the problem ourselves.

"Look Jean, I have a doll. Isn't she pretty? If you give me the pen and the wooden glider, I'll give her to you," Jimmy said.

"How come you get two gifts?" I asked.

"Because stupid, she's bigger than the other two gifts put together." Jimmy replied, which made sense to me.

"Okay," I agreed, handing over the items.

Soon the piles of gifts were very unevenly distributed. Being the youngest and most easily duped, my pile was the smallest. Out of guilt, my siblings gave me the gifts they really hated, even some they had taken on trade earlier to get rid of something they wanted even less. Besides the doll, I got a calendar organizer, a little address book, some cheap plastic opera glasses, and a copy of the Book of Mormon.

Back in my room, I introduced my new doll to my old stuffed mouse. Together we crawled into the safety of the closet. It was hot and stuffy and smelled of dirty socks. For a moment, I was comforted by its familiarity. I tried to lose myself in a fantasy adventure between the doll and the mouse. Sadness crept into our game, and I put them both aside. I felt disappointed that Santa didn't come. Santa used to come when Dad lived with us. Santa at least knew what I wanted, and Mom didn't cry on Christmas. Sitting there in my sanctuary, I wondered if Dad was ever coming back.

***

A month or so after Christmas my father did come back, but just briefly. I was surprised by his visit. My parents didn't fight, so I guess Mom knew he was coming and why. They talked in the kitchen. A bit later, Mom called me in and told me my Dad wanted to take me out alone. The news made me very nervous.

"What about Jimmy and Joanne, can they come too?" I asked.

"No Jean, your Dad just wants to take you out," Mom replied.

"Come on Half-Pint, I'll get you a cream soda. I know it's your favorite," Dad said.

He took my hand and led me out to his truck. Mom waved from the steps as we backed out of the driveway. She looked really sad. Snow still lined the road in shaded areas. As we drove, I was unable to shake the shyness I usually experienced with strangers.

"How you been, Kiddo?" Dad asked.

"Okay," I replied. It was a lie, but I didn't want him to think that Mom hadn't been taking care of me.

"Whatcha been up to?"

I stared nervously down at my lap and said, "Nothing." Dad gave up trying to get me to talk, and we drove in silence until we reached our destination. Gravel crunched under the tires as we pulled into the driveway of Dad's friend Charlie's house. I knew the house because I had been there a couple of times before. Charlie was older than my Dad and had a white beard. I remembered him as being nice. Still, I was surprised that Charlie's was where Dad had decided to take me.

Charlie came out of the house to greet us. The men shook hands. "Martin! What a surprise. It's good to see you. It's been awhile. And look who's with you—a cute little princess. Come on inside and get warm," Charlie said with a big smile.

Inside, Christmas lights still hung in the windows. The room was warm and smelled of burning wood.

"Sit down. Sit down. What can I get you and this pretty little thing?" Charlie asked.

"Got any cream soda?" Dad inquired.

"Sorry Martin, I don't. But I've got root beer."

"Jean, how about a root beer?" Dad asked.

"Okay," I agreed, with a tinge of disappointment.

We sat down on stools in front of a small wooden bar. After we got our drinks, Dad and Charlie spent some time catching up. I stared at the blinking Christmas lights and the fake snow sprayed on the windows. Eventually, Dad leaned over and said something quietly to Charlie.

"Oh, I'm sorry to hear that, Martin. I'll be in the kitchen. Just yell if you need anything else," Charlie said, before retreating into the back of the house.

Dad scooted his stool closer to me and said, "Jean, I came to visit you today because I need to tell you something important." Then he paused and looked around the room as if he was uncomfortable. I waited. He began again.

"You know your mom and I aren't living together anymore. Sometimes people do that and they go live in different places. That's what's happened with your mom and me."

"Are you ever coming back to live with us?" I asked.

"No Half-Pint, that won't ever happen again. I live far away now with someone else."

"Will I see you again?"

"Sure you will Honey, but maybe not so often. But I promise, I'll be back to visit you and you'll come visit me," Dad said.

I didn't say anything and dropped my head to stare at my lap. For some reason the conversation made me feel sad. Though Dad scared me, I still missed him. I also knew that Mom missed him too.

After that visit, my father never returned like he said he would. There were no letters or phone calls. Mom, if she talked about him at all, used only swear words like "bastard" to describe him. His presence was replaced by a string of other men, and after a year or so, I had difficulty remembering what he looked like exactly. Sometimes, I would ask Mom when he was going to come visit me again. Usually, she just got mad and cursed him, so I stopped asking. On my 8th birthday, hoping that somehow the special occasion would make him appear, I asked Mom again if he would come visit me. She told me he was dead. After that I tried to not think about him at all.

Chapter 4: Smiling Faces Sometimes

The day I left Juvy, I was dressed in my personal clothing, minus my earrings, which I clutched in my hand because the holes in my ears had closed. Seeing them in my hand made me feel so mad. A detention worker I had never met before led me through several locked doors to a waiting room near the entrance. I was feeling uncertain, but in high spirits thinking my mother had finally come to get me. Before we entered the waiting room that led to the exit, I peered through the thick glass windows and saw a woman I didn't recognize waving to me. She had an outdated bouffant hairdo, long nails, and gobs of gaudy jewelry. Although she was smiling broadly, something about her made the hairs stand up on the back of my neck. I would have this feeling again years later when I first saw Tammy Fae-Baker on TV, a painted-on smile while the face underneath emoted something far different.

The woman handling my release introduced the dreadful woman as my new foster mother. She explained I would be leaving Juvy for a temporary placement known as shelter care.

"This is Mrs. Gibson, Jean," the detention worker told me, as she pushed me in front of the stranger.

"You go ahead and call me Mom, sweetheart. That's what all my foster kids call me," the Tammy Fae look-alike told me quickly.

Calling her "Mom" was the last thing on earth I wanted to do. I had only been motherless for a short period, and I didn't think I should trade in my real mom for a strange woman. Yet, I wasn't brave enough to ignore the woman's demand.

"Nice to meet you—Mom," I replied. I felt like a traitor saying it.

I was officially passed from the care of the detention center staff to the woman. My new "mom" helped me pick out a few outfits from the donation bin because I had arrived at Juvy with nothing but what I had on when the cop came for me. I was used to hand-me-down clothes, so I didn't mind that part so much, but the things in the box felt unlike me somehow. Once we had a few outfits, the woman led me to her car and we left Juvy behind.

Following a short trip through the city, we pulled into the driveway of single-story ranch-style home. Getting out of the car, I glanced at the other carbon-copy homes lining the street of the lower middleclass neighborhood. They all looked the same. The neighborhood was so different from my small mountain community; there, every house was somehow unique. Not even an hour out of Juvy, I already felt misplaced. It was not a good feeling. It didn't help that thick smog blanketed the city and hid the mountains where I had grown up. When I looked to the horizon where they should have been, it was as if they had been erased. A lost feeling came over me. *Will I ever go home again?* I wondered.

We entered the house through the side door; the front door was reserved only for guests. Once inside, I was introduced to the other foster children, a girl a few years older and two boys younger than me. My new foster father was at work. I later learned his presence was rarely felt around the house, that is, until harsh punishment needed to be doled out. "Mom" told me to go with my new "sister" so she could show me our room and explain the rules. Turns out there were lots of them.

"You can't speak unless you ask permission first. You are not allowed in the living room until Mom or Dad invites you. That's yours," she rattled, as she pointed to the bed that was to be mine. "You can never go into anyone's room except your own. You must do all of your chores every day. There is a list posted on the refrigerator. This is your dresser,"—again, she pointed—"It's really important you remember what I'm telling you or you will be in trouble. Every day you must also make your bed. Do you know how to make a bed with military corners?"

I shook my head.

"Okay, I'll show you. You have to do this right or you'll be punished, so watch closely," she said, as she pulled the blanket and top sheet off the bed. Quickly, she remade it military-style, folding the corners of the sheet and blanket tightly into a crisp seam and then tucked them under the mattress.

The next morning, I learned that somehow I missed a critical step in her demonstration. Standing next to my bed, I found myself unsure what to do so I made it the way I used to when I helped my mom. I carefully smoothed out the wrinkles in the top sheet, tucked it in straight at the bottom and folded it over a few inches at the top. Then I put the blanket over the sheet, followed by the bedcover, leaving enough at the top to carefully cover my pillow. It looked nice, but during the mandatory morning chore check, my new "mom" angrily pointed out my failure to make the bed correctly with military corners. After lifting up the bottom corner of the bedcover, she told me to come and stand right next to her.

"Didn't you learn to make a bed right at home?" she asked.

"That is how I make it at home," I said, confused that there might be only one correct way to make a bed.

"Well, it's wrong! I'm going to show you one time how to make it right. Then you'll make it by yourself, and you won't get breakfast until it's perfect," she said, before remaking the bed the "right way" with lightning speed. "Now, you do it!" she said, and stepped back to watch.

I repeated the process of smoothing the sheets and blankets perfectly the way she did. Starting with the sheet, I folded the bottom corners and then the sides in crisp lines and tucked them under the mattress. Again it looked nice, but there was a small wrinkle in the middle of the bed and she made me do it again.

On my third try, I was able to do it to her satisfaction, and I was permitted to have breakfast.

Making my bed correctly was not the only rigidly dictated chore I was required to do. Bathroom cleaning, dish washing, dusting, vacuuming—all had to be done each day with military precision. Poor performance meant punishment; repeated failure meant severe punishment. There was something scary about my new mom's obsession with perfect cleanliness. The most frightening exhibition of her sickness appeared about a week into my stay. As my foster sister sat coloring on the couch while I sat on the living room floor playing a game with my two younger foster brothers, our "mom" came into the room, extremely irate.

"Who used the toilet last and forgot to flush it?" Mom asked, holding a folded leather belt in one hand.

Palpable fear crept across the faces of all us kids and no one replied. Our silence only made her angrier. With mounting fury she pressed us for an answer.

"Who? Who did it? Tell me right now who forgot to flush the toilet!" she shouted.

We stared at her, fearing punishment and simultaneously each of us blurted out a jumble of almost the same words: "It wasn't me! I didn't do it! It must have been someone else."

Unsatisfied, she pressed us harder. Her tone was flat and cold as she spoke through gritted teeth. "I know one of you is lying. Someone left a BM in the toilet. I suggest you tell me who did it. Speak up, because I know one of you did it," she hissed.

Again, we were silent. I was confused about what a "BM" was, but I didn't dare ask for clarification.

"I suggest that if any of you know who didn't flush the toilet, you tell me. Otherwise, I will punish all of you! I'll get the truth one way or another. If someone doesn't speak up, I will give each and every one of you enemas. I'll match what's inside you with what's in the toilet," she said.

There was total conviction, in her voice and I knew she wasn't joking. With a kind of chilling clarity, I suddenly understood what a BM was—it was shit. I already knew what an enema was because my mom had been badly constipated once and had borrowed an enema bag from my auntie. Knowing what an enema involved, I was sure I didn't want one. Churning with fear and revulsion, I waited, hoping one of the other kids would confess to their crime. We were individually paraded into the bathroom to look into the toilet and asked if it was ours. Before my turn came, I silently begged for the culprit to fess up. *Come on...just tell her.* But, each remained silent.

When I came back from my turn, one of the boys was pulling at a thread in the rug and the other sat frozen, staring into his lap. My foster sister remained silent too. *It's not mine, but I'm not getting an enema,* I thought in disgust. I decided to take responsibility. Somehow I found the courage to tell my new foster mother I had done it, because I couldn't imagine her giving me or the poor little boys a forced enema. "I did it Mom. I didn't mean to. I just forgot to flush. I'm sorry," I said repeatedly. As I spoke, I kept hoping that my confession would draw the real culprit out due to guilt, but I wished in vain. My foster siblings just looked away.

I knew I would be punished. Still, that was preferable to an enema administered by a crazy woman. My imagination ran wild thinking about what that would be like. I could envision us waiting as cries from the current enema recipient echoed through the bathroom door, with each of us desperately hoping the guilty party's poop would match before our turn came. The images in my head left me feeling sick. Although I was upset I had to take the blame for someone else's poor bathroom habits—one of the younger boys probably—I did not want an enema! Perhaps that's why my false confession came out easily.

Following a whipping with the belt, I was forced to clean not just the toilet, but also the entire bathroom using a toothbrush and bleach. Long after the other kids had gone to bed, I was still on my hands and knees scrubbing. During the hours of cleaning I thought about my real mom. I wondered how come people thought I was better off with this woman rather than with her. This woman wasn't treating me better, she was treating me worse. Even if my foster mom didn't drink, I felt less safe with her than I did at home with my real mom. It was a terrible feeling.

* * *

Sometime during my first shelter placement, my 9th birthday came and went unnoticed. The only special thing we did during my entire stay there was go to the beach. I had never been to the beach, at least not that I could remember, so as beach day approached I became very excited. My favorite show at that time was the *Undersea World* with Jacques Cousteau. When I lived with my mom, I never missed an episode. So I couldn't wait to see the ocean. The trip was the only thing I had to look forward to in my terrible new life. When beach day arrived, I woke early and quickly went through my morning chores. When they were finished I went into the kitchen. Our foster mom was in the midst of preparing breakfast. As the other foster kids filed in, I helped set the table. Oatmeal was bubbling on the stove. As I was putting silverware and napkins on the table, I saw my youngest foster brother staring morosely at the oatmeal. "Is that for breakfast?" he asked me quietly. I nodded. "I don't like oatmeal. Do I have to eat it?" he asked again in a desperate whisper. I nodded one more time.

Hearing our exchange, "Mom" piped in, "Of course you have to eat it."

"But I don't like it. It makes me sick," he told her cautiously.

"I don't care if it makes you sick! That's what we are having for breakfast, and you will eat it, period! Now stop arguing and eat. The sooner everyone finishes, the sooner we can go to the beach," she told him, placing a large bowl of oatmeal on the table in his spot.

"Dad" arrived at the table shortly after, said the prayer, and we began to eat. While we ate, my foster brother listlessly moved his spoon around in the bowl. I felt bad for him. He was only four or five years old and seemed scared all the time.

"Eat that right now young man!" our foster father yelled at the boy, startling the rest of us kids because he usually wasn't around, and when he was, he was quiet.

"Please, I can't. It makes me sick," the little boy begged.

"You eat it right now, or you'll get the belt!" replied Dad. I watched with a horrible sinking feeling as tears welled in my youngest foster brother's eyes.

"I can't," he whispered weakly.

"We'll see about that. The rest of you kids finish quick and go outside," Dad ordered.

We gulped our food down and went out the kitchen door into the backyard. I sat on the small swing set feeling awful for the boy, as well as frustrated that our trip to the beach might not happen. My other foster siblings took up positions around me, but none of us talked. Inside we heard our foster parents yelling.

"You'll eat that or else," Mom said sternly.

"Please, I can't," the boy whimpered.

"You have ten minutes. When we come back in here your bowl better be empty. If it's not, you'll get the belt," Dad yelled.

Then it was silent except for my foster brother's sobs. We waited, the minutes going by at an agonizingly slow pace. My older foster sister became annoyed with the wait. "What a stupid baby! Why doesn't he just eat it so we can go to the beach? He's ruining it for the rest of us," she said. I agreed with her but said nothing. I thought about when I got hit with the belt the night I had to clean the bathroom. I wanted to go to the beach so bad, the wait was awful. Finally, my foster sister could stand it no more.

"Jean, go find out what's going on," she demanded. "It's already been ten minutes."

"No, you go! You're the oldest," I replied, holding on tighter to the chains of the swing.

"Come on, just go. If you do, I'll show how to catch sand crabs when we get to the beach." *Sand crabs*, that sounded cool. I knew how to catch snakes, lizards, spiders, and even bees in a jar, but I didn't know how to catch crabs. I pondered her offer for a few seconds.

"Okay, I'll do it. But you have to promise cross-your-heart that you'll really show me how to catch crabs," I told her.

"I promise," she said, making the sign of the cross over her heart.

"You better not be lying!" I said, staring hard at the girl. "Okay, I'll go, but I want my swing back when I'm done."

"Be careful, Jean," my other foster brother cautioned.

I got up and moved toward the small window in the back door that looked into the kitchen. I ducked down, trying to keep out of sight. Slowly I moved my head up to peer in. Just as I did our foster parents re-entered the room. A belt was clutched in our foster dad's hand. They looked at the untouched bowl of oatmeal. "I told you to eat that! You're going to eat it!" screamed Mom, as she snatched the spoon from the bowl. Grabbing our foster brother by the hair, she forced a large spoonful of oatmeal into his mouth. He tried to swallow but gagged and vomit rushed out. "Oh, no you don't!" she screamed, forcing vomited oatmeal back into his mouth with the spoon. Choking on oatmeal and vomit, he began to cry very hard. Our foster dad pulled him from his chair. In one swift move he ripped down his pants and began beating him with the belt. I couldn't watch and moved away from the window. His screams echoed through the walls out into the backyard. My foster siblings looked at me, but no one asked what was going on inside—they didn't have to. I no longer cared about the beach. I only cared about going back home. I sat in silence and wondered if that was ever going to happen.

* * *

About a month later, a social worker arrived one day to pick me up and take me to my new placement. I felt immediately safe with the woman because she was not even five feet tall. There was something comforting in being with an adult about my height. She introduced herself as Mrs. Hill and shook my hand with a warm smile on her face.

She said, "Jean, I'm going to be driving you to your new home today."

"Will my mom be there?" I asked.

"No Sweetie, she won't. She can't take care of you right now. But guess what? I am taking you live with someone you know. Walter and Greta Baker have agreed to take you while your mother is getting better. You remember them, don't you? Greta was your mother's foster mom when she was a girl and now she will be yours. Does that sound good?"

The news made me sad, but I nodded. I wanted to go back home and be with my mom. Still, I was willing to take Grandma and Grandpa Baker over my current crazy foster parents any day. Enemas and beatings over tiny infractions were not something I felt I could survive for long.

My soon-to-be ex-foster mom helped me put what few clothes I had into a garbage bag, an item destined to become my luggage for the next eight years. As we packed, my foster siblings hung back in silence, looking morose. Our enema-wielding foster mom talked to my new case worker in a sunny voice, making comments about how sad she was to see me leave. I wanted to scream—"*Stop it; you're just pretending to be nice!*"—but I couldn't make the words come out because of the fear that seemed to live constantly in my belly.

My new social worker helped me put my things in the car. I got in and fastened my seatbelt. Then we pulled out of the driveway. As I watched my first foster home recede into the distance I felt intense relief.

It wasn't long into the drive that I started to think about where I was going. The thought of living with Walter and Greta Baker caused me both joy and apprehension. There was no way I wanted to stay with the crazy family I had just left, but I saw Greta and Walter so infrequently that it was hard for me to judge whether I would like to live with them. And truthfully, I was kind of scared of Greta.

Greta was a tall woman, made even taller by an outdated graying beehive hairdo. She wore black cat-eye glasses that might have looked cute on someone else, but on her, they gave the impression of a very angry librarian. She was trained as an accountant, but the year I went to live with them, she and Walter were selling vitamin supplements in some sort of pyramid scheme to make a living. Both were deeply religious, especially when it led to personal gain. Walter used his title as an ordained Baptist Minister to make extra money whenever could. His tall physical stature, firm handshake, and easy smile made people like and trust him almost immediately. He counted on his charm to make a living and it worked. His and Greta's endeavors provided them with a sound middleclass lifestyle: two nice cars awarded for selling product and inducting others into the pyramid scheme; a big three-bedroom home in a good neighborhood; and a house full of expensive antique furniture.

Greta had been married to someone else before Grandpa Walter. It was during that prior marriage that she became an unofficial foster parent to my mom. Greta never had children of her own. I'm not sure if this was by choice or because God kept the gift of pregnancy from her. My mother always felt that Greta had taken her in more to raise her standing in the church as a saintly sacrificing woman than out of any sincere parental instinct. According to my mother, Greta's emotional coldness, along with frigidity in the bedroom caused her first husband to leave her. It was that same unfeeling nature that Greta exhibited that made my mother miserable too, and I felt it myself whenever she visited us. I'm sure that in her own way, Greta did care. She just wasn't good at showing it.

It was some years later that Greta met Walter and married him. By that time my real maternal grandmother had been permanently institutionalized, and so to have some kind of family connection, my mother kept in touch with Greta through the years. I never met my mother's father, though my mother always claimed that the man listed on her birth certificate was not her real father anyway. I knew nothing of my father's parents, not even their names. That meant that Greta's husband Walter would become the only grandfather figure I ever knew. In contrast to icy Greta, Walter could be affectionate and funny when the mood struck him. As possible surrogate grandparents go, I guess it could have been worse. We didn't see Greta and Walter that often, maybe once a year.

Because we didn't see the Bakers often, I had never been to their new house. So when Mrs. Hill and I pulled into their driveway, I looked around carefully. From the outside the house looked very nice. Fruit trees provided shade in the front yard and a vegetable garden grew in a large lot to one side of the house. The house was so much nicer than any of the ones I had lived in previously. It made me both uncomfortable and excited at the same time.

Mrs. Hill helped me get my garbage bag filled with clothes from the car. As we walked up the sidewalk toward the front door, Grandma and Grandpa Baker came out to greet us. Grandma hugged me roughly, like she was trying to break my bones. It was a painful hug. She released me, and Grandpa picked me up and hugged me with softer sincerity. Grandpa put me down and then invited us all into the living room. We all sat down on cream-colored antique furniture. Feeling anxious, I sat with my hands clasped tightly in my lap and stared at the cream-colored carpet, every child's nightmare. All the white gave me terrors about getting it dirty like the time I had gotten the blue stain on my dress. I really just wanted to go home and be with my mom. Tears began to leak from my eyes as I sat imagining what my new life might be like.

Perhaps to put me at ease, Mrs. Hill explained to everyone that she hoped my stay would be temporary; that it was really her job to reunite children with their parents whenever possible.

"When can I go back to Mom? Will it be before school starts?" I asked, feeling a moment of hope.

"Sorry Jean, but your mother is still very sick and I don't think she will be able to take care of you that soon," Mrs. Hill explained.

"What kind of sickness does she have? When I get sick I'm always better real soon. How come she won't be better by then?"

The adults looked at each other. Grandpa Walter intervened before anyone could answer.

"Jean, do you know that you have a friend waiting for you in the garage?"

"Really Grandpa, who is it?" I asked, confused and excited.

"Why don't you come with me and find out?" Grandpa said.

I jumped up from my seat and looked at Mrs. Hill because she seemed to be the person in control.

"Is it okay?" I asked.

"Sure Jean. I need to talk to your grandma for a bit anyway," she replied. "Then I have to drive back. I'll be coming again soon to see how you're doing. Have fun!"

Grandpa took me by the hand and guided me through the large house. Besides the living room, there was a formal dining room, a spacious kitchen, and a gigantic backyard. Three bedrooms were spread out over a long hallway at the back of the house.

Leading me down the hallway, Grandpa pointed out the rooms and explained their purpose.

"This is my office. You're not allowed in here by yourself, okay, Honey?"

I nodded.

"This is your room. Why don't you step inside for a second?" Grandpa said, guiding me inside and pointing. "Look, you have a bed all your own. All the furniture was mine when I was a little boy. Do you like your new room, Jean?"

I nodded again but it was a bit of a lie. My room was the smallest bedroom in the house with a wooden cross hanging over an old antique twin bed that smelled of dust. The mattress was lumpy but everything else was impeccably well cared for. There was a museum sensation to the room that left it feeling like people lived there long ago, but not now. It just didn't seem like a room meant for a little girl.

We stepped back out of my room and moved across the hall. "Right next door is your bathroom. I put a nightlight in for you in case you have to go at night," Grandpa said before he turned and opened the door to his and Grandma's room. He stepped back to let me enter ahead of him. The room was larger than the other two bedrooms put together. A huge king-size bed sat in the middle of the room with still enough space around it to fit all the furniture from the living room. There was a large master bath off the main room. Next to it was the laundry area with a door leading to the garage. I would soon learn that this door was the best shortcut to the garage if I didn't want to go out the front door and all the way around the house to get in.

Grandpa led me though the master bedroom to the garage, but before he opened the door he said, "Close your eyes Honey." Then he took my hand and led me carefully through the doorway. I could hear a kind of worried squealing and the rustling of newspaper. "Go ahead Sweetie, open your eyes." There in front of me was a cage containing my guinea pig, Sam.

"Oh my god Grandpa, how'd Sam get here? I thought I would never see him again. Do you have my other pets too?" I squealed.

"Don't use God's name in vain, Honey. God doesn't like it and it means Satan is in your heart. Understand?" Grandpa replied.

I nodded, feeling worried that I was in trouble already.

"After your mother got sick and it was clear she would not be back to your old house, homes were found for the other animals. Luckily, your nearest neighbor kept Sam for you just in case. When we knew you were going to be living with us, Grandma and I went and got him and brought him back for you. Now you have to promise to take good care of him. Do you promise?"

I promised until I was sure Grandpa would not change his mind. He left me in the garage to play with Sam. I took him from his cage and held and kissed him. He didn't really like it. I thought about the dogs. I was really going to miss them. While I was in Juvy, and then the shelter home, I tried very hard not to think about the life I left behind because it hurt too much when I did. Sam reminded me not just of the other animals now gone, but of life with my mom and siblings. The happiness of being with Sam again was tainted by that loss. I cried a little while sitting on the cold cement rubbing Sam's musky fur against my cheek. Then I remembered that my father hated crybabies, so I bit the inside of my mouth until it bled. That distracted me from missing my family, and I was able to make my tears go away.

* * *

Unfortunately, Sam would be the cause of an event which would forever cement in my grandparents' mind that I was a "heathen." It was an emergency that led to my fall from grace, an emergency with Sam. The horrifying experience happened not long after I moved in. When frightened, Sam's squeals were loud enough to echo from the garage, through my grandparent's room, and across the hall into my bedroom. Early one morning, I was woken up by blood-curdling squeals. Thinking that a cat or raccoon had gotten into the garage to kill Sam, I raced out my door and across the hall to my grandparents' room. Then, without knocking, I threw open their door to utilize the garage shortcut. I was just into the room when I was stopped dead in my tracks by the sight of my grandfather's nude body. His foot was propped on the edge of the bed, a toenail cutter in his hand. My grandmother was lying under the covers. Her eyes suddenly popped open. Grandpa looked over at me with shock upon his face. I saw his large testicles hanging down from between his legs like hairy udders on an old cow. Sam was quickly forgotten as shame and embarrassment reddened my cheeks. Grandma, becoming quickly aware of what was happening, stared at me with intense hostility from the bed. I stammered—"I'm sorry!"—but for some reason I was too confused by what I was seeing to leave. My paralysis was broken when Grandpa finally yelled, "Jean, get out! Don't you ever come in here again without knocking first! Do you understand?!" His words startled me out of my confused daze. I nodded and ran from the room.

As I closed the door behind me I heard Grandma say, "What have we gotten ourselves into? She's a little heathen."

"Heathen" became a theme. I could do nothing right in my foster grandmother's eyes. Religion was all-pervasive in her world, and so, each time I didn't do as she wanted I was reminded that I was a heathen. There was no room for doubt—I was a heathen, plain and simple.

As punishment for my mistaken entry into their room, my grandparents decided I had to give Sam away. I cried and begged them to let me keep him, but they would not budge. A little heathen could not be trusted. Grandma told me that it was the will of God. She believed everything that happened was God's will. If it was a bad thing that happened, then it was God's punishment for being a sinner. God didn't want me to have Sam because I was a sinning heathen. According to Grandma, my mother's sickness (still undefined to me at this point) was also God's will. Some of the time Grandma said that Mom's sickness was caused by her immoral behavior; except when I was bad, then Grandma blamed my mother's illness on my behavior. "You kids made your mother sick because you don't behave," she would say. Both implications made me feel terrible. I was either a terrible daughter or my family was possessed by the Devil and deserved God's punishment.

Secretly hoping I might get Sam back, I tried to be good. I wore the silly clothes my grandparents bought me without complaint: polyester dress pants, frilly long-sleeved shirts, and large hair ribbons. I wore them even though they made kids pick on me at the bus stop and at school. I used good manners, at least as often as I could remember to. I went to church. I tried to listen very closely during Sunday school. I said prayers each night at dinner and before bedtime even though they often felt meaningless to me. I tried so hard to be good, but I just couldn't ever seem to be good enough. While my grandparents prayed for my salvation, I sat praying I would go home to my mother.

When my foster grandparents heard that the great Reverend Billy Graham was coming to town, they saw a divine opportunity for my redemption. They got tickets to the show at San Diego Stadium and praised the Lord. On the day of Reverend Graham's sermon, we dressed in our best church clothes and headed out to be redeemed in God's light. The stadium was packed. Everywhere devout Christians milled about. They stood in long lines at the bathrooms, concession stands, and tables set up for the sale of religious paraphernalia. We waded through the crowd to find our seats—center, but in the nosebleed section. Choir music was pumped through loudspeakers as people found their places. Then down below Billy Graham leaped onto the stage and began to preach salvation. From where I sat, he looked and moved much like a miniature puppet. Hoping to improve my view of the miraculous man I had heard so much about, I narrowed my eyes into squinty slits. Still, I could not clearly make out his features. To get a clear view of his face I had to look at the large projection screens placed around the stadium; Billy's own holy Diamond Vision. His voice boomed through the loudspeakers. My foster grandparents listened in rapture.

I tried to take in his words, but like most 9-year-olds, I was totally uninterested in the ceaseless talking of adults. I sat bored. I fidgeted. "Jean, sit still!" Grandma admonished, slapping my thigh to get the point across. Twirling my hair around my finger over and over again, I stared at the crowd. The people were uninteresting. They all looked the same: women in church dresses, men in nice shirts with ties. I began sucking on a thin strand of hair. "Jean, get that out of your mouth, that's disgusting." Again Grandma slapped my thigh. I removed the hair from my mouth and began biting my nails. Billy Graham droned on. I stared down at the baseball diamond. I examined the pristine white lines that made a square from base to base. *What are the lines made of? Are they grass? Can you grow white grass?* I wondered as I stared down.

For some reason, I became obsessed with the lines. When I played baseball at home or school with other kids, we just drew lines in the dirt with a stick or the heel of our shoes. Our lines were never straight and when we ran the bases they disappeared. These lines were different though; they were perfect. I knew that something special must have been used to make them, but I didn't know what it was. Every conceivable possibility for their production ran through my head. *Perhaps it's paint? Could be some kind of special tape? Maybe it's like the fake snow Mom sprays on the windows at Christmas?* I thought. I was fascinated, and I just had to know what the lines were made of. Then Billy Graham, or maybe God himself speaking through Reverend Graham, gave me my opportunity to figure it out. Reverend Graham called the unsaved members of the flock to the stage to be saved. Now he had my attention. As I remember, his words were passionate and full of hope. They were something along these lines: "God gave his only begotten son to save us sinners. You can be saved. All you have to do is receive Jesus into your heart. Are you a sinner? Have you not yet accepted Jesus? Today, right now, you can receive the Lord and be saved. Just ask for forgiveness and be born again in Jesus Christ."

From high in the nosebleed section I watched as people left the bleachers and headed out across the baseball diamond. They stood on the grass in very close proximity to the white lines that held my curiosity. I knew right then that I too, wanted to be saved.

"Grandma, Grandpa, can I go down and meet Billy Graham? I want to accept Jesus. Please, can I go?" I begged.

"Jean, you can only be saved if you know what it means and truly want it. Do you know what it means to be saved?" Grandma asked, looking intently into my face with skepticism in her eyes.

"Oh yes Grandma, I know what it means. I must accept Jesus into my heart and he will save me. Then I will be a true Christian just like you and Grandpa," I replied.

"Jean, I think you are too young to really know what it means to accept Jesus as your personal savior. I just don't think you're ready yet," Grandma said.

I saw my chance to get down onto the field slipping away, so I quickly shifted my plea from Grandma to Grandpa.

"Grandpa, I am nine now, don't you think I'm old enough? I love Jesus! Please let me go!" I pleaded, while taking his hand and holding it in both of mine.

"Do you really want Jesus to enter your heart?" Grandpa asked.

"Oh yes Grandpa, I really do!"

"Okay then Honey, that's good enough for me. Let's go down," Grandpa said, as he stood and lifted me from my seat.

Grandpa took me to the aisle and set me on the stairs. We moved through the crowd—down, down, down toward the infield stage. Religious rapture had taken over. Everywhere people were standing and swaying. Prayers and testaments to the Lord echoed through the stadium. People touched me as I walked by, saying, "Praise the Lord! God bless you child." Grandpa beamed with pride. I felt a twinge of guilt. I knew in my heart that I couldn't care less about Jesus or being saved; I just wanted to see what made the white lines of the baseball diamond.

We joined others moving out of the bleachers. They filed down the baselines like God's own grand slam heading to home plate for redemption. On the large projection screens I saw Billy Graham holding hands with each new convert. His prayers for their salvation echoed over the loudspeakers. I began to wonder if I might just go to Hell for pretending to have an interest in being saved. Fear intruded on my excitement. You couldn't live in a house with religious fanatics and not wonder if Satan was real. As we approached the infield, getting ever closer to my goal, I switched my thoughts back to the lines. Just a few more feet and I would have my answer. The line going from third base to home plate was the first one we came to. I kicked at it with my new black dress shoes. *Chalk! It's just chalk!* I screamed internally. I couldn't believe it. With trembling hands I reached down and touched it just to make sure. The white gritty substance coated my fingers. Yes, it was only chalk. I wanted to cry. I was going to go to Hell for sure, and for what, stupid chalk!

Grandpa pushed me forward toward the stage steps. I was petrified and my legs didn't work properly. Billy Graham loomed above me. An assistant to Reverend Graham took my hand and pulled me up the stairs onto the stage. Someone handed me a pamphlet and some sort of registration card. I was moved along with the other converts and soon was standing in front of Reverend Graham. I was terrified. "Do you take Jesus Christ as your personal savior?" he asked. I felt his firm grip on my hand. I looked into his intense eyes and was speechless. I nodded my head, knowing that "yes" was the correct answer but I was unable to utter the word. Reverend Graham began to pray for me. As he did, I imagined the door to Hell opening wider, and there waiting for me were demons dancing along lines of chalk.

* * *

As the end of the school year and my 10th birthday approached, I arrived home one day to find an unfamiliar truck with a camper-shell parked in the driveway. The truck made me apprehensive for some reason. I walked up the sidewalk toward the front door. The scent of fresh-cut grass filled the early summer air. Looking next door, I saw the friendly old couple who sometimes gave me pieces of homemade strawberry-rhubarb pie working in their garden. I felt a compulsion to go to their house instead of my own. Hoping for an invite, I shouted over a hello to them. The sound of my voice caused the front door of my house to open. Grandpa pulled me inside. "Jean, look who's here!" he said, pointing into the living room. I looked in that direction and saw Grandma sitting on the couch. A stranger sat in a rocker nearby. He seemed familiar but I wasn't sure. I stood stiffly in the entryway holding my empty lunch box against my knees. Grandpa gave me a little push, forcing me to step down into the living room from the entryway. I stared at the stranger, not sure what say. Everyone was staring at me, expecting some reaction.

"How you been, Half-Pint?" the stranger asked.

"Dad?" I asked hesitantly. Everyone in the room nodded. I was stunned. Ever since Mom told me my dad was dead, I had stopped thinking I would see him again. In fact, I rarely thought of him at all. As Grandpa pushed me in Dad's direction, I examined him more closely. The blue eyes, the gray hair, the large body—the man seemed a bit like my dad, but I wasn't 100 percent sure. This man was different from the person who had left me more than four years ago. This man had graying hair and was a lot heavier. He also had a beer belly that I did not remember on my father. My dad had been only lines of hard muscle. It was strange for me, because the man in the rocker appeared a bit soft, which was not how I remembered my father.

"What Jean, aren't you happy to see me?" he asked with a laugh. I saw the distinctive gap between his front teeth and heard the familiar baritone in his voice. It was my Dad all right. *Happy, should I be happy?* I wondered as I stared at him mutely. Grandpa came to my rescue.

"Sure she's happy, Martin. She's just a little shy. Give her some time to warm up. Jean, why don't you run and change out of your school clothes. After that, you and your dad can catch up," Grandpa said, guiding me toward the hall. I nodded and walked to my room. Emotions overwhelmed and confused me. I was happy, sort of. My dad wasn't dead after all, which made me feel a little bit good. He had left us though, and the man I remembered was violent. Mom also hated him, even if she sometimes said he was the only man she ever loved. I wondered if I was a traitor to Mom if I was happy to see him again. Sitting down on my bed, I felt torn. After all, he was my dad and not a complete a stranger. Maybe I didn't like the kind of dad he had been, but he was better than no dad at all.

I changed out of my frilly school clothes into an old pair of blue polyester pants and a shirt authorized for playing in. I walked back out to the living room and sat in a chair across from my father. Grandpa and Grandma excused themselves to go find a camera.

"So Jean, how have you been?" Dad asked when we were alone.

"Fine," I replied.

"How's school?"

"Fine," I lied.

"What do you do at school?" Dad asked, shifting his legs. I wondered if he was feeling as uncomfortable as I was.

"Nothing really, just school stuff."

Feeling too uncomfortable to look him in the face, I stared at the painting of a stormy sea on the wall near his head.

"So hey, you have a new brother. He's name is Billy. He'll be two in the fall. I hope you'll get to meet him soon, along with my new wife Bridget," Dad said with a big smile.

I didn't know what to say to his revelation. While my mom was sick; while I was living through hell in Juvenile Hall; while I was being shuffled from home to home, my dad was off having another family. Even though I had sort of forgotten him, I felt like he had betrayed me. I wanted to scream—*I hate you!*—but I was too terrified about what he might do to me. So I just sat quietly, staring at the painting and feeling awkward. I could see that my silence was making him tense. Our reunion was not going well.

Grandma and Grandpa came back in with the camera, saving me from having to think up a response to his happy news. At Grandpa's request I went over and stood next to Dad's chair. I was reluctant to get too close. Fortunately, my father did not try to put his arm around me or touch me. I stood awkwardly at his side while the picture was taken. When it was over Dad stood up and said, "Well, I better hit the road. It's a long drive back." He shook my foster grandparents' hands. We all walked him out to his truck. After he got in, he told us he'd be back for another visit as soon as he could. "Good to see you Half-Pint," he said, before backing out of the driveway. I waved goodbye as he drove off. I realized as the truck slipped from view that he never asked me how my mom was doing. It made me sad, like he really didn't care about us anymore. I also wondered if I'd ever see him again, or would it be like the last time he left and never came back again. Turning from the street, I realized it didn't matter;

my mother was the person I wanted to see. Everyone else was unimportant.

PART TWO

Survival

Chapter 5: Another Brick in the Wall

As a kid I was terrible student—a *really* terrible student. By the time I was in 4th grade, I was still struggling to read; in mathematics I was hopeless. Whenever the teacher would ask me to read a passage, I stammered and needed help with almost all the words. When she asked me to give the answer to a mathematics question, I could do little more than guess. I was frequently kept after school to finish assignments. To others I was stupid, but they didn't have to tell me. I already knew.

My stupidity drove my mother to desperation long before I went into my first foster home. She tried to help with my school problems, but when she did, she quickly became frustrated. Her frustration only made me feel worse about myself.

I remember one terrible day when she tried to tutor me. "Jean, are you stupid? Spell *kiss*!" Mom yelled, with my weekly third-grade spelling list clinched tightly in her hand. We were only on word three of the list and my attempts to spell the previous words hadn't gone well. "What is the first letter, Jean?" Mom demanded.

"Ka-Ca-Cay...Is it *C?*" I asked, trying to sound out the word. I had difficulty picking out consonants and vowels that sounded similar, which drove my mother crazy. While she quizzed me, I looked down at the blue-green variegated rug underneath my feet to avoid her hostile stare.

Mom crumpled my spelling list as she squeezed it more tightly in her hand. "*C?* Are you kidding me? You must be kidding me!" Mom said impatiently. I sensed her anger and knew if I didn't spell the word right she was going be really pissed. Reluctantly, I tried to sound out the word again.

"Ka-Ee-Ee...Ka-Ee-Ee-Sss. Is it *K, E, E, S*-?" I asked tentatively, hoping I was right.

"No! I can't believe you don't know this. Are you pretending to be stupid? Just spell the fucking word!"

"I can't! I don't know how to spell it. I'm stupid. You're right, I'm stupid." I sobbed, as I ran up the stairs to my bedroom.

Ripping the blankets off the bed, I threw myself onto it and pulled the covers up over my head. I lay there sobbing. Heat built up around me until it seemed like I might suffocate. "I'm stupid! I'm so stupid!" I muttered tearfully. Losing control, I kicked at the blankets and pounded the bed with my fists. I hated myself. When I heard Mom coming up the stairs a short while later, I quickly wiped the snot from my nose with the back of my hand and tried to pretend I was fine. When she pulled the covers back and looked at my face I saw that she wasn't angry anymore. In fact, she seemed sad.

"Jean Honey, are you okay?" she asked.

I didn't answer.

"Sweetie, please don't be mad at me. I'm just not a good tutor. Let's get Joanne or Jimmy to help you next time, okay?" She said, sitting next to me on the bed.

I began to sniffle.

"Please don't cry, Baby! I'm so sorry," she said, taking me into her arms.

"I'm stupid. I'm so stupid," I said, and cried into her chest. She stroked my hair and told me it was going to be all right.

* * *

Throughout my childhood evidence of my stupidity showed up over and over again—at home, at school, and while playing games like Scrabble with my siblings. I just couldn't do what other children my age could, and as a result, I was teased ruthlessly for being dumb. My teachers were frequently frustrated with me. I was accused of not trying. Eventually, I began to hate anything educational in nature like school, books, and games that required reading or math. I even hated Sesame Street. Always shy with strangers, I began to find myself terrified of teachers, even those I knew. My fear only made things more difficult. I became unable to speak in class, even when I had the correct answer. Worse, I found myself unable to ask for help, especially when I most needed it. Each time teachers asked me to talk, all I could do was stare, paralyzed, at the top of my desk while the kids around me whispered and laughed. My fear made me stand out when all I wanted was to be was invisible.

Fear began to rule my life. I remember one particularly upsetting incident in the school auditorium. I was with other children rotating through art activities supervised by different teachers. Stations were set up for finger painting, macaroni necklace building, matt weaving, and art made from eggshells and pasta. Kids from different grades and classes were mixed together at the various stations. I was at the easels finger-painting a picture for my mom. I tried to concentrate on my stick figures of a mom holding the hand of a little girl in a blue dress, but I was distracted because I had to pee—very badly.

"Can you please ask the teacher if I can go to the bathroom?" I whispered to another first grader standing next to me. The girl turned and looked at me as if I was an alien.

What?" she asked, confused.

"Can you please ask the teacher if I can go bathroom?"

"No, you ask!"

"I can't. Please, you ask," I replied desperately.

"No! You do it! Geez, you're such a baby!"

I stood at my easel, terrified. Looking over at the teacher frequently, I hoped she would somehow miraculously sense my need and give me permission to go the bathroom. I wasn't brave enough go without permission. I begged the girl again to ask for me, but she wouldn't. I stared at the auditorium door. I couldn't see the bathroom, but I knew it waited for me just outside.

Prancing from one foot to the other, I tried to distract myself with motion. It didn't help. I stared again at the teacher as she moved around our art station. Her long brown hair swayed as she leaned down to help one of the other students. I had seen her before but had never had her as my teacher. Teachers were scary enough, but teachers I had never talked to were petrifying.

As I returned my gaze to the row of finger paints sitting on my easel, a feeling of dread came over me. I couldn't wait any longer. Pee, which I was helpless to control, ran down my legs. I tried to stop it but it just kept coming and created a pool on the floor beneath me. My neighbor yelled, "Eeew, she's peeing her pants!" The teacher finally turned and looked at me. Embarrassed and ashamed, I began to cry.

"Why didn't you go to the bathroom?" the teacher at my station asked, walking over to me. My cheeks darkened with shame and I stood mutely as the wetness in my panties began to go from warm to clammy.

The woman called another teacher over and asked him to watch the other students at my station while she took me to the bathroom. Taking my hand, she led me as I cried across the cavernous auditorium. Kids from the various stations turned and stared as we walked by. Some boys from my class yelled as I walked by, "Hey Jean, you forget your diapers?"

Inside the bathroom, the woman told me to go finish in the toilet but there was no point. What pee I had was now sitting pooled on the auditorium floor waiting for the janitor to come with a mop full of disinfectant to clean it up. Pointlessly, I went into the stall and sat on the toilet with my pants down. After a few minutes the teacher asked if I was done. I pulled up my disgusting wet undies and pants, then fearfully exited the stall. It worried me that I was going to get paddled for peeing in public. I knew I was old enough to know better.

The teacher led me out of the bathroom and down the long hall to the office. Again she asked, "Why didn't you just go to the bathroom?" Her question only made me feel worse. I didn't want to admit to her that I was too scared to ask. Being scared showed others you were weak. I walked bowlegged down the hall trying to keep the wetness from my skin. The smell of urine permeated the air around me. Kids giggled as I walked by.

I was handed over to the secretary with a brief explanation of what had happened in the auditorium. The secretary took my hand and led me to a plastic chair.

"Well, Jean Honey, let's see if we can get a hold of your mom so she can bring you some dry clothes. Do you know your number or do I need to look it up?" the secretary asked. I shamefully recited my phone number to her between sniffles. She smiled at me as she dialed and then listened into the black receiver. Every now and again she silently mouthed, "It's okay!" Her tenderness made me feel better.

After a few minutes, she put down the receiver and said, "No answer, Honey. I'll try back in a little while. Why don't you go sit in the Nurse's Office until I can get ahold of your mom, okay?"   I moved into the Nurse's Office and lightly sat on a hard blue plastic chair, trying not to feel the wetness on my butt. Across from the chair hung a poster of a wet cat clinging to a stick by its front paws. Words were printed across the bottom but I couldn't read all of them. The poster was both sad and funny. I felt the cat's panic. I felt sorry for it. I wondered what the words said. I stared at them for a long time trying to sound them out. The first and third words I had no idea of, but the second and last I read out loud, "[ ]...in...[ ]...baby!" Soon the urine soaking my undies and pants began to irritate my skin, and I gave up trying to read the poster. I wiggled uncomfortably on the hard blue chair. I grabbed the legs of my pants just below the wetness and pulled them away from my body. *When is Mom coming?! I bet she's at the bar*, I thought impatiently.

An hour passed, but still my mother hadn't arrived to pick me up or bring me dry clothes. The nurse came in and told me she needed her room to see a sick student. "But Nurse, I don't want to go out there. The other kids will make fun of me. I want to stay here until my mom comes," I whined. The nurse talked to the secretary to find out where my mother was, but the secretary still hadn't gotten any answer on the phone. Since my mother couldn't be located, they decided I would have to go back to class. The secretary went off in search of dry clothing but all she could find was a pair of white and brown plaid bell-bottom pants that had already been peed in by another kid. "Sorry Honey, that's all we have," the secretary said, as she handed them to me. A clearly visible dried urine stain spread out from the crotch and across the back of the pants. I looked at them in horror.

"They got a big urine stain on um. I can't wear those," I protested.

"Sorry Honey, that's what we have. You can either go back to class in your own pants wet, or you can wear these dry ones," the nurse said. "So what'll it be Jean, wet or dry?"

"Dry," I replied, feeling worse than the cat in the poster.

After the secretary and the nurse stepped out, I peeled off my wet items and slipped into the pee-stained pants. They were a little tight so the urine stain stretched snugly and obviously across my butt. Shamefully, I walked out of the Nurse's Office with my butt hugging the wall hoping to keep the urine stain hidden.

"Great Jean, you're all dry now. Until I can get ahold of your mom, let's get you back to class," the secretary said, writing me out a hall pass to take to my teacher.

When I entered my class some of the kids giggled and pointed. "Hey, let's be respectful. It's not nice to tease other kids. I don't want to hear anyone giggling. Just focus on your assignment," my teacher said, as he took my hall pass and led me to my desk. For some reason, once I was back in my chair, I felt even more ashamed. I lifted my desk and pretended to be looking for something. Angry, silent tears slid down my cheeks. As my shame deepened, I couldn't help but be furious at my mother for not bringing me dry clothes. It was her fault I was forced to sit in someone else's disgusting pee; her fault I was forced to be sitting there dirty and embarrassed. *She's the one that wants us to be clean and pretty, so why hasn't she come?* I wondered. For just a moment I hated her. I hated myself even more for being too chicken to ask the teacher in the auditorium if I could go to the bathroom.

* * *

As my school struggles continued, my teachers began to be alarmed. In class, I was falling further and further behind the other kids. It was my third grade teacher who finally asked that I be tested to see if there was something wrong with me. She saw how frustrated and timid I was. She could also tell how much I hated school, and she wanted to help. She asked for my mother's permission to have me tested by a psychologist for learning disabilities. Because we lived in a small mountain town, a special psychologist had to be brought in to do the testing.

For about a week, I was taken out of my regular class each morning for various types of tests. I was asked to complete block puzzles while being timed; copy images from cards; repeat words and numbers; I was also given an eye exam. At the conclusion of testing, the educational psychologist had determined several things: 1) I needed glasses; 2) I was dyslexic; 3) I had a disorder called dyscalculia. Of the learning disabilities I was diagnosed with, the dyslexia was my worst disability. Since I didn't really understand what "dyslexic" meant, I began to fantasize that I had some sort of disease that might kill me. The psychologist told my mom to get me glasses, and that the school would put me special classes to help me catch up to the other kids.

While I waited for my prescription eyeglasses, I took to wearing sunglasses to school. When my teacher asked me to take them off, I told her I had to wear them to keep my eyes from getting worse—doctor's orders. She looked at me skeptically but didn't force me to take them off. By that time, my mother was starting to become unhinged again, and each time she came to the school she managed to cause a scene. I don't know if my teacher indulged my habit of wearing sunglasses out of pity, or out of fear of my mother's erratic behavior.

* * *

When I moved to the home of Grandpa and Grandma Baker, I was nine years old and ready to start 4th grade. At my new school, I was put into special education classes for part of the day. The rest of the time I spent in the normal classroom with the other kids in my grade. But, even with support, I struggled to keep up with my classmates. In an attempt to help me make up some of my deficits, my new teacher required me to stay after school several times a week until I learned all my multiplication tables and improved my reading to grade level. Grandma Greta and Grandpa Walter were already frustrated by my learning difficulties. Their frustration was not helped by the fact that I missed the bus to the babysitter's house each time I was forced to stay after school, which meant they had to take time off work to pick me up.

I hated staying after school. I hated sitting next to my teacher's desk like some sort of baby. I hated the lonely feeling I got because all the other children were gone. I hated the work I was supposed to do because it was all so difficult for me. Afternoons passed but my academic improvement was incredibly slow. I just wanted to finish so I could once again leave at the same time as the other kids. After my teacher read us *A Wrinkle in Time* by Madeleine L' Engle in class, I felt more motivated to read since the girl in the story was like me and didn't seem smart to the other kids in school, but she really was. With a huge amount of effort, I got through the reading exercises assigned to me, but I couldn't, no matter how hard I tried, learn my multiplication tables. I wrote them down over and over. I repeated them over and over. I quizzed myself endlessly, but they just didn't stick. When we were given quizzes on our multiplication tables, I failed. The teasing by other kids intensified with each failed math test, and I was left with no choice but to cheat.

In my room at home, I secretly spent hours copying the entire multiplication table onto a strip of paper about as wide as an old-fashioned gum wrapper. Then I took it to school, ready to do whatever was required to pass my multiplication tables and be freed from my after-school torture. The day of our next multiplication test I got out my pencil, and closed the lid of my desk carefully to make sure the small strip of paper was barely sticking out from beneath the lid. By looking straight down into my lap and giving a gentle pull on the paper's corner, I was able to read the answers I had written with minimal obvious motion. Miss Howell started walking around the room to pass out the tests. My hands were sweating and my heart beat wildly as she came by my desk. I looked down to make sure my cheat sheet was not visible. It wasn't, but I suspected my teacher already knew that was a big fat cheater. Miss Howell dropped my test and walked on. My heart slowed a little but I felt like I was going to be sick.

"Okay class, let's begin. Remember, eyes on your own paper. Also, the first one to finish gets a lollipop," Miss Howell said, as she sat down at her desk.

I started mumbling the questions on the test sheet in front of me quietly. "7x9...?" I carefully pulled out my list and scanned for the answer—*7x9 = 63,* I read. I jotted the answer down and moved on. "7x6 equals...?" I mumbled, then scanned my list, and jotted the answer down. I repeated the process over and over. My cheat sheet was so efficient that after just a few minutes I was done. Looking up, I realized no one else had handed in their quiz. I really wanted the lollipop, but knew if I finished first Miss Howell would be suspicious. Perhaps I was stupid in math and reading, but I was smart enough to know I couldn't go from being the dumbest kid in class to the smartest one in just a week. I lingered over my last problem for a very long time, erasing and rewriting the answer several times. I changed two others to make sure I passed but didn't have a perfect score. Other kids began handing in their papers. When all the really smart kids and a few average kids handed in theirs, I took my test to the front. Miss Howell smiled at me broadly. I dropped my eyes.

When I received my graded test back a few days later, *Good Job!* was penned across the top with several gold stars stuck on either side. I felt both proud and ashamed, but my shame didn't keep me from repeating the process week after week. I was tired of staying after school. Also, I liked feeling like the other kids who did well, even if it was a lie. Once, I was even brave enough to hand in my test first to win the lollipop. I kept expecting to get caught, but I never did. I was kept after school less and less often, which was a relief. Kids also picked on me less frequently. Cheating eased a small bit of the fear I had about going to school, which was an incentive to continue, even though in the long run, I would hurt myself more when I was expected to apply skills I didn't really have in more difficult grades.

* * *

Though things at school began to improve with my creative approach to solving math problems, life at home with my foster grandparents changed little. In their eyes, I was still a heathen—and stupid. Greta remained constantly critical of me. When she was around I felt like I could do nothing right. This feeling was intensified by the fact that she seemed to enjoy pointing out my flaws to others. One incident in particular, really sticks in my mind. It was a Saturday afternoon and as I sat playing quietly in my room, I heard Grandma calling me.

"Jean, come in here. I want you to meet my cousin Sally and her son Ben," Grandma called from the dining room. Reluctantly, I stood and walked down the hall. Entering the dining room filled with antiques too precious for me to sit on or to touch, I found a heavyset woman and a boy about six years old with dark hair and glasses much thicker than my own.

"Ben, this is Jean," Grandma said. We nodded and said hello.

"Jean, Sally was just telling me how well Ben does in school. They have already put him ahead a grade. Isn't that impressive?"

"Yes," I said, as a hard pit formed in my stomach.

"Ben, why don't you show Jean what a great reader you are? How about you read to us out of that encyclopedia over there on the shelf? Jean, go get it for him!" Grandma continued, without even waiting for Ben to answer. I walked over and pulled the large book off the shelf and extended it to Ben.

"Jean, why don't you read something to us first?" Grandma said, examining me with a gleeful, yet cold, look in her eyes.

"That's okay Grandma, I don't mind if Ben reads," I replied quickly.

"No Jean, I want you to read first," Grandma commanded, as she took the book and opened it to a page about the formation of the United States Government. She handed it back to me. I looked at the words on the page and immediately knew I was in trouble.

"The le...the leg...i-i...the legi-is, la-a-ay...t..." I stammered, struggling particularly with each vowel sound.

With her eyes never leaving my face, Grandma said, "Ben, can you help Jean read the passage?"

Ben sat next to me and began to read flawlessly, "The legislature has the responsibility and power to make laws for the country...." Each word was crisply accentuated by his annoying nasal tone. It was exactly what you would expect from a little boy genius. My face flushed from the humiliation. Ben was six years old and I was going on 10, which only served to remind me of my ongoing failure to be like other kids.

"Perfect, Ben! You're so smart. Can you spell 'legislature' without looking?" Grandma asked, all-too ready to rub failure in my face.

"Sure I can," Ben said, closing the book. "Legislature: L, E, G, I, S, L, A, T, U, R, E."

Sally and Grandma clapped their hands and cooed over Ben as if he had just won the National Spelling Bee. Sally and Grandma beamed proudly at Ben while I quietly nursed my hatred for him.

"How come you can't read like me, Jean? Aren't you a 4th grader?" Ben asked, his dark eyes full of surprised curiosity.

"I don't know. Maybe I don't want to," I replied hotly.

"Mom, is Jean dumb?" Ben asked.

"Ben! That's not nice. Apologize!" Sally admonished, in an embarrassed tone.

With a hint of sadistic satisfaction, Grandma replied, "Oh, it's okay, Sally. He doesn't need to apologize. Jean is in special classes, Ben. Just like you are ahead in school, Jean is behind. She can't do lots of things that other kids can do."

The heavy pit in my stomach grew into a sharp pain. I asked to be excused and walked morosely down the hall lined with pictures of dead relatives unrelated to me. *Strangers, I'm so tired of strangers,* I thought as I passed under their vacant stares. Back in my room I laid down on the lumpy bed smelling of dust and mold. I wanted to cry but couldn't.

Ever since I was sent to Greta and Walter's house—ever since Juvenile Hall—ever since leaving my family, I couldn't seem to cry when I most needed to. When I was yelled at, when my feelings were hurt, when I was hit—my eyes stayed dry. Inside me something had changed but I wasn't sure what. When something awful happened, it was like I just wasn't there anymore. I wasn't trying to go away; my mind simply wasn't connected to my body any longer. During painful moments, I found myself thinking nothing, hearing nothing, feeling nothing—for some reason I was totally numb.

*　*　*

The months with Greta and Walter passed. I went to church. I went to school. But unlike when I lived with my mom and siblings, I was treated as an outcast and made few friends. I was teased for wearing glasses, for being dumb, and for living with old people who were not my parents. Kids picked on me relentlessly.

"Look, it's four-eyes!" Ricky, the meanest boy in my neighborhood yelled one cold morning. He pointed so all the kids at the bus stop would look in my direction. "Hey four-eyes, read any good books lately? Oh sorry, I forgot you can't read," Ricky snickered. All the kids laughed.

I moved down the road away from the group without saying anything. In the past, my brother and sister would have stopped other kids from picking on me, but they weren't around anymore. I stared in the direction the bus would come, trying to will it to arrive while ignoring the name-calling and laughter that echoed toward me. Trying to look uninterested in the kids shouting insults, I scuffed at the dirt with my shoes, pretending to be mesmerized by the rocks and sticks I uncovered. Out of the corner of my eye I caught movement. I turned defensively but it was too late. Ricky and another boy threw snails into my hair before I could duck. Stumbling back away from them, I fell onto the dirt, cutting my hands. Instantly, I was horrified that I had gotten my school clothes dirty. I jumped up and shook my head hard, desperately trying to dislodge the snails from my hair. The boys laughed, and even the girls joined in. Seeing that the bus was about to arrive, the other kids quickly gathered their things and lined up to get on. The bus door opened and they entered, acting as if nothing had happened.

Holding back tears of hot anger, I gathered my things from the dirt where they had dropped and got on the bus last. I sat in the front seat near the bus driver and ignored the giggles behind me. My hands stung. I dug my fingernails into the cuts while hating every kid on the bus—hating my foster grandparents—hating the stupid frilly clothes I was wearing—hating my glasses—hating the ribbons in my hair—hating every single thing about my existence. I wanted to scream and throw things—to curse at the kids and anyone else who got near me—but I didn't. I just stared straight ahead while pushing all thoughts from my mind. Then, as if I had entered a dark tunnel, I wasn't on the bus anymore. I wasn't in my body. I was nowhere. I didn't exist.

.

Chapter 6: Take Me Home, Country Roads

Mrs. Hill had given instructions to my foster grandparents not to let me have any contact with my mother for the first month I lived with them. Mrs. Hill said the no-contact rule was there to help me adjust to my new life. Not talking to Mom was hard. Greta and Walter said Mom was still in a special hospital, so even if they wanted to let me talk to her, she wasn't able to do so. I felt as if my life was in limbo, and my thoughts revolved around how soon I would be able to speak to my mother again.

Sometime in the following month, Mom got out of the hospital and I was allowed to call her under my grandparent's supervision, i.e. they listened in on our conversations using the phone in their bedroom. Mom cried a lot and told me how sorry she was. I said it was okay. She told me how much she missed me and that she was working really hard to get me back. She also said that my social worker Mrs. Hill might let me come visit her soon. I asked if she had heard from Joanne and Jimmy. I had only seen them once since I had entered foster care. They were living at their dad's but they didn't seem very happy, particularly Joanne. Mom didn't know much about them either, still she clung to the hope that they would be back to live with her soon, too.

I also told Mom that I had to get rid of my guinea pig Sam; about being kept after school; and about how much I missed her. Even though I felt like crying, my words were without much emotion because I didn't want to make her feel bad, especially since Grandma and Grandpa were listening in on the other phone. It was so important to me that I not be the kind of bad kid who would make my mother go to the hospital again. Before we hung up I told Mom that I wanted to come home. She started to cry and said, "I know, Jean, I want you to come home too."

Just before Thanksgiving, I was granted permission to spend the time with Mom. If the visit went well, it was big step toward going home permanently. It would be the first time I had seen her since she'd been released from the hospital following her breakdown. She didn't have her own place yet. She had rented a room she could afford in the house of a woman she had met at one of her AA meetings. Pam was an artist with a daughter the same age as me named Sara. My foster grandparents drove me the hundred or so miles back up to the mountain for the visit. I had never met Sara or Pam before, so I was nervous. I also worried about seeing Mom again. She often sounded emotional over the phone, and Grandma kept telling me to be good or I would make Mom sick again. I still wasn't exactly sure what kind of sickness Mom had, but I was certain I didn't want to make her worse.

When we arrived at Pam's house after a long drive, Mom ran out as soon as our car pulled into the long dirt driveway lined with pines. I could see her running toward us, waving both arms. She looked so excited and happy. Relief washed over me. "Mom!" I cried with excitement. As soon as the car stopped, she pulled open the door and smothered me with hugs and kisses. "Jean! Oh my god, Baby, it's so good to see you," she said. I looked at Grandma and Grandpa, wondering if they were mad because she used God's name in vain. They either didn't hear or decided it was best not to say anything. I almost couldn't breathe as Mom squeezed me against her chest. It felt so good, and I was so happy. We had almost two weeks of Christmas vacation to make up some of the lost time we had experienced—and I couldn't wait to begin.

Mom asked us all to come in. We entered through a side door that led into a warm kitchen where we were introduced to Pam and her daughter. I wanted my foster grandparents to leave but they decided to stay for a little while. While Pam made hot chocolate for everyone, Mom showed me around the house. It was not exactly what I had expected from the outside. While quite large and lavishly furnished, the place was actually very dark inside, both in lighting and décor. Pam's paintings crowded every wall. Some were very beautiful, but others were terrifying. There were plaster casts of faces attached to large canvases, and painted in swirling circles of black and red like they were falling into Hell's abyss, or trying to get out. There were also many paintings with the theme of a bloody hand coming out of the ground. The scenes and seasons changed in each painting, but the bloody hand clawing its way upward was always the same in each. I got goose bumps on my arms looking at them. It was still daylight out and I was frightened. I knew that when night came I would be terrified.

The tour of the house ended back in the kitchen where Pam and Greta were looking very uncomfortable with each other. Greta and Walter used my return as the moment to make their escape. "Be good, Jean! You know how stressful you kids can be on your mother, and you don't want to make her sick again," Grandma said, as she pulled on her jacket. Pam glared at Greta and my mother looked embarrassed.

"Have fun, Pumpkin! We'll miss you," Grandpa Walter said quickly, before anyone could respond to Greta's insinuation. I hugged them both, and Mom walked them to the door. Tension went from the room once they were gone. Pam and Sara asked me about what things I liked to eat and do; all the while, Mom squeezed my hands and touched my face like she couldn't believe I was real. I sighed deeply and for the first time in a long while I felt like I was exactly where I was supposed to be.

It was a few days before I got used to the house and its dark décor. It also took me a few days to get used to my mother again and to stop worrying that I was going to make her sick. Once that happened I became a kid again and spent the visit acting both naughty and nice. Mom indulged my every whim. Her guilt over getting sick and causing me to go into foster care kept her from punishing me—for anything! With my foster grandparents, I had no control, but suddenly with Mom, I had all the control. Like any normal kid, I took full advantage of the situation.

* * *

"Jean Sweetie, go brush your hair. It looks terrible," Mom requested about four days into my stay.

"I did brush it," I said, knowing it was a boldfaced lie.

"Jean, are you sure? It looks really bad."

"Yes Mom, I really did brush it!" I pouted.

"Okay Honey, but next time you brush it try to get those rats out of the back, okay?" Mom said, hugging me. I agreed and then immediately forgot her request.

The next morning her questioning was more intense and direct after I showed up for breakfast looking as if a family of mice had camped in my hair.

"Jean, did you brush your hair?" Mom asked.

"Yes Mom!" I lied again.

"Jean, you did not brush your hair. It looks worse than yesterday. You need to go brush it, please!"

"Mom, I did!"

"Jean, do you think I'm stupid? Please go brush it right now," Mom said, pulling a cigarette out of the pack on the table in front of her. I noticed her hands shook as she lit it.

"Fine! But I did brush it already," I said, unable concede to having lied.

I stomped off to the bathroom. When I looked in the mirror I could see Mom was right, my hair did look worse than the day before. Picking out the softest-looking brush from the cluttered bathroom drawer, I tried to get the mess under control. With a moderate amount of effort I got the front smoothed out. When I got to the back though, I was shocked by what I found. A tangle of ratted hair bigger than a golf ball lay just above the nape of my neck. I tried to run the brush through it but it just went over the top of the tangle without changing it at all. I pulled a harder brush from the drawer and tried again. "Ow, ow, ow," I moaned, as the brush snagged in the tangle and ripped clumps of hair from my scalp. After a few more strokes it hurt too much and I gave up. Using a hand mirror to see the back of my head in the medicine cabinet mirror, I carefully pulled the brush over the tangle until just enough hairs were released to cover the rat in the smooth hair.

The tangle grew each day of my visit but somehow I was able to smooth just enough brushed hair over the top to keep it from Mom's detection. On our last day together, Mom wanted to make sure she sent me back in good condition, to prove to my foster grandparents she was indeed a good mother. Much to my dismay, she insisted on brushing my hair. The first brushstrokes went okay, but then she hit the tangle on the back of my head. She was shocked at its size and began to brush it as I whined about how much it hurt.

"Jean, why did you let your hair get like this? We have to get this out!" she said, as she brushed harder.

"It hurts, Mom! Please don't brush it," I cried. Normally she would have just forced the brush through my hair whether I cried or not, but something had changed. She dropped the brush on the couch next to her and stood up to get a cigarette.

"Please Baby, I don't want to hurt you. Can you try to get most of this out yourself?" she asked. "I'll cut the rest with the scissors."

It was such an unusual response from my mother that I turned from where I was sitting in front of the couch and looked up at her face. There was nervousness in it, like she didn't know what to do. It was a shift that made me feel shame and pity. I took the brush, and while tears sprung to my eyes, I ripped clumps of hair out of my head. When I could get no more of the rat out, Mom, her shoulders drooping as she sadly heaved a sigh, took the scissors and cut out a large tangled section from my honey-blonde hair. The gap in the back of my hair was obvious. Dismayed, Mom said, "Oh Jean, I don't know why you let your hair get so ugly when you know Greta will tell Mrs. Hill that I didn't take care of you. I won't get you back if people think I'm a bad parent."

I looked at one of the bloody hand paintings hanging on the wall across from the couch. It was a message. "I'm sorry Mom. I promise I will tell them it's my fault," I said, swallowing the knot of fear that had suddenly formed in my throat.

* * *

Not long after the visit with Mom, Mrs. Hill came to see me. She explained I would be going to court with her to see if a judge was going to let me live with my mother again. She said that my mother had gotten her own apartment and that Jimmy and Joanne were already living there. Given how well my mother was doing, Mrs. Hill wanted to know if I would like to go home to live with her again. I was so excited by the prospect I could not sit still. "Yes! Yes please!' I said, biting my nails nervously. Mrs. Hill explained that it was up to the judge, and she couldn't promise anything.

A few weeks later, the Bakers and I traveled to the courthouse for what would become an annual pilgrimage to my custody hearing. My mother was already there, sitting on a bench outside the courtroom. I hadn't seen her in months. She was dressed in her best jeans and a nice shirt printed with small flowers. She looked terribly nervous while frequently touching her hair, smoothing her clothes, and tapping her fingernails on the wooden bench. As usual, when she saw me she got up and hugged me like the world was going to end. My social worker, Mrs. Hill, came to greet us all. Then she took my foster grandparents to speak privately, just as she had done with my mother before our arrival.

Mom pulled me down to sit next to her and then dug coins out of her purse. "Do you want a snack, Honey? There are vending machines over there," she said, pointing toward the back wall behind the benches. I nodded and took the change she gave me. From one of the vending machines I selected a package of Bugles, a corn snack shaped like little dunces' hats. I walked back to the bench. Sitting down, I then proceeded to put the Bugles on my fingers to make them like long witches' fingernails. Mom grabbed one of my hands and quickly ate all my play fingernails. We both laughed.

After my worker and grandparents returned, Mrs. Hill left us to give her report to the judge. Twenty minutes later the courtroom door opened again and a bailiff called my mother and the Bakers inside. Mom started to tremble and looked like she was going to faint. She grabbed my hand and squeezed it before walking into the courtroom. I tried to follow her, but Mrs. Hill told me to wait outside on a chair nearby. I sat down and played aimlessly with the chips. Five minutes passed, then ten, then thirty. *What if they don't let me go home again?* I wondered, with a growing sense of terror.

After what seemed like forever, the courtroom door opened and my mother came out smiling with Mrs. Hill. She rushed over to me and said, "Baby, you get to come home!" A river of relief washed over me. I wrapped my arms around my mother's waist and didn't let go.

Mrs. Hill was cautiously optimistic. "Yes, Jean gets to go home, but remember, her staying is conditional upon you meeting all of the requirements outlined by the judge. You do understand that, Joy?" Mom nodded nervously, hugging me tightly in front of her like some sort of protective shield. I looked at Mrs. Hill, so tiny she was almost like a child, and wondered why she made my mother so afraid. My grandparents told Mrs. Hill they would bring my stuff to Mom's apartment the following weekend. Then we all said goodbyes. I tried not to look overly happy, but I couldn't wait to go home to be with my real family.

* * *

We left the courthouse and returned to the mountain. My mother had moved from the house she had been sharing with Pam, the artist, into her own small apartment in another town about 15 miles from where Aunt Ginny lived. The apartment building was very run down. It was actually an L-shaped building, but the long side of the "L" was never completed and sat there decaying. In the completed section of the L-shape there were seven apartments: three on the bottom and four on the top. Our apartment was upstairs in the middle left part. It had two bedrooms—a larger one upstairs and another smaller one downstairs next to the bathroom. My brother had already moved into the bottom bedroom. Next to the kitchenette was a small staircase that led to the upstairs bedroom. Mom had managed to squeeze in a full-size bed and a twin. My sister had the twin, while I shared the full with Mom. There wasn't a living room exactly. After you came in the front door there was barely room for a kitchen table in what was supposed to be the kitchen/living room combo. The kitchen was just a small countertop with a sink and four electric burners with a small refrigerator slipped in.

That night when we crawled into bed, everyone was happy to be together again. It was very crowded, but I was so happy to be home again it didn't matter. I snuggled up against Mom while she created static electricity under the covers and then leaned across the gap between the beds and shocked my sister with her electric touch. My sister screamed and then tried to do it back. Soon we all erupted into giggles and crazy play-fighting. No one could sleep. After we exhausted ourselves with tickling, shocking, and pillow fighting, we began to talk about things that had happened just before my mother had gone into the hospital and we were taken away. Joanne talked about how Mom had brought strange men home and took us to nudist places. I reminded her about the time she picked up two Hell's Angels when we were walking home one day and getting them to bring us back to the house, using the promise of a six-pack of beer as an incentive. Then, after the ride home she started talking about sex really graphically, the burning of Jesus, and her witchcraft powers. The Hell's Angels got uncomfortable and abruptly left with my mother screaming that they were "worthless pussies" as they drove off.

Mom denied the stories at first. "I didn't do that! Did I? No, no, I wouldn't have done that!" she said with a kind of confused desperation.

"But Mom, you really did," I said.

"Yep," Joanne chimed in.

"Oh my god! I can't believe it. Oh kids, I don't really remember very much of what happened before they put me in the hospital. What else did I do? No, don't tell me, I'll be too ashamed,"—she paused and then said with dreaded anticipation—"Okay, tell me. It's better that I know."

So we told her. She would respond to each story with shock and shame. Through all the tales, we somehow managed to laugh. Each story was like a painful comedy skit, the kind where someone gets hurt and you don't think you should laugh at their pain—but you do. We lay in bed that night and laughed at all the hurt, insanity, and fear that her breakdown had brought into our lives. Over and over again Mom said, "Oh my god, I am so sorry."

* * *

We settled into life back on the mountain the best we could. I started school again in the new town. The school didn't have any special education teachers, so I was mainstreamed for the whole day into the regular classroom. Though the time I spent in Special Ed at my previous school had helped me to catch up some, I continued to be behind the other kids in some areas.

This meant I still hated school and kids picked on me for being dumb. Mom felt sorry for me and began letting me stay home sick when there were assignments due that I wasn't good at. Then she would write me a note reading, *Jean was too sick to come to school today. Please excuse her from the assignments she was unable to complete.* On the days I played hooky we would go places together, like the local diner, donut shop, public library or one of the town's touristy gift shops. Sometimes we would hike down to the creek not far from our apartment and go swimming. Staying home from school made me really happy, not just because I hated it, but because I had really missed Mom the year we were apart.

For several months everything felt perfect, then little things began to happen that shattered the safe serenity I was building inside. My brother Jimmy began fighting a lot at school, stealing things, and coming home wasted. He and Mom argued often. During a soccer game at his high school, a guy he had fought with intentionally ran at him full-force and kicked him in the thigh. The kick broke his femur. At the ER they put him into a full leg cast and excused him from school for an extended period. Over the course of several weeks, Jimmy seldom left his bed and we all had to help take care of him. This put a lot of pressure on Mom, which she didn't manage well. Soon she was drinking again. When she was drunk, Mom was a lot meaner to my sister Joanne, and soon they were fighting all the time too. Mom's drinking led to bars, the bars led to men, and soon life began to have the old familiar awfulness I hated. As we disintegrated, everyone found their own ways to cope. Joanne stayed away from home as often as she could, with friends or doing stuff at school. Jimmy continued his drinking and drugs. I decided it would be cool to follow in his footsteps.

* * *

I was in 5th grade when I learned how to roll a joint. I used to steal the pot from one of Mom's boyfriends, a guy named Doug who was first introduced to us as Mom's brother. Doug was about 10 years younger than Mom and was actually the adopted son of Walter, Grandma Greta's second husband. Mom never lived with Doug as a girl because he was adopted by Walter and his first wife. Back then, Greta was married to someone else too, so Doug didn't enter Mom's world until after she had run away from Greta. Mom stopped referring to Doug as her brother when they started having sex. Still, it was weird for us kids to accept that Mom was sexually involved with someone we were used to calling uncle.

Fortunately, Doug didn't come to town very often, but when he did he always brought big bags of pot with him. This was a fortunate turn of events for Jimmy and me since we were seeking escape from our world. Mom and Doug weren't the only ones doing drugs. Lots of people did drugs in the apartment building where we were living. It was 1977, disco was big, and everybody liked to party. All the kids I hung out with were latchkey kids due to their parents' drug habits. It was a honed skill to mill about keeping yourself entertained and out of danger while your parents and their friends got wasted. Most of the kids just ran around the neighborhood unsupervised, throwing rocks at stuff, building forts, or getting into fights with each other. I did plenty of that too, but stealing pot from Doug was my key to a kind of previously unfounded coolness.

While other 10-year-olds were off playing army or hide-and-seek, I would sneak into Mom's bedroom where Doug kept his stash. With an attentive ear toward the door, I would creep to the dresser for the dark wooden box where I would find a supply of drugs. The contents of the box varied. Usually it was just the loose green aromatic leaves of marijuana—low quality stuff really—but I didn't know that at age 10. Sometimes there would be pills of varying colors: pink, black, blue, and even white powder. I didn't touch those, but to seem grown up, I told my friends about them as if I knew what they were. I was so clueless I made up names for the pills or used the ones I had heard the party people talking about.

Whenever I stole Doug's pot, along with several carefully removed rolling papers, I would head back outside to impress the neighborhood kids with my goodies. "Hey, come here! I got something I want to show you," I would say to the first kid who crossed my path. Sometimes I was unlucky and got a really young or naive kid, one who didn't appreciate what I had.

"What's that?" they would question.

"It's pot, Dummy! You wanna smoke some?" I would ask, expertly pulling out a rolling paper and filling it with green leaves. I had watched Jimmy for weeks to figure out just how he did it. At first, rolling a joint had been really hard. I would always spill the pot on the ground or end up with a big lump in the middle, making the joint impossible to smoke. The young and naïve kids didn't really appreciate how hard rolling a good joint was. Plus, they usually got scared and told me I was bad. Then they would run off to tell on me or play some stupid kiddy game. "Big babies!" I would scream after them.

The big kids were another story. They were my preferred target group. They would seek me out for free weed, and praised me for being bad. I loved the attention. While I had pot, I was cool enough to be part of the teenage crowd, but the minute I didn't, I was just a little kid again. I felt especially cool when I received praise from the cute older brother of one of the 5th grade girls I sometimes hung out with. All I had to do was tell my friend Stacy that I had pot, and a day or two later her brother Steve would come find me.

"Hey Jean, what's going on?" Steve would say, sauntering up to me, his green eyes twinkling with amusement.

"Not much," I would reply, trying to act really cool even though I might have just been making mud pies in the field near my house.

"Not much, huh? I heard your *Uncle* Doug is in town. Oops…I mean I heard your Mom's *boyfriend* is in town," Steve usually said, with a weird smile spreading across his face. Something about that smile made me angry and embarrassed. I was torn between wanting his attention and feeling the need to protect my family.

"Are you making fun of my mom?" I asked, turning away quickly to show him I was ready to walk away.

"Hey, settle down, Tiger! Of course I'm not. I was just ask'n because I thought you might have some weed. You know how cool my friends and I think it is that you can get weed from that dude," he said, grabbing my arm to keep me from leaving.

"Oh, okay. Just as long as you're not making fun of my mom. I hate that," I said, relieved. "Yeah, I got weed! I just got to run home a sec to get it."

I ran home and pulled one of the joints I had so painstakingly rolled from the inside of one of my socks in my dresser. When I got back Steve took the joint and held it up to look closely at my handiwork.

"Nice job! You're just 10 like my sister, right?" he asked. I nodded and smiled. "Not bad!" he said, lighting the joint with his lighter before walking off. I beamed with pride.

In addition to trying to supply teens in the neighborhood with Doug's pot, I sometimes took it to school. There weren't too many other kids in my fifth grade class who had as much exposure and access to drugs as I did. For most of the other students my age, drugs were something only bad kids did. However, there were two girls in my class just like me: one was Stacy (the girl whose brother sought me out when I had pot) and the other was Tammy. Tammy was short and squat with brown hair and freckles. She had a strange voice that made kids give her the nickname "The Frog." Stacy also had brown hair, but she was taller. She might have been pretty if not for the large red birth mark spread across her forehead and right cheek like some sort of alien parasite. Like me, they were from families who didn't pay a lot of attention to where they were or what they did. So when I brought the pot to school the first time, I asked them to come smoke it with me in the girl's bathroom. Without any hesitation they agreed, but it turned out to be more complicated than we had anticipated.

Our first plan was to smoke a joint together in the bathroom during recess. While I dug the pot out of my pants pockets, Tammy and Stacy stood watch near the door. "Come on Jean, hurry up," Tammy said, her freckled face pressed against the cracked bathroom door.

"Keep your shirt on!" I replied, my hand fumbling nervously around in my jeans to pull out a crumpled joint.

"Maybe we should go into one of the stalls to smoke it," Stacy suggested.

"Good idea," I replied, moving past the sinks and toward the gray stalls.

"Oh my god! Quick, put it away! Here comes that prissy blonde girl from the other fifth grade class. She'll tell for sure," Tammy blurted out while quickly shutting the bathroom door.

Panicked, I stuffed the joint back into my pants. Looking like the Three Stooges, we ran around bumping into each other until we settled ourselves into a cluster near the sink. When the girl entered we tried to look casual.

"How come you're all just standing in here?" the intruder asked, her eyes narrowed suspiciously.

"None of your business!" we shouted in unison.

"Yeah, just mind your own business. Come on guys, let's get out of this stink-hole," Stacy said snidely. Wanting to get out before a teacher came in, I led the charge back out of the bathroom. Out on the playground we agreed to try again later.

Around 2:00 p.m. the three of us secured hall passes from our teacher, claiming we needed to go to the library to get books for one of our assignments. With nervous anticipation, we headed to the bathroom once more. I leaned casually against the bathroom wall while Tammy sat on one of the sinks and Stacy stood lookout near the door. Pulling the mangled joint from my pocket, I tried to light it but was having difficulty.

"You have to puff it hard," Tammy said, her legs swinging back and forth as she sat on the edge of the sink.

"I know that, Tammy!" I said, but I didn't really know how I was supposed to puff. That was because although I rolled joints to look cool, I had actually never smoked one before.

I sucked in a large breath, expanding my cheeks rather than inhaling it into my lungs. The lighter I had stolen from my mom got hot under my thumb as I held the flame to the joint. Thick smoke filled my mouth. It tasted terrible. I quickly expelled the smoke and passed the joint to Tammy. Tammy did the same. Stacy was next. I moved over to watch the door while she took a hit. Just like me, her cheeks ballooned out while she made several loud puffing noises. None of us coughed, I'm pretty sure because none of us inhaled; and certainly none of us acted like the people I had seen get high.

After the joint went around one more time, we decided to get back to class before we got caught. We walked down the hall saying how high we were, but I didn't feel any different. We all quit laughing when we saw a girl walk past us on her way to the bathroom. We paused and looked back toward the bathroom. "Eeew, it smells funny in here," the girl said as she entered. We all laughed nervously.

We were bad. We were tough. We were grownup—and so terrified of getting in trouble.

***

In the months leading up to my 11th birthday, my mother's behavior began to change more dramatically. I had been home from foster care for less than a year. Instead of trying desperately to show everyone that she could be a good mom by constantly showering us with love and attention, her actions became frantic, her speech fast and uncontrollable, and she rarely slept. Just like when I went into foster care the first time, she began to frequent bars late into the night, and when she came home at all, it was often with strange men. She developed kleptomania and would empty her purse the next day of an excessive array of shot glasses, ashtrays, lighters, and other bar oddities.

Unlike the other times she when she had been sick, something subtly shifted between us, and I did not enjoy being her constant companion as much. When she would take me on wild spending sprees (usually paid for by our rent money) or let me stay up with her at all hours in order to bear witness to her varied fancies, I felt worried. The worry became how I felt most of the time. Her intense speeches about anything and everything that never let you get a word in edgewise didn't seem so normal anymore. I felt embarrassed when she talked about how beautiful she was and how much men wanted her. I stood silently beside her while she screamed insults at waitresses, store clerks, and managers for mostly imagined slights and insults. When they finally asked her to leave because she was bothering the other customers, I felt anxious that she would just get worse—and usually she did—screaming something like, "How dare you! My father is the leader of the Mafia. I will bear the Second Coming of Christ. You think you can treat me this way? I'll have you killed and condemned to Hell."

Her ranting would sometimes lead to the cops being called. I hated it all, but I went with her anyway, because I wanted to keep her from being arrested. Her being arrested would mean I would have to leave home again.

"Come on Mom, these people aren't worth your time. You deserve better. Let's go find a nicer place," I would say, catering to her sense of self-importance. If I said anything else, something that sounded like criticism, or in defense of the other people in the room, she would turn her anger toward me. I didn't fear her anger as much as I feared my father's anger, but I felt hurt and betrayed when she took things out on me.

June approached and things continued to go downhill. Mom was demanding and unpredictable. Everyone else in the house was on edge.

"Jean, come on! Let's go for a drive. I need to get some soil samples for my experiments. I think the best spot is out by the Forest Service fire lookout," Mom said to me one afternoon.

"I was going to go play at my friend Kristy's. Do I have to go?" I asked respectfully. Like my sister Joanne, I was beginning to feel the need to gain some protective space. Going to a friend's house seemed like a better idea. Mom had kept me up all night with her rants, and everything got edgy when that happened.

"You're not playing with that little slut! Now go get your ass in the car," Mom said, pointing one of her long crimson nails in the direction of the door. Knowing better than to argue, I picked up the paperback book I was reading and shuffled toward the door. I was tired. I was hot. I was irritable. All I wanted to do was escape from her—but there was no escape.

Mom collected her purse and walked out the door. I followed her across the dilapidated wooden porch and down the stairs to the dirt lot that served as the parking area for our building. By the time I reached our old red Plymouth, Mom had already started the car and was screaming at me

"Hurry the fuck up! I don't have all day," she yelled. With a feeling of dread, I opened the car door and climbed in. Before I could slam the door shut, mom started backing out of the parking lot and onto the road.

"Shit, Mom!" I yelped, and closed my door quickly.

"Don't you fucking swear at me! You think you're big enough to take me on? Is that what you think? Well, come on then!"

"No, no! Sorry, it just slipped out. I was scared."

"Well, you better watch it in the future! No one talks to me that way!"

As we drove toward the fire lookout nestled high in the National Forest near our house, Mom ranted nonstop. "I need soil. Africans don't get this disorder. Fucking shrinks! They think they know what I have. I think they're full of shit, trying to make me take that poison hidden in those pills. I'm not taking that shit anymore because the real cause is the soil. I know it's the soil because Africans don't get it. I'll get our soil and compare it to some African soil; then I'll prove to those bastards that I'm right!"

"You stopped taking your medication? Wasn't it supposed to help you?" I asked with concern.

"It wasn't medication! It was fucking poison!" Mom shouted, pounding the steering wheel.

I turned away and stared silently out the window while Mom continued to rant. The pine trees flew by at a dizzying pace as she raced at dangerous speeds over the mountain roads. I focused all my energy on not throwing up.

"You know that people in Africa don't have these disorders, don't you? The government doesn't want us to know that but it's true," she said, digging with one hand into her purse to get a cigarette. "I just need dirt samples to prove it. I need to get some African dirt."

We pulled off the pavement onto a logging road. Feeling nauseous and irritable, I couldn't help myself from saying in a voice dripping with sarcasm, "Well Mom, I don't think they have African dirt on the shelves of the store here." I immediately regretted my words. Her response was electrifyingly fast. In one fluid movement she slammed on the breaks, slapped me hard across the face, leaned across me to open the door and shoved me out of the car. I landed hard on the dirt. It was the first time she had hit me in a long while. Shocked, I sat stunned for a few minutes, watching the car disappear up the logging road. When it was out of sight I got up and began to walk the reverse of the route we had just driven. There was no way for me to pretend that everything was normal now. Things between us had changed so much since those first months of bliss when I came back home from foster care.

I was beginning to admit to myself that sometimes I hated her. It was a feeling I wasn't used to—a feeling that also made me hate myself for being a terrible daughter. I had walked about a half-mile when the car pulled up behind me and Mom commanded me to get in. I did, but during the rest of the drive home I sulked in silence. It was a rare moment of acting my age, rather than acting like the protective parent.

* * *

That first year I was back with my mother, my dad started to make more frequent contact. Over Easter break, I had actually gone on a vacation with him and his new family. We all spent a week camping and fishing at a lake. The experience was mostly good, though I did get grounded for taking a small boat far out into the lake. I wanted to go around a strand of land that kept me from seeing how big the lake was. No one had told me how far I could go from shore when they said I could row the boat alone. It seemed like an unfair punishment given the failure of any adult to give me clear direction. Still, my dad hadn't hit me for it, and that was an unexpected first.

The vacation led to an agreement with my mother and the Court that I would stay with my father for part of the summer. With Mom's behavior becoming more erratic, I was looking forward to spending time with him and his family. Dad picked me up for the authorized visit shortly after my 11th birthday. The drive to his house was hundreds of miles from the mountain. He had two houses—trailers actually—both far away from the mountain and Mom. One was a single-wide trailer permanently installed in a tiny farming town nestled among the rolling hills of central California. The other was a 27-foot travel trailer that he moved from town to town in search of work as a trucker. The vacation started out at his permanent trailer where I was left in the care of my stepmother while Dad travelled for his job. I liked my stepmom and found it fun to play with my little half-brother.

While I was away, Mom's behavior became more bizarre. When the time came for my father to take me back, it was clear she had had another "breakdown" and would need to be hospitalized again. My siblings were sent back to their dad's house, and through an agreement with the Court, it was decided I would go live with my father until my next annual custody hearing. I wasn't really sure how I felt about it, especially since it meant I would be switching schools and friends once again.

* * *

"Come get your shit! You have three days, after that it's going to the dump," then the phone went dead.

Those were the last words my father ever spoke to me. I remember holding the phone in disbelief. "Dad, Dad?" I asked into the dead line, hoping I had only imagined that he had hung up. I hadn't. I tried calling back. He didn't answer. On my second, third, fourth, and fifth attempts the phone line was busy. For the next few days, I kept trying but continued to get a busy signal, as if the phone had been left off the hook. Then I got a message that the phone number had been disconnected. I didn't cry. I was just surprised. *How could he be mad at me? I had protected him during the custody hearing. Didn't that count for anything? Couldn't he see that I had done him a big favor?* I wondered. His anger surprised me, but after all that had happened I was just too emotionally numb to feel hurt by his rejection.

Dad's second abandonment happened just after my 12th birthday. I had been living with him for one year—one more year away from my mother. As in the previous years, it was time for my annual custody hearing where a judge would determine my fate. We rode on my father's motorcycle the 160 miles to the courthouse that the held jurisdiction over my case. By the time we got there, my legs were stiff and my butt was sore. I sat down on one of the hard wooden benches and looked around for my mom. She wasn't in the room. Dad sat next to me. I moved over so his body wouldn't touch mine. I tried to avoid making eye contact with him. The butterflies in my stomach felt terrible. Dad noticed my nervousness. "Don't worry Kiddo, they won't take you away from me," he said, squeezing the back of my neck. I tried not to cringe.

Mom came out of a door to the right of the waiting area that led to interview rooms. She was with my social worker Mrs. Hill. Before I stood up to go to her, I asked Dad's permission. "No, wait here," he said. I put my hands above my head and waved frantically in their direction. Mom and Mrs. Hill came over to us. Mom was once again dressed in her best clothes: a black sweater and a pair of new jeans. Her makeup was perfect and she looked a lot better than she had the previous summer before I had been sent to live with my father. Suddenly, I was embarrassed about my motorcycle hair and tried to smooth it down.

"Oh Baby, it's so good to see you," Mom said, reaching for me. I stood up to hug her. During the past year, I had grown a lot and it was awkward to realize I was taller than her. We squeezed each other tightly. She smelled reassuringly familiar, a potpourri of cigarette smoke, perfume, and hairspray. After the greetings, Mrs. Hill asked to speak to my father in one of the interview rooms. When they left, I sat snuggled up to my mom on the bench. "Oh Baby, I'm so scared they won't give you back to me," she said, stroking my hair.

Later, Mrs. Hill came back with my father. He looked irritated and gave her a menacing look when she asked to speak to me. Mom gave my hand a reassuring squeeze as I stood up. I could feel my parents' eyes on my back as I walked across the room with my head down. A bailiff appeared as we walked past, and recited a list of names of those who needed to report to Courtroom A. The butterflies in my stomach increased, as I knew that our names would be called soon.

Mrs. Hill directed me to an interview room at the end of the hall where she had just met with my parents individually. As we entered the small interview room, I twisted a strand of dirty hair, put it into my mouth, and began sucking on it nervously. Mrs. Hill motioned me to a seat saying, "Jean, now that you are 12 years old the judge will factor in to his decision your preference regarding where you would like to live." Never had I been considered before in the decision. My preference would matter. It was a huge relief to me, but also overwhelming because I knew I would have to betray one of my parents. I sat down across from Mrs. Hill and looked around the room, trying to avoid eye contact with her. I was worried she might know by looking at me that I was about to lie.

My case file already sat on the table. It was thick—really thick. Page after page contained each and every detail of my defective family life. Sometimes I felt curious about what was written on those pages, but I was never allowed to read them. There was something ominous about the file—the file that determined everything that happened to me. As I looked at it on the table, hate welled up inside me. All the police reports; all the hospital reports; all the psychiatric reports; the judge's opinions and rulings; Mrs. Hill's recommendations; all those documents bloated the file like a leach swollen with my blood. I was staring at the file when Mrs. Hill spoke to me.

"Jean, how are you feeling?" she asked, reaching over to pat my hand.

"Fine," I replied, shifting my gaze away from the fat folder.

"Jean, you understand that today the judge will determine whether or not you live with your mom, your dad, or go back into foster care. He will make his decision based on a number of things, including my recommendation. That's why it's really important that you answer all my questions honestly. Can you do that for me?"

I nodded, avoiding her eyes.

"Great! So tell me about the past year living with your dad," she said, opening the yellow legal pad in front of her to take notes.

My palms were sweating as I began to recite the story I had been rehearsing for weeks. Deciding what to tell, and what not to tell Mrs. Hill had been excruciatingly hard. I removed the strand of hair from my mouth and began twisting it around my finger over and over again.

"Well, Dad's gone a lot. Sometimes when he has a long delivery run he'll be gone for days. When he goes he leaves me alone," I said, which was only a partial lie. Dad's truck driving job did require that he be gone for days. He would leave me alone, but I always had a neighbor to check on me and I could go over to her trailer to stay if I really wanted to. Usually I didn't, because she had cockroaches that swarmed the walls even during the day. I really hated cockroaches and it freaked me out, especially if I had to stay the night. Then the roaches would crawl over my body as I tried to sleep on the couch.

"When he's gone sometimes there's no food in the house. So I go hungry a lot," I continued. This was a complete lie, but I was worried that being left home alone wasn't a serious enough reason to give me back to my mom. When Dad left on a long run I was often forced to eat things I didn't like, but there was always food.

"Where are your stepmother Barbara and your half-brother when your dad leaves? Don't they make sure you get fed?" Mrs. Hill asked.

"Dad and Barbara split up. But even when they were together, we didn't live with them. I thought you knew that," I said, looking into Mrs. Hill's eyes for the first time. That was not a lie.

"Where have you been living?" Mrs. Hill asked, confused.

I explained that Dad and I lived in his travel trailer together in a trailer park near his work. The travel trailer was too small for all of us, so Barbara and Pete lived in the other trailer that I originally thought I would be living in also. That trailer was bigger, but since it was a two-and-a-half-hour drive from Dad's trucking hub, we hardly went there. Once Dad and my stepmom split, things started getting weird.

"How small is the travel trailer you and your dad are living in?" Mrs. Hill asked, her dark eyes narrowing.

"Small! I think Dad said it is 27 feet." Again, I wasn't lying.

"Twenty-seven feet is pretty small. Where do you sleep?" Mrs. Hill asked, her tone was warm but it had taken on a commanding edge. It was her "tell me everything" tone.

"On a little fold-down couch in the front of the trailer," I replied cautiously. I knew she was looking for incriminating information. Again, I was telling the truth, but I hoped she wouldn't ask me any more questions about my living arrangements. There were lots of things that went on in that trailer, things I didn't want to tell her about. I blamed the trailer for a lot of what happened.

*　*　*

When I learned it was just going to be me and him living in the travel trailer, I was disappointed. I liked my little brother Pete and my stepmom Barbara, but also, I sensed that things between Dad and me would be different if they weren't around. When Dad first took me to the small trailer, I felt apprehensive. The trailer was newer than all the other trailers in the rundown trailer park, but it was also really small. You could walk the length of it in less than a minute. Dad had the only bed, which wasn't even a full size. It sat tightly squeezed into the middle of the trailer in front of a miniature bathroom at the very back. A narrow hall ran between Dad's bed and a built-in dresser to the left. A brown plastic accordion-style door separated Dad's bed from the kitchen/living room area. That's where I slept on a small plaid couch that you could fold down into a square, which was not really long enough for a person to stretch out on. The kitchen contained just a sink, a two-burner stove, and a miniature fridge. Crammed between the kitchen counter and the folding couch was a small dining table with upholstered benches. On the opposite side of the dining nook was a tall narrow shelf with drawers below. On top of this sat a small color TV. It was a compact efficiency space not meant for more than one person. If a couple were going to share it, they would really have to like each other a lot, because there is no privacy in a space that small.

I had just turned 11 when I moved into that trailer, and was already going into puberty. My body was changing rapidly. I went from an A-cup bra straight to a C-cup in the first few months. It happened so fast there was little time to adjust to the changes in my body. At school, I looked much older than all of the other 6th grade girls. Men noticed, my dad noticed. We shared a 10x27-foot space—it was hard for him not to notice. The attention he gave me started to feel different. He also gave me more direct attention than he normally did—like I suddenly existed.

At first I liked the attention I got from my dad. We would sit close together on the little couch watching TV. He would pull me close and we would snuggle. I loved the smell of his Brut aftershave and the way his big calloused hands felt when he held one of mine. After years of separation, it felt good to have a dad again, not one of my mom's sleazy boyfriends—but a real dad, my dad. The affection was at times confusing. Sometimes it felt too nice the way he ran his hands slowly up and down the skin on my arms. Since we'd been strangers for so long, sometimes I didn't feel like he was my dad. Maybe he didn't feel like I was his daughter. I don't really know. It was just all very confusing.

"Jean, come here and lie down with me," Dad said one day after we'd been living alone together for several months after he and my stepmother split up. He was reclined across my couch bed. I went over and sat down on the edge since there wasn't really room for two to lie down. Dad grabbed my arm and pulled me down on top of him. At first, I thought we were just going to snuggle. Dad began tickling me, pulling my shirt up to tickle my bare skin. I laughed while he held me against him. Then he pulled his white T-shirt up and pressed my bare skin against his. I could see the salt-and-pepper hair on his chest. I stopped laughing and began to feel nervous. I didn't mind the feel of his skin but the way he was looking at me seemed strange.

He pushed my bra up so that my bare breasts were resting on his chest. He began kissing me on the mouth. His kisses weren't like the kind he had given me before. My feelings turned from nervous to ashamed as he began gently licking my lips and sucking them into his mouth. As he pushed my shirt up further to expose my breasts, I could feel his erection rise against my pelvis through his jeans. Terrified, I didn't know what to do. He began moving my body up and down against him by grabbing my hips with his hands. Then he slid his hand down the back of my pants until one of his palms rested on my butt. With the other, he began to unzip his jeans.

I knew I needed to make him stop. "Dad, I have to go pee really, really, bad," I whined. He stopped rubbing his body against mine and looked at me skeptically. "Honest Dad, I have to go pee really bad," I said, smiling. I knew it would be a bad idea to make him mad. Very quickly I gave him a kiss on lips and jumped up, pulling my shirt back down. With a big smile, I blew him a kiss and raced to the back of the trailer as if nothing weird had just happened.

In the bathroom, I sat on the toilet with my jeans up for a long time. I felt sick to my stomach. When Dad came to the door, I told him I had diarrhea. I felt so ashamed. When I finally came out, Dad was cooking dinner and acted like nothing had happened. We never talked about it. Over the next three months leading up to my annual custody hearing, I began the complicated ballet of a sexualized child trying to navigate safely through the world. I did everything I could to avoid his advances, yet flirted with him when it seemed like I had done something to make him mad so I could avoid getting into trouble. I contrasted false flirtatious behavior with being as unappealing as I could. I stopped washing and combing my hair. I wore only my baggiest clothes. I avoided sitting next to him whenever I could. I told him I had started my period even though I hadn't and made him buy me pads. At school my grades dropped from A's and B's to D's. I had really been trying to be a better student, but after the incident on the couch, I began playing at friends' houses all the time rather than going home to do homework. When Dad did touch me, regardless of how, I used all kinds of excuses to extricate myself quickly. Making it to my next custody hearing, three months away, without ending up having sex with my father became my only goal.

* * *

As Mrs. Hill continued asking questions about the last year living with my father, I scrunched up smaller and smaller in my chair.

"Jean, can you please look at me? I can't see those nice eyes of yours if your head is down. Do you have anything else you would like to tell me about your dad?" Mrs. Hill asked gently.

I glanced up briefly and then looked away while shaking my head.

"Okay Sweetie, but I need you to know that since you are now 12 years old, the judge is going to let you in the courtroom. He will ask you questions before he excuses you, and it is important that you tell the truth, okay?"

I nodded again.

"All right, we better get your parents and go to the courtroom. I need to meet with the judge for a few minutes before the hearing," Mrs. Hill said, as she got up and held the door for me.

Joining her at the door I pleaded, "Please let me go back to my mom."

"That's not up to me, Jean. It's up to the judge," she said firmly before walking out into the hall.

As we moved toward the courtroom, I imagined killing myself if the judge didn't let me go back to my mom and made me stay with my Dad. Just as I entered the waiting room, I heard the bailiff call our case. Mom and Dad stood up. My heart felt like it was going to break as I looked at my mother's terrified face. Life with her had been so terrible at times, but life without her had been worse. My parents walked toward me. I avoided looking at my dad. When we all met in the center of the waiting area, my father reached up and grabbed me by the back of the neck, steering me with his hand in the direction of the courtroom. I wanted to scream and wrench myself away, but I passively let him guide me in silence.

Mrs. Hill motioned me to the front of the courtroom to sit next to her. Mom and Dad sat on opposite sides of the bench behind us. Mom looked terrified. I ached to be with her. Dad looked smug. After a few minutes, the judge entered and court was called to order. We all stood and sat again as told. Then he opened my file. I dropped my head so my hair covered the sides of my face. The judge spoke into the microphone, giving the standard greetings, case information, etc. He then asked me the question I was dreading: "Jean, I just have one question for you today. Before I make my ruling in this case, I would like to know which of your parents you would prefer to live with. Mrs. Hill has put into her report that your preference is to live with your mother. Is that true?"

The judge looked down on me from his elevated podium. I found his presence intimidating, my father's presence even more so. It was terrifying to me that I had to make my choice in front of him. I opened my mouth to speak but nothing came out. The rapid beating of my heart made me feel faint. Mrs. Hill reached over and squeezed my hand reassuringly. "Yes, I would like to live with my mom," I said barely above a whisper, but the microphone on the table made my words audible to everyone. My father began to mutter angrily. The judge thanked me and then asked me to wait on a bench outside the courtroom until the rest of the proceedings were finished. I avoided my father's stare as I walked past. My mom reached out and brushed my hand as I was leaving. Terrified, I left the courtroom and sat on the bench outside.

For a long time, I sat biting my fingernails until they bled. When they did, I began sucking on my hair. I knew I was too old for that but I couldn't help myself. Just as the clock on the wall moved to say 4 p.m., my father stormed out of the courtroom and right past me. "Dad?" I called. He ignored me. His face was red with rage. Mrs. Hill quickly followed after him. My mother came out of the courtroom jubilant. "Oh Baby, they're going to let you come home with me!" she said, pulling me into her arms. I was so happy—but also worried about how angry my father seemed. I let her hold me awhile and then said I should go talk to Dad about going home with him to get my stuff. I didn't have much, but I really wanted to get the hamster he had bought me when I first moved in. I was worried he wouldn't take care of it.

As I approached, I could hear my father arguing with Mrs. Hill. Before I could reach them my father angrily left the courthouse. "Mrs. Hill, where is my dad going? Shouldn't I go home with him to get my stuff?" I asked.

"No Jean, I don't think that's a good idea. You'll be going home with your mom today. You can call your dad and make arrangements to get your stuff later."

Reluctantly I agreed. Shaking off my worry for my hamster and the hurt I felt at my father for not saying goodbye, I walked over to my mother and took her hand. Relief seeped through my body as we walked out of the courthouse. I was going back home. Looking up at her beautiful face, I prayed that this time it would be forever.

* * *

The tone of my father's voice during that final phone call, the one where he said I had three days to get my stuff, told me he was serious. He was not a man who made idle threats. I knew if I didn't manage to get my things before the time was up, he would take my stuff to the dump just like he said. The problem was, my mother didn't have a running car. She managed to get one of her friends from her AA meetings to drive us the couple hundred miles to his trailer on the third and final day of the allotted time he had given me. When we got there, my stuff was sitting outside the trailer in garbage bags. There were only a few bags and that seemed like too few. I quickly pawed through them and saw a number of items were missing, including my hamster Teddy. Also missing was the 10-speed bike my uncle had bought me on my last birthday and the few clothes my father had bought me over the preceding year. I didn't care about the bike or the clothes very much, but I did not want to lose Teddy. I loved my hamster. He was one of the few things I could care for and receive something nice in return.

My dad's truck was parked in the yard, so I went and knocked on the trailer door. There was no answer, but I could hear someone moving around inside. "Please Dad, open the door. I just want Teddy," I said. He didn't answer. "Please Dad,

I'm begging. I just want Teddy, nothing else. Please!" I cried, with a rising sense of panic. I put my ear against the door. I no longer heard him moving around, but I could hear him whispering to his new girlfriend, the one he had cheated on my stepmom with before they got divorced. I began to pound on the door over and over crying, "Please, I don't want anything to happen to Teddy. Just let me have him. He's mine!" When Dad still didn't answer, I started screaming and pounding the door as hard as I could. Nothing happened. I collapsed onto my knees, cutting them on the metal step in front of the door and began to sob. My mom came over and pulled me away.

"I'm sorry Baby, he's not gonna open the door. We're just going to have to leave Teddy behind," she said, wiping tears from her eyes. Her friend silently put the garbage bags in the car. Then she turned and looked at me with pity. I climbed into the car and stared at my father's trailer, feeling full of hurt and hate. My mom and her friend got in the car with the air of people just returning from a funeral. We backed out of the driveway.

"How are you doing, Honey?" Mom asked, turning in her seat.

"I'm fine!" I snapped and stared out the window waiting for the numbness to finally take over. *You bastard, I hope you die,* were my final thoughts as the trailer vanished from sight. We drove back to the mountain in silence while images of my father killing my hamster swam in my head.

ABOVE: My mother as a teenager (left). My mother shortly after she married my father in what would be her third of six marriages (right).

BELOW: Me (center front) with my half-siblings a few years before the oldest two returned to live with their father permanently.

ABOVE: Me at age nine shortly after being taken from my mother and placed in foster care (left). Me with my father during our first awkward visit following four years without contact (right).

BELOW: Mom during the good period following my return from foster care at age 10 (left). Me at age 12½, and Mom a few months before I was permanently removed from her care and placed again with my foster grandmother.

ABOVE: Me at age 17 with my daughter and my mother during the period when she was living in a board-and-care home for the severely mentally ill (left). Me and my daughter around the period when we were homeless (right).

BELOW: Me and my daughter the day of my PhD graduation ceremony (left). Me and my daughter (right) the day of her MSW graduation ceremony.

Chapter 7: You and Me Against the World

When I returned from my father's house to live with Mom once more, it was shortly after my 12th birthday, just in time to start 7th grade. Back with Mom our lives took on a familiar pattern that was comforting. She doted on me, and I took all she gave. Memories of my father receded into the past as I consciously blocked all thoughts of him from my mind. Later, I would learn from my ex-stepmom that when people asked him about me, he told them, "She's dead to me!"

Mom was still living in the same rundown apartment complex I had returned to after living with my foster grandparents. The only difference was that during the previous year, Mom had moved from the small two-bedroom apartment we had lived in into a larger three-bedroom. The larger apartment allowed for Mom to have her own room, which was in the back of the apartment near the only bathroom. Mom's room was the largest, while we kids had small loft bedrooms tucked into the steep pitch of the A-frame roof. Jimmy had one to himself, while Joanne and I shared the other. Really it was pretty much Joanne's room alone, because I quickly returned to sleeping in Mom's bed whenever she felt sad or lonely. We kids' bedrooms looked out onto the living room. They did not afford us much privacy since there was only an open wooden railing, similar to the bars on a crib, between us and a potentially nasty fall down into the living room. A steep staircase led up from the living room to the lofts. Because of the placement of the staircase, whenever anyone walked up it, a loud echo was sent through Mom's room. There was also a small kitchen about the size of a walk-in closet with a narrow wooden breakfast counter and two bar stools. This sat directly under Jimmy's loft and opened onto the living room.

Red carpet was laid throughout the house and was the reason the place was called The Red Carpet Lodge. Mom had capitalized on the red carpet to make the place look somewhat like a

Spanish brothel or a matador's den. Black wrought-iron lamps and furniture collected from various thrift stores filled the house. Everything was black or red. Mom draped lace shawls on the furniture to enhance the Spanish theme. The décor made the apartment feel dark and dungeon-like even though large windows lined the living room on one side. I both loved and hated the way Mom had decorated the place. Sometimes it scared me and sometimes it made me feel like I lived in an exotic country full of mystery.

Mom's sickness made it hard for her to work, but while I was living with my father, she had managed to become the apartment building manager. The building owner lived hundreds of miles away and was too cheap to hire a realty company. He hired Mom because she worked cheap; in fact, he paid her nothing. She rented out the apartments, mailed the owner the rents, did the gardening, and tried to do the maintenance when things broke. In return, she got the three-bedroom apartment for the same price as the two-bedroom. Without the position, she would not have been able to afford the bigger place, and she needed to prove to the Court she could provide appropriate housing—meaning we kids (males and females) had separate rooms along with my mother having her own.

The apartment complex was as rundown as when we first moved there, but Mom did everything she could to make it nice for us. She planted flowers, raked up old pine needles, made sure all the tenants kept their trash picked up, and washed the wooden porches and cement walkways until they were spotlessly clean. She tried hard, but honestly, the place was too much of a shithole to ever look nice.

As always, the first four or five months went really well. Mom and I spent every spare moment we had together. It was not unusual to hear us laughing and talking late into the night.

"Do you know who's hot, Baby? Tom Jones," Mom would say.

"Yuck! He is not hot! Oh puke!" I would scream.

"How about Barry Gibbs, Jean? You think he's cute?"

I'd laugh and say, "Maybe just a little, but he looks like a sissy."

"Mom, you know who I think is cute?

"Who, Jean?"

"Peter Lorie!" I said, trying to gross Mom out a bit.

"Oh my god Jean, really? He's horrible," Mom laughed.

"No, he's cute. He has nice eyes!"

I wasn't even lying because I did somehow find him cute, along with other slightly weird actors such as Gene Wilder, Marty Feldman, and the guy who played the character Tatoo on *Fantasy Island*. Something about their big eyes made me like them. They made me think of animals. I liked animals so much.

"Jean, there's something wrong with you. Maybe it's time to get you new glasses!"

Eventually, we would find someone we both liked, such as young Elvis. Then we would giggle and talk about what kind of boyfriend they would be.

Our connection went beyond talking about who was hot and who was not. We were similar in many ways. We even ate the same things, one of our favorites being a glass of buttermilk seasoned with black pepper and accompanied by a lard and green onion sandwich. The combo completely grossed my siblings out. We were weird, but totally like each other in our food tastes. We loved to be in the kitchen together, where much to my siblings' annoyance, we cooked and ate all kinds of things only we found yummy. Mom and I liked liverwurst sandwiches; my siblings liked bologna. We liked poached eggs; my siblings liked scrambled. Fried liver and onions—we loved that dish; my siblings hated it. They liked eggnog; we preferred our buttermilk. Often we would rave about how good something tasted while my siblings would say it was disgusting. Food became another place where Mom and I bonded, once again leaving my siblings out.

Per the usual routine of previous years, given any excuse, Mom would let me stay home from school, which was really about keeping her company more than anything. I just had to ask, and if she was lonely or in a good mood, I could stay home. Sometimes though, I didn't ask because in 6th grade, school got a bit easier for me as my reading excelled, and I developed a love of history and geography; but Mom didn't understand that so well. When she was feeling down she would say, "Baby, why don't you stay home from school today." I would always agree because I knew Mom sometimes wasn't safe when she was left alone. Most of those days I stayed home, we did our usual things—walking together in the forest; eating our favorite dessert at the only restaurant in town we could afford; looking at pretty items in the local gift shop. It didn't really matter what we did; as long as we were together, things felt safe and okay.

Unless Mom was too depressed to leave the house and sent me out alone with a note to buy her cigarettes, we were constant companions around town. We found comfort in being physically connected. We walked hand-in-hand while pressing our shoulders against one another. We would press just hard enough that neither person was thrown off course; we became a single being in perfect balance—if I wanted it that way. During the year I lived with my dad, I had grown taller than Mom and almost as heavy, which meant that if I pressed too hard with my shoulder against hers, she would veer off to one side a little bit. To keep us in a straight line she would then press harder against me to bring us back into balance. It became a kind of game of push and shove shoulder-to-shoulder. Sometimes, to be funny, I would suddenly move aside so that she would stumble in my direction. "Stop it, Jean!" she would yell. It only made me laugh and do it more. "Jean, why do you want to be so mean to your poor mother?" she would ask, pouting. Then I would stop being silly.

"I love you Mom, you know that!" I would say as I gently touched my shoulder against hers again. When we came to a steep hill—and there were lots of them in our mountain town—we would take turns pushing each other up from behind. It was in these moments when we were completely connected that one of us would start singing the lyrics from the song *"You and Me Against the World"* by Helen Reddy. We would squeeze hands a little harder while we sang. We felt those lyrics so deeply—it was Mom and me against the world. Sometimes, while we were singing, one of us would start to cry. There was a terrible truth neither of us wanted to admit—we couldn't really protect each other from the ugliness of the world.

* * *

Mom had been doing pretty well when she got the job as the Apartment Manager. But, like a rerun of a terrible movie, as the year wore on, she became increasingly unstable and bizarre. My anxiety increased as the familiar pattern unfolded. The type of tenants she rented apartments to, began to change. As the poor but relatively normal people moved out, Mom replaced them with drug addicts, crazies, and criminals. They all fed off each other's sickness and created an unhealthy environment for any kid.

Mom's and my relationship became different too. Whereas she had been warm and loving to me in the beginning, she sometimes became harsh and irritable. She was even worse with my siblings. During that period, Mom seemed like she was always on my sister about something. Joanne, like most 16-year-olds, was becoming more and more willing to fight back. Her reasonable defiance in many cases created a lot of tension in the house.

"Joanne, what the fuck are you doing in there?" Mom screamed early one morning as I sat at the table eating cereal.

"I'm cleaning the bathroom," my sister yelled back at her in an annoyed tone.

"Bullshit, you're staring at yourself in the fucking mirror again."

My sister came out of the bathroom holding the toilet brush in her hand. "I'm cleaning!" she yelled, as she waved the toilet brush around. I could see the anger in Joanne's eyes.

"Don't you fucking talk to me that way! Get your ass back in the bathroom!"

I stopped eating my cereal and held my breath. Joanne turned and headed back toward the bathroom muttering "Bitch!" under her breath. My heart began to race as I watched Mom to see if she had heard. She had. Mom picked up the coffee cup sitting on the table in front of her and launched it at the back of Joanne's head.

"You fucking slut! Get the hell out of my house!" Mom screamed as the cup left her hand. Joanne ducked into the bathroom just as it hit the edge of the door frame. The force split the cup in half. One side bounced off the wood and was deflected into my fish tank—the fish tank I had bought less than a week before with money it took me over six months to save. Water and fish cascaded onto the carpet. I jumped up from my chair and ran over to save the fish. Mom continued to scream obscenities at Joanne. "See, you little bitch, see what you've done!" Mom yelled when I began to cry over the fish flopping around on the carpet.

Joanne came out of the bathroom to help me. She managed to grab two of the fish but one had flopped across pieces of broken glass and was bleeding. Crying, I ran into the kitchen to get a bowl to put them in. "See Joanne! See what you have done! Your sister is crying because of you," Mom screamed. Unable to take the abuse any longer, Joanne retreated upstairs to the loft. I continued my attempt to save my beloved fish.

"Flush those fish, Jean. They're only going to die anyway," Mom said, standing over me as I picked up the final fish from the carpet. I looked into the rescue bowl. The fish that had been bleeding was floating on its side at the top. I knew she was right, but I couldn't bring myself to put my new pets into the toilet.

Mute, I just stared at the fish thinking about the day a few months ago when Mom had been playing with us. We had all been chasing each other with squirt bottles of ketchup and mustard. We were laughing and having so much fun until Mom accidentally stepped back onto the head of my new 6-week-old kitten. His name was Wolfie and he was trying to follow us around as we played. The kitten was still so small that the accident broke its neck. Mom's reaction then was so different when I began to cry. She felt terrible and took the kitten immediately to the vet even though we couldn't afford it. The kitten died anyway. Mom apologized to me over and over again. I didn't understand how my mother's reaction to my fish could be so different. They were my pets just as the kitten had been. I wanted to cry but something felt stuck inside me.

"Give them to me, I'll do it," Mom said, as she grabbed the bowl from my hand. She leaned around the door frame of the bathroom and dropped the fish into the toilet.

"Please don't!" I cried—but it was too late. Pushing the handle, she flushed the beautiful fish I had worked so hard to buy down the toilet. "Why? Why did you do that? I might have been able to keep them alive in a bowl."

"Jean, quit being a crybaby! I'll get you a new tank and some better fish." Mom said, before turning and going back to finish her makeup.

I knew she wouldn't be able to afford a new tank or fish. Mom had been spending money in weird ways and we were behind on the rent. Buying fish would be the last thing on her mind if we were given an eviction notice. My saving six months for the tank and fish was a total waste of time.

Upset, I ran upstairs to join my sister in the loft. When I got there Joanne was in the middle of packing her things.

"I can't stay here anymore," she whispered angrily.

"What are you going to do?"

"I'm going to the store and call Grandma Greta to come get me. She told me I could live with her if things got bad here."

Out of us five kids, Joanne had always been our foster grandmother's favorite. Thinking about her options, I realized that going to Greta's house was probably the best alternative. Mom had never shown Joanne a lot of love, and with the way Mom was behaving right then, it was clear that Joanne could not live with us anymore.

"You should come too, Jean," Joanne said, grabbing my shoulders.

"No, I'm staying with Mom." I replied, thinking about the last time I lived with Grandma. She treated me a lot like Mom treated Joanne. I didn't want to live like that even if Mom was responsible for the deaths of my kitten and my fish. Greta would never be a woman I voluntarily chose to live with.

While Joanne slipped out and called Grandma from the store, I stayed out of Mom's way. She was keyed up, and I was worried she might explode again at any minute. She was cleaning the house in a manic frenzy when Grandma called later to tell her that she thought it would be best if she came to pick Joanne up.

"Come get the ungrateful bitch. I don't care," Mom replied.

Since it was going to take several hours for Grandma to arrive, Joanne and I went outside to wait. We didn't talk much and it seemed awkward. After a long period of silence Joanne asked me why I didn't want to leave.

"Mom's getting sick again, Jean, it isn't good for you to stay here. Why do you want to stay?" she asked. I looked at her and tried to explain why.

"Joanne, I can't go. Grandma wasn't nice to me when I lived there before and Mom needs me. I don't want to leave her here alone with Jimmy. Maybe it's a mistake, but I have to stay."

Not long after Grandma Greta pulled up to take Joanne away.

* * *

Something inside me was changing. I don't remember what Mom was talking about when I realized that something inside me was different. During that period there was so much talking. Mom would talk and talk and never shut up. The words exhausted me. It was like having a heavy wind pushing against you while you tried to climb up a hill slick from rain. The words—all those words! The key to surviving was to make sure you did not look away or bored while she was talking.

"Jean, do you think those black babies know what it is to be rich? No, rapes! They know the rapes, white men violating them. That's why I'm half black. My mother was raped by a Moor. I'm little Sambo, a slave to the white man. If I were back in Africa I would not need those fucking doctors. Fuck doctors! They are selling poison. Fuck your father, that bastard! But, you know, Jean, your father was the only man I ever loved. But he's not the one. Did you know I'm going to bring the second coming of Christ into this world, Jean? Did you know that? I've been chosen. Burt Reynolds is going to be the father of Christ resurrected. Jean! Jean, are you fucking listening to me?"

Mom's harsh use of my name brought me back to the moment. It was the point in her rants that she would suddenly focus her all her attention on me, waiting for an answer. That would be the moment when I would quickly come back from the zoned-out space I had learned to survive in. *Shit*, I would think, quickly trying to rearrange my face so that it was scoured of any expression that was less than rapture. Then I would search her large blue eyes to see if I had managed to save myself. "I'm listening, Mom," I would reply tentatively, hoping she believed me.

The words—I don't remember all the words—there were just too many. What I cannot forget, however, are those moments when I did not respond the way Mom expected me to.

Like the words, there were just too many mutable and ever-changing expectations for me to always get it right. What I still remember was my failure and the consequences that came from not responding the way she wanted—the sting on my cheek; the water welling up in my eyes; the blood in my mouth where I bit back the pain, the shock, the embarrassment. It was a conquest over the hurt, more emotional than physical. *You're not a baby, do not cry*, I would tell myself, echoing the voice of my father inside my head. In that entire struggle, in the killing of my own emotions to avoid escalation, there remained a love for my mother that was drowning me.

* * *

In the months leading up to Mom's final breakdown and my return to foster care, my brother Jimmy was also unraveling. Joanne had gone to Greta's house, so only he and I were still living at home with Mom. He was 17 and I was 12. He drank and did drugs like lots of teens, but something else was going on, something darker. He was unpredictably violent. Sometimes for days at a time he wouldn't come home. He converted his closet into a growing room for marijuana, and the drugs he couldn't produce himself, he robbed houses to pay for. He was out of control. Mom, even if she weren't coming apart herself, was in no position to stop him from doing what he was doing. I gave him a wide berth and tried to stay invisible the best I could.

Mom and I were asleep in her bed one night when Jimmy came home from partying. The slamming of the front door startled us both awake. My heart raced. I heard Jimmy's voice utter obscenities as he bumped into furniture in the dark. Worried, Mom got out of bed to see what was going on. She put on her robe and went into the living room leaving the bedroom door slightly open behind her. I could hear Jimmy's and Mom's voices clearly through the opening. Lying in bed with the blankets pulled tightly to my chin for security, I hoped they wouldn't fight. But from the sound of their voices, it seemed likely a fight would happen.

"Jimmy, where the hell have you been? Are you drunk?" Mom asked accusingly.

"I'm gonna kill him, Mom!" Jimmy slurred.

"What? What are you talking about, Jimmy? Kill who?"

"I'm gonna kill um! I'm gonna fucking kill um!"

I could hear Jimmy's voice rise with a kind of uncontrollable hysteria.

"Jimmy, what are you talking about? You're drunk, why don't you go on up to bed and sleep it off?" Mom said in a tone that was less accusing and more concerned. I could hear Jimmy's feet on the stairs going up into the loft, but he kept screaming about killing some guy. A few minutes later, I could hear Mom's voice more muffled above me in Jimmy's room.

"Jimmy, please calm down. Are you high on something? Did you take anything tonight, any drugs?" she asked.

"No, the scum slipped something in my beer! I'm gonna kill him!"

"You mean someone put drugs in your beer? Do you know what it was?"

"Fuck! Leave me alone. Maybe it was acid, maybe PCP. I'm gonna kill someone for this!"

Then Jimmy started shrieking like a wounded animal.

Mom's voice rose over him. "I still don't know what you're talking about, but I think you're having a bad trip Jimmy. You need to sleep it off. Please just try to lie down," she pleaded. I could hear the fear in her voice.

"I love you, Mom! Where is Jean? I want to talk to her," Jimmy said, ignoring Mom's pleas.

I lay frozen in the bed and stared at the crack in the bedroom door. A narrow beam of light illuminated the red carpet in the hall. I heard footsteps on the stairs again above me. In the beam of light from the cracked door, I saw Jimmy moving down the hall closer to me. His blond hair was matted with sweat and his eyes were open wide with a frightening intensity. Mom ran quickly ahead of him to pull the bedroom door shut. A knot formed in my stomach. I slid further under the covers and closed my eyes pretending I was asleep.

"She's sleeping, Jimmy. Don't wake her up. Please go on up and lie down," Mom begged. In the bed, I tensely waited for Jimmy to push Mom's bedroom door open again, but their conversation became slightly muffled as they moved back into the living room. Soon I heard footsteps one more time on the loft stairs. Shortly after, Mom came back in to the bedroom and got in bed with me again.

"What's wrong with him, Mom?" I asked.

"He's just drunk, Honey," she explained, as we lay side by side. I could feel that she was trembling. I squeezed her hand, hoping to reassure her. For a little while, the house was quiet. I was about to drift off when Jimmy's screams shattered the silence. Again, they were not ordinary screams, but high-pitched shrieks as if he were possessed. Interspersed between the shrieks, Jimmy yelled, "I'm gonna kill someone." Mom told me to stay in bed while she went back upstairs to try and calm Jimmy down. I crept out of bed and stood next to the bedroom door listening as Jimmy's screams grew louder, "I'm gonna kill the mother fucker. You can't stop me. I'm gonna kill him!"

"Jimmy, calm down! The neighbors are going to call the police. Please, go back to bed."

Jimmy ignored her and abruptly switched his interest to me. "Where's Jean? I'm going to kill Jean," Jimmy yelled.

"Jimmy, stop it! You're not going to kill anyone!"

Jimmy just kept screaming he was going to kill me. My heart began to race wildly. Up above, I could hear the sound of someone rummaging around in one of the closets. I heard Mom's voice again, "Jimmy, put that gun down or I'm going to call the cops." She sounded terrified and helpless. I could tell by her tone, I was in danger.

Survival instincts took over. I ran from the bedroom into the bathroom, the only room in the house with a lock on the door. As quietly as possible, I closed the door and locked it. Heavy steps thudded fast down the loft stairs as I crouched, terrified, in the bathtub behind the flimsy plastic curtain. My body shook uncontrollably. I pulled the shower curtain closer to my body as if it might protect me. Through the bathroom door I could hear Mom screaming, "Jimmy, put the gun down! Put the gun down!"

"Get out of my way, Mom!"

There was a scuffle outside the bathroom door. Then I heard a heavy thud as if someone had fallen.

"Little sister, where are you?" Jimmy yelled maniacally. The image of the lead character in the book *The Shining* flashed into my head. From the loudness of his voice, I could tell Jimmy was close. The silver knob of the bathroom door wiggled back and forth. Whimpering, I thought, *Please don't let me die.*

There was no window in the bathroom—no way to escape. I looked around for anything that might hide me or protect me better than the flimsy shower curtain, but there was nothing. Seconds later the door burst open. Slivers of wood flew toward me as the door frame cracked under the impact of Jimmy's boot. I stood up abruptly in the bathtub. Splinters stung my skin as I stared at my brother. The barrel of his 22-caliber rifle was pointed directly at my face.

Time became distorted. I felt like I was in a slow-motion movie scene. The moment seemed to drag on, but really only a fraction of a second had passed. I watched, paralyzed as my brother squeezed the trigger. The movement was so clear, so intentional. I heard the click of the hammer engaging. I briefly closed my eyes and waited for the bullet to kill me.

Like time, reality was also distorted. I heard someone screaming uncontrollably. I wondered where it was coming from. It took a moment to recognize it was coming from me—yet, even when I did, I couldn't make myself stop.

After a few seconds more, I realized there was no pain. I opened my eyes again, confused. My gaze was immediately drawn to Jimmy's finger, which was still on the gun's trigger. I watched, completely unconnected from my body, as he pulled the trigger a second time. The same click I heard before repeated. "Fuck!" Jimmy shouted as he turned and ran from out of the bathroom. I was still screaming. Over my screams, I could hear Mom in the background fighting with Jimmy over the phone. Still standing in the tub, I watched through the shattered bathroom door as the phone landed in the middle of the living room with a crash, its guts spilling everywhere.

I could hear Jimmy's steps as he loudly pounded up the stairs to his room again. I was still standing paralyzed in the middle of the tub staring into the living room. Mom stepped into directly into my line of vision. "Jean, run! Get out of the house, he's upstairs getting ammo! Run now! Go next door and call the police! Go!" Mom shouted at me in a panic before heading back towards the loft stairs. Quickly, I leapt from the tub, sprinted out of the bathroom, and ran through the living room to the front door, jumping over pieces of the broken phone in the process. As I turned the deadbolt and pulled the front door open, behind me I heard the metallic clinking of bullets being loaded into the rifle chamber. Mom ran up the loft stairs and tried to block Jimmy from coming back down.

A cold wind blew through the thin fabric of my pink nylon baby-doll nightgown as I ran. The rough boards of the porch stung my bare feet as I moved toward the outside stairs leading down to the yard. Leaping two steps at a time, I hit the cement walk—which turned and led underneath the porch—at full speed. I was halfway down the cement walkway to the street when I heard Jimmy's feet thud across the porch above me.

Mom was screaming for him to stop, and for me to run because Jimmy now had a loaded gun.

Staying close to the wall of the apartment complex, I made a hard right along the building out of Jimmy's line of sight. Pine-needles and rocks crunched under my feet as I ran for the closest house. Once I reached the house's dark porch, I began pounding on the door and screaming for help. Normally, I would have avoided this house because the guy who lived there gave me the creeps and hit on all the young girls in the neighborhood, but Jimmy chasing me with a gun gave me little choice. The light came on and the neighbor, a man in his forties with a pot belly and balding head, came to the door. He opened the door a crack and looked out at me. I couldn't remember his name, but he knew mine. "Jean, what's going on?" he asked. His eyes glided down my body and lingered at my newly developed breasts showing through the thin material of my nightgown. His leers made me feel gross. I wanted to leave again, but I heard my mother screaming in the background for Jimmy to stop.

"Please, my brother's got a gun and he's trying to kill me. Please call the police!" I said urgently. The man hesitated and moved his eyes from my breasts to my face. "Please! He's right behind me. We need to call the police! I'm not lying," I cried.

"I don't see anyone else. Are you sure he's chasing you?" the neighbor asked, looking cautiously behind me into the night.

"Yes, yes! He's coming with a gun! I need to call the police!"

Taking my hand, the neighbor pulled me inside and locked the door. He led me over to the brown-and-white plaid couch and told me to sit down. I sat while he walked to a small table near the door. He opened a drawer and took out a phone book. Frantic inside, I didn't understand why he just didn't call the operator and ask for the police. Looking up the number seemed slow and stupid. My body was keyed up like a deer scenting a mountain lion. I was sure that at any second Jimmy was going to burst through the door and kill me. After what seemed like forever, the man picked up the phone and dialed the police from the number in the phone book.

"Hello, I live at 1825 Indian Flat Road. I have a neighbor girl here from the Red Carpet Lodge apartments next door, and she says her brother has a gun and is trying to kill her," he said, and then paused to listen.

"No, I don't know what kind of weapon he has. Do you want me to ask her? Maybe it would just be best if you talk to her directly."

The neighbor handed me the phone. As I took it, my hands were trembling, and I felt like I was hyperventilating. I told the police what had happened and that my brother had a rifle. The police reassured me there were cars on the way before I gave back the phone. As the guy went to hang the phone back up, I moved toward the door.

"Jean, where are you going?" he asked, hastily hanging up the phone.

"I need to see if my mom's okay."

"No, that's not a good idea. She'll be over here soon. The police seemed very concerned. I think you should stay inside. Come here and sit on the couch next to me."

I hesitated by the door. My mom was still out there, and the guy was looking at me in a really disturbing way. I wanted to leave but he came over and pulled me by both hands so that I fell onto the couch just as he sat down. He put his arm around my shoulder and moved his body so that it was right next to mine. I sat stiffly, my mind numb again. The man turned toward me and began stroking my hair with his free hand.

"It's all right, Jean. You're here with me now. Has anyone ever told you what a pretty girl you are?" he said, putting his lips close to my ear. I could smell alcohol on his breath. He moved his other hand onto my bare thigh. I couldn't believe what was happening. I sat frozen as he began to move his hand up my leg toward my crotch. Outside, gunshots rang into the night. I began to shake uncontrollably. The neighbor moved his hand farther up my thigh until it was resting at the edge of my panties. "It's okay," he whispered and began kneading the inside of my thigh, making sure his fingers brushed against my crotch. I didn't know what to do. I felt gross and afraid, but I was more afraid of going back outside. The neighbor started to pant heavily and began trying to slip his fingers under the elastic of my panties. Just then someone pounded on the front door. The neighbor jerked his hand from my crotch and almost stumbled as he jumped up. I heard my mom's voice outside. Before unlocking the door, he said, "You don't want to make your mom more upset, do you, Jean? That would cause more problems for you." His meaning was clear to me—I better keep my mouth shut. Mom came in and ran over to me.

"Jean, thank God you're safe."

"She's okay. I've just been trying to calm her down. I think she's cold, I'll go get a blanket," the guy said before he left the room. I had the disgusting image of him going off to masturbate. Mom was too preoccupied to notice he was acting weird.

"Oh my god, Jean, the police are everywhere. Jimmy's in the field with the gun. I think they're going to kill him," she cried.

I stared into Mom's terror-filled eyes. Her pain was overwhelming. No longer did I care about the sleazy neighbor's hands in my crotch; I just didn't want my brother to die. Next to me on the couch, Mom began rocking back and forth. After what seemed to be a long time, the neighbor came back out into the living room and gave me a blanket. I wrapped it around myself to hide my body from his leering eyes.

Sirens continued to wail outside, some still in the distance, but coming closer. Mom went and opened the door a crack to hear what was going on. We heard the police say through a bullhorn, "Jimmy, you need to put the gun on the ground in front of you and step away with your hands raised above your head." Then there was a short pause. "Jimmy, if you do not drop the weapon, we will be forced to shoot." I thought the voice from the bullhorn sounded like the dad of one of Jimmy's friends—the friend whose dad was a cop.

Mom began whispering the same thing as the police, but in a tearful way. "Put the gun down Jimmy! Please, put it down," she repeated over and over. After a few minutes, she came and sat with me again. I put my arms around her, trying to reassure us both. Then a single gunshot rang out. "Oh my god, he's dead. Jimmy's dead," Mom said as she jumped up again and ran to the door. She flung it open and ran out into the night. I dropped the blanket from my body and followed her.

There in the field next to our apartment building, illuminated in spotlights aimed from police cars, stood Jimmy. He was facing away from the police with the rifle clutched across his chest. I reached for Mom to keep her from running into the field to protect Jimmy. She pushed me back toward the neighbor's door. More gunshots rang out. Mom screamed, and we turned again toward my brother. He was firing the rifle away from the police into the darkness. Like a record on repeat, the cop reissued the order for Jimmy to drop the gun. Other officers were stepping forward with their own guns raised. By then, more police had arrived, and about seven cops were pointing their weapons at my brother from three sides of the field. Mom was begging the cops not to shoot. "Please, he's on drugs. He doesn't know what he's doing," she cried.

The neighbor called me from his doorway to come back in. I ignored him. I pulled on Mom, but there was another shot into the dark. Mom cried out and ran toward the cops. An officer intercepted her and held her by his car.

Like so many times in my childhood, I was once again invisible. No one seemed to notice I was standing there shivering in a thin nightgown. Moving quietly to the edge of the apartments, I stopped and watched the scene unfold in a kind of numb trance. Jimmy ran out of ammo and dropped the weapon. It wasn't long before the cops were dragging him across the field with his hands cuffed behind his back. They roughly dropped him onto the center of the asphalt road running next to the field. Mom was kept from him by force. Then she calmed down a bit and began talking to an officer with a notepad in the yard of our apartments. Her words came out fast and were tinged with hysteria.

Jimmy was in his own state of frenzy. He was screaming obscenities about the cops; about the guy who slipped him the drugs; about me. Frustrated at being cuffed and on the ground, he started to frantically kick at the cops nearing him. Several of the cops moved in to restrain him. They managed to grab his legs and put plastic cuffs around his ankles, pinning his feet together. Jimmy tried yanking his legs back and forth while twisting his body. It was a wasted effort; there were too many cops holding him. They turned him back onto his stomach, and dropped his legs. Then several officers began kicking his feet while another cop kneeled across his back with a hand holding my brother's head to the ground. Jimmy began screaming even more hysterically.

Observing the beating, I felt bad for Jimmy, but numbness kept the feeling from expanding beyond a momentary thought. I was watching a movie—not my life. I could hear Mom crying harder in the yard, but she didn't try to intervene. The tall officer with the pen took her arm and led her back up the stairs to our apartment. I remained standing against the edge of the apartment building, watching as the cops kicked Jimmy's feet to gain his submission. Eventually, Jimmy's struggles to kick the officers stopped, but he continued to scream. Then he stopped even that.

Once he was passive, they picked Jimmy up under his arms and dragged him to one of the squad cars parked in the driveway of our apartment building. When he was finally locked into the backseat cage, I decided to go back to the apartment and join

Mom. To get to the stairs leading to the second floor I had to pass by the police car. It was my hope that Jimmy wouldn't see me, but as soon as I passed near the car he began to kick the rear passenger window with his cuffed and bloody feet. My heart beat faster as Jimmy screamed, "Jean, I love you! Don't forget I love you!"

* * *

Jimmy was taken to Juvy that night. He got out after his court hearing in which he agreed to join the military as soon as he turned 18. If he didn't agree, Jimmy would be sentenced to time. He could barely walk. Most of his toes were broken and his feet were black and blue. Mom was relieved he would not go to prison, but the fact that he was leaving in just a few months put her into a depressive state. For several weeks, she cried constantly and seldom left her bed. I did the best I could to cheer her up, but nothing I did seemed to help.

One evening when Jimmy was out of the house, Mom tried to kill herself. Most of the day she had been agitated, fluctuating between anger at how horrible life was and sadness that made her weep. After trying to talk to her and getting only anger at my attempts, I went upstairs into the loft that was now mine alone. There I sat, quietly watching her through the open railing. Once the sun went down, she started saying she wanted to die. She often said that, so I wasn't overly worried, but then she went to the front door and put on the deadbolt. She sat at the kitchen bar with all her medications in front of her, along with a bottle of booze. She began swallowing the pills from the bottles one by one and washing them down with whiskey. I stood up and leaned over the railing and cried, "Mom, please don't!" She looked up at me and swallowed another pill. I came downstairs and tried to leave the apartment to get help. She grabbed me, and I began yelling as loudly as I could for someone to help. Jimmy had come back and was hanging out with friends in the yard. He heard my cries and soon he was pounding on the door, screaming for Mom to let him in. He was pounding and pounding, begging, ordering and pleading, but Mom ignored him. Not sure what to do, I went back upstairs and began screaming out the window for someone to call the police. Mom calmly went back to her pills and swallowed a few more. Then, she took a lighter from the countertop and began to light the curtains on fire. "Jean, this is the best way. Don't be afraid," she said, looking up into the loft. Just as the curtains began to smolder, sirens rang out in the distance.

In a numb state that seemed to be my new normal, when Mom went into her bedroom to light those curtains on fire, I went downstairs and opened the front door to let in Jimmy and whoever else might be coming. Outside the door, I found Jimmy collapsed on the porch in a fetal position with his hands bloody from pounding. He was trembling, and his face was clammy to the touch. It seemed like he was in a state of shock or something. I tried to help him up, but he was too heavy. I asked a neighbor who had come out of their apartment if they could help him. The neighbor lifted Jimmy up. "You shouldn't be here, Jimmy. Go to your friend Dave's house and stay there until somebody comes for you. I don't think it's a good idea for you to be here when the cops arrive," I said, remembering the last time our small-town cops and Jimmy had met. With the neighbor's help, he staggered off the porch. I ran back into the house to try and help Mom. Moments later the police, paramedics, and fire department pulled into the yard.

Mom lay weeping in the middle of the living room floor. Christmas lights, still hanging in the window, blinked green, red, and blue over her limp form. The fire department rushed in with a fire extinguisher and quickly stopped the fire from spreading beyond the curtains. The paramedics went over and tried to examine my mother. She went crazy. The police officer who was with them suggested I go upstairs. I nodded and retreated to Jimmy's loft, which had the best view of my mother in the middle of the living room. As I took in the scene, I felt so detached. It was like my body wasn't even mine.

One of the paramedics was talking calmly to Mom, "I need to know how many pills you took. Did you only take the kind in these bottles? Is there any alcohol in your system?" Mom didn't answer. He asked her if he could take her blood pressure. She didn't answer that question either. He lifted her arm and Mom started screaming and swinging at him with her fists. The other paramedic got out a straightjacket. With the help of the firefighter and the cop, the men held her down to put the straight jacket on. As she was being pinned by the fabric and straps she was screaming, "I know you want to fuck me! Admit it, that's what this is about, you want to fuck me!"

The paramedic trying to take her vitals looked up at me in the loft. I could see on his face deep concern and pity for the girl he saw. I didn't understand why he felt bad for me, because truthfully, I felt nothing at all. Feeling was something I was finding harder and harder to do. I was only 12, but I could no longer cry. Life was painful, whether you liked it or not, the best thing was to just accept it.

Chapter 8: A Horse With No Name

Returning to foster care after Mom tried to kill us both meant going back to my foster grandmother, Greta. Joanne had already been living with her for going on a year. I didn't want to leave Mom, but I had no choice. Greta did seem a better choice than going with random foster parents again. I was dreading it though, because Greta was never very nice to me, and worse, she and Grandpa Walter had divorced in the years since I had last lived with them. The divorce was on account of the Devil. According to both Grandma and Grandpa, the Devil had gotten into Grandpa and made him have an affair with a much older woman, one with lots of money. After divorcing Greta, he married the other woman. When the woman died just a few years later, Grandpa inherited her wealth. Grandma then forgave him for the affair, because after all it wasn't really his fault, "the Devil had made him do it." Greta and Walter would later remarry, both benefiting from the woman's money. I wasn't around for that though; the year I came back to Greta, Grandpa was nowhere to be found. I knew that without Walter as a buffer it might be worse for me. The only thing that made me feel a little bit better about the situation was that Joanne was living there.

Leaving Mom also meant leaving 7th grade before the end of the school year. I had already changed schools yearly since 2nd grade, but starting at a new school again while the year was still in progress was particularly hard. Especially since in junior high, everyone seemed to go around in cliques formed early in the year. In the first few weeks, I was befriended by some of the popular girls on the cheerleading squad, likely because I had developed early and looked more like an adult than any of them. For girls trying to act so grown up, my adultness must have been kind of fascinating. It was an unexpected social group, since I had never been popular with kids like that. They even invited me to try out for the cheerleading team. I explained that I could not even do a cartwheel, so unless they wanted me as a mascot, I would have to decline.

For a while they accepted that I was not like them. We went to the mall as a group after school, where I taught them how to shoplift makeup. Then I tried to graduate them to stealing large knick-knacks from the Hallmark store, but that proved to be more terrifying than they could handle. My inclusion in the group was reversed after I stole an expensive porcelain music box and gave it to one of the girls too scared to steal anything. I couldn't take it home myself since Greta knew I didn't have any money, and as a general rule, didn't trust me. The girl's parents wanted to know where she got it from. She said I gave it to her, but even her parents knew it was too expensive a gift to come from a 12-year-old. In the store it sold for almost 70 dollars. When they pressed her about where I got it from, she spilled her guts about all the thefts. The school was called, then Greta. Then other girls distanced themselves from me for fear of getting in trouble for hanging out with a thief. I didn't mind the ostracism too much since they were all too shallow for my taste.

When I started 8th grade at the same school a few months later, I had again fallen fully into the category of *weird unpopular kid*. It didn't help that the school put me into all regular classes. I was still behind in math, and Special Ed might have been a better place for that subject. Instead, in regular math I found myself once again behind everyone else and the kids in that class started teasing me about being dumb.

Greta also began to nag me constantly about my grades and pretty much anything else she could think of. Joanne tried to act as a buffer, but she had started dating and was rarely around. Greta didn't like that either, but Joanne was getting straight A's in school so she didn't nag her much. After Joanne moved out just before her 18th birthday because of a fight with Greta over her boyfriend, things went from bad to worse for me.

***

"Jean, didn't I tell you not to use the flour," Grandma said one night as we sat down to dinner.

"Sorry Grandma, I was hungry after school. I just used it to cook something."

"I don't care what you used it for. I told you not to cook when you get home. You can wait for dinner."

"Okay, sorry, I won't do it again," I promised, as acid from my stomach rose in my throat.

I tried not to eat when I came home, but Greta had not applied for me to get free lunch at school because she said that people who took charity were disgusting. She was very restrictive about food in the house, so I often spent my day hungry. Sometimes I stole food from the lunch line, but that stopped after I got caught stealing a burrito. The lady who caught me felt bad for me when I explained why I stole it. Instead of reporting me, she made me promise never to do it again and I didn't. In fact, getting caught stealing in the lunch line stopped me from stealing anything after that.

Without food in my growing body, I spent a lot of time listening to my hungry stomach grumble. I could have brought something from home, but Greta never bought much in the way of lunch-making items. So I went to school with nothing and usually came home starving. To make sure I didn't cook after school, Greta started drawing lines on the outside of containers of flour and other staples to show how much was in there. She would also leave notes inside of bags and jars telling me not to eat whatever it was. There was something so annoying and sad about being nagged on paper. Even when I didn't eat things she was saving, she badgered me about other stuff. Dinnertime was when I could expect the worst of it, especially after Joanne was no longer there to act as a buffer.

"Jean, didn't I tell you not to wash your clothes until you have worn them more than twice?"

"Yes, you told me."

"So why did you do laundry today?"

"I don't know. I forgot I guess," I said.

I hadn't forgotten. That day I had been called into the school counselor's office to talk about my hygiene. Greta's policy of not washing clothes to save money left the things I wore stinking of teenage BO. The snotty cheerleading crowd that were no longer my friends had complained about my smell, which resulted in a shameful and embarrassing talk with the counselor where she explained about showering, soap, and underarm deodorant. For some reason, I was too ashamed to tell her I wasn't allowed to wash my clothes after I had worn them. Perhaps the thing that keep me silent was the embarrassment that I could not do the thing that was so important to my mother—to be clean.

Greta was also very cruel to me after anyone said things to her about her parenting. I didn't want the counselor to call her to discuss the fact that she didn't let me wash my clothes as often as needed. I knew if that happened, she would find some way to blame me and make my life even more miserable, which was actually pretty hard because she was already so good at it. Every night at dinner and also throughout the weekends when I was forced to be with her, Greta spent time telling me how bad I was; how I was going to go to Hell; how Mom's mental illness was my fault; how I didn't clean the house right; how trashy I looked in my clothes; how wearing makeup made me look like a slut; how I was bad because I ate her food and wasted her water. The constant criticism left my stomach full of acid all the time and I bit my nails to the quick. I dreaded coming home as much as I dreaded going to school. All I wanted was to escape, but I was trapped. So I turned to anything I could get that would alter my state of mind.

* * *

I was old enough by then to know how to actually smoke pot, but it was hard to get. Alcohol was easier and I already had a lot of experience with how it could make you feel. When Dad was still around he used to let me sip his beer. After their divorce, Mom would sometimes give me a glass of the cheap rose wine she drank. My getting drunk was a kind of entertainment for her and her boyfriends. They found it funny to watch me stagger around the room even though I was only six or seven. By age 12, it wasn't so funny anymore because I had a drinking problem. Alcohol was an escape from the horrible nature of my life. During the year I lived with Greta after my sister moved out, my only goal was to be wasted as often as possible.

In order to feed my alcohol addiction, I became the babysitter from hell. I didn't babysit for money. I did it for booze, but of course I never told the parents who gave me the jobs that. If a family didn't have a well-stocked bar, I turned down the job so I would be free to sit for families who did. At first I didn't drink while I was babysitting. I had a pint bottle that I would bring with me that I would fill from all the booze bottles in the house. I never took much from any one bottle. Instead, I would make a deadly concoction from small amounts of vodka, whiskey, tequila, gin, rum, brandy, all types of liqueurs, and anything else they had. The taste didn't matter to me. All that was important was that it could make me forget. At home, I would hide the bottle underneath my mattress and take swigs of it just before Greta came home. In the beginning, I hit the pint bottle only once or twice a week, but as the year wore on and my unhappiness increased, so did my drinking.

One of the kids I babysat was a 4-year-old named Tommy, who had a Star Wars addiction. Seriously, he had more Star Wars toys than I knew were even on the market. Normally my sister Joanne babysat Tommy, but when she moved she didn't live close enough to do it anymore. When Tommy's mom called the house looking for Joanne to babysit; I politely explained that Joanne was unavailable but that I would be happy to do it for her. Since I had only just turned 13, she hesitated at my offer. Seeing the opportunity slipping away, I laid it on thick about how responsible I was. Given that she was in a bind and had no other alternative, she reluctantly agreed.

Greta was quite happy to get rid of me, and she believed that kids should make their own money, so she not only agreed to let me sit, but offered to give me a ride. Greta dropped me off and Tommy's mom quickly walked me through the large house, explaining along the way where things were and who to call if there was an emergency. Then she left for work. Tommy and I were alone. Everything might have gone just fine if Tommy hadn't asked for some juice almost immediately. Leaving Tommy in the large den area with his vast array of expensive toys, I walked into the kitchen and opened the fridge. It was crammed full of food, condiments, and drinks. Not the cheap stuff, either. There was ham, expensive lunchmeats, lots of cheeses, name-brand sodas, and two different kinds of cheesecake. I felt a large wave of envy as I looked at the refrigerator's contents. I had never lived in a house with a fridge that full.

On the top shelf, I found a pitcher of what looked like orange juice. I poured some into a glass. When I picked up the glass to carry it to Tommy, the seductive scent of alcohol wafted up. I lifted the glass to my nose and sniffed; yep, it was booze. Sipping a little from the glass, I determined that what was in the pitcher was premixed Screwdrivers—one of my mom's favorite drinks. At the thought of getting drunk, goose bumps rose on my arms and saliva filled my mouth. I lifted the glass again and was about to down it when Tommy came into the kitchen.

"Where's my juice?" he asked. I jumped and quickly put the glass down on the counter next to the pitcher. Tommy eyed me suspiciously.

"That's not juice! It's Mom's special drink. I can't have that. Were you going to drink it?" he asked.

"Oh it's your mom's special drink. Sorry, I didn't know that. I thought it was orange juice, so I was pouring it for you. I'll get you something else if you can't have it," I said as I opened the fridge again and took out a container of apple juice that was partially hidden behind the milk. Grabbing a fresh glass from the cupboard, I poured the juice and handed it to Tommy. He gulped it down while I reluctantly put the pitcher of Screwdrivers back in the fridge. I directed Tommy out of the kitchen and away from "Mom's special drink."

We went back into the den. "Here, you be Darth Vader. I'll be Luke," Tommy said, as he handed me an action figure. We sat down close together on the beige carpet. He began making up some imaginary dialogue while he thrust Luke in Darth Vader's direction. Tommy was a really cute kid, but I aimlessly moved Darth Vader around because my attention was really focused on the booze waiting for me in the kitchen. How badly I wanted the numb bliss that a couple of Screwdrivers would give me.

"Darth Vader has to tell Luke he's his father! How come you're not playing Darth Vader right?" Tommy asked, kicking his heels on the floor in frustration.

"Sorry Tommy, I'm not very good at playing. I saw a boy your age next door. I bet he's really good at being Darth Vader. Why don't you go next door and play?"

"Craig? He's not my age yet, but he's okay to play with. I guess I could go play with him," Tommy said, as he collected his figurines.

I walked him to the large oak door and opened it. I followed Tommy as he moved down the sidewalk and across the lawn to the adjacent house. After a brief delay, Craig's mom opened the door. "Hi! I'm Tommy's sitter and I was wondering if it would be all right for him to come over and play with Craig?" I asked.

"Sure! Come on in, Tommy. Craig's in the family room watching cartoons. I'm sure he'll be happy to play with you," she said, opening the door wider for Tommy to come inside. I smiled broadly at the woman and waved goodbye. Tommy was safe at the neighbor's, which meant I was safe to get drunk.

In a flash, I was back at Tommy's house with the front door closed and locked. I excitedly rushed to the kitchen for Screwdriver heaven. Without hesitation I picked up the full glass I had left sitting on the countertop and downed it. The sweet liquid burned my throat. Mom's special drink was heavily laced with vodka. I laughed, thinking about Tommy's perfect mousy mom having a drinking problem. I waited just a few minutes for the warmth in my throat to subside, and then I opened the fridge for another refill. I figured I could have one more without much risk of being caught, especially if I added water to the pitcher to hide what I had taken. By the time I walked back into the den to watch TV, the numbing bliss I was looking for had begun to take effect. I sat on the couch awkwardly and laughed at my poor coordination. While absently watching the TV, I sipped my refill. A relaxed, happy feeling radiated through my body—it was bliss. When my glass was empty, I stared at it, wondering where my drink had gone. I was sure I hadn't drunk it *all*. Since I couldn't remember drinking it, I figured the best thing to do was get another refill; the room swam as I stood. Falling twice, I staggered into the kitchen.

A loud banging woke me later. Confused at the noise, I opened my eyes but I didn't know where I was. Thinking I was dreaming, I closed my eyes again, but the banging continued with loud urgency until I was forced reluctantly back into reality. I opened my eyes again and looked around more carefully. Contours took shape. I realized I was lying on the floor with my body halfway in the hallway and halfway in the bathroom. It frightened me that I didn't know how I got there. I tried to sit up but wave of nausea wracked my body. Holding the doorframe, I stood and staggered toward the toilet in front of me. As I puked I remembered Tommy. "Shit, Tommy! I forgot Tommy," I said, as I wiped the vomit from my mouth. I staggered out of the bathroom and moved toward the front door. The banging grew louder as I neared. On the carpet in the hall and in the living room there were pools of orange-tinged vomit. I had no memory of how the vomit had gotten there. Confused, embarrassed, and sick, I opened the front door. Tommy stood on the porch crying.

"Tommy, what's wrong? Did Craig hurt you?" I asked.

"Where were you? I've been knocking and knocking. Craig's mom made me come home a long time ago because they were leaving," Tommy replied, with large tears running down his cheeks.

"It couldn't have been that long, Tommy. I was right here and I didn't hear you knocking," I said, concentrating on the shapes my mouth was making as I tried not to sound slurred.

"I've been knocking forever! You didn't come. You're mean. I hate you!" Tommy screamed as he walked past me, arms folded across his chest.

"I'm sorry, Tommy. I'm sick. I think I have the flu. I'm going to have to go home. Let's go call your Mom at work, okay? I said, as I moved toward the phone in the kitchen.

I noticed the clock on the wall as I dialed Tommy's mom. Several hours had passed since I had sent Tommy next door. My heart filled with shame, knowing he really could have been on the porch for hours. Guilt mingled with my fear of being found out. After a few rings, I got Tommy's mom on the phone. I explained to her that I had been stricken with the flu. I asked if she could come home immediately. She reluctantly agreed. While I waited for her return, I went around the house cleaning up the vomit on the carpet and in the bathroom. As I scrubbed I tried to remember throwing up, but for the life of me, I couldn't. The only memory I had was sitting on the couch drinking. My head pounded as I cleaned, and after few minutes of scrubbing I was forced to go to the bathroom again to puke. Tommy's anger at me was replaced with concern. He stood in the bathroom door and asked if I was okay. His worried eyes only made my shame worse.

* * *

After the incident at Tommy's house, things went downhill quickly. I was getting a lot of babysitting jobs, which meant that I was also drinking a lot. Sometimes after dinner when Greta had really laid into me, I would go back to my room and drink more than just a shot from my pint bottle. My 13-year-old body was not great at processing the alcohol and I began to have blackouts. I would wake up in the middle of the night frequently in a pool of vomit, yet I had no memory of getting sick. Though I was too embarrassed to ever babysit Tommy again, I babysat other kids and started drinking at those houses too.

One night, I got so drunk after the kids were in bed I decided it was a great idea to steal steaks from the freezer. Steak had always been a rare luxury for me, and the rich family I was sitting for seemed to have so many in their freezer. It seemed unfair to me they had so many steaks when I often didn't even get lunch.

Drunkenly, I dug through the freezer pulling out only the best cuts. Once I had four large Porterhouse steaks I took them into the living room and made a pile on the coffee table. For a long while I contemplated how I would sneak them out of the house without getting caught. Then I had a brilliant idea, the kind of special idea God reserves only for drunks. I put on my coat and stuffed steaks into the sleeves. My arms took on a lumpy Popeye look, like after he ate the spinach. I was sure no one would notice—no, I was just too slick for that. Convinced at my brilliance, I went back to the freezer and pulled out a couple of filets mignon. Those I zipped up inside of the jacket over my chest. In the four hours I had been babysitting, I had magically grown in size, but I was still sure no one would notice anything unusual.

When the couple arrived home, I was sitting on the couch already zipped into my jacket. They looked at me oddly and then at each other. "I guess you're ready to go, Jean," the wife said. I nodded, my eyes heavy from alcohol.

"Come on then, I'll take you home. See you in a little while Babe," the husband said, as he pecked his wife on the cheek and headed toward the garage. I got up from the couch very carefully, cradling the bulge in my jacket like the stomach of a pregnant woman. I waddled to the car like a penguin, trying to keep the steaks from falling out. In the car, the husband once again looked at me oddly but said nothing. On the ride back to Greta's he made a few attempts at conversation. I replied rather incoherently and then he lapsed into silence.

When he dropped me off at Greta's house, I felt smug. I knew I had gotten away scot-free with some high-quality beef and a newly filled pint bottle. I put the steaks into Greta's freezer. When she came out of her room to see what I was up to, I told her that the family had given us steaks because they had so many. Greta was pleased. I excused myself and went to my room to sleep before she could smell the booze on me. I giggled at my talent as a thief and a liar. Then I fell into a hard, black sleep.

My smugness lasted only until morning. The couple called Greta to say their steaks were missing, and also, that I was acting strange. All hell broke loose. "I can't believe what you've done. Not only did you lie to me, you stole! You embarrassed me. You are a filthy sinner, Jean, and I can't believe I ever took you in! No wonder your mother ended up in the hospital. You are a shameful heathen," Greta seethed. The berating went on for a very long time. I was used to her telling me how worthless I was, so most of it didn't sink in. The only words that really stung were those related to my being responsible for my mother's sickness. Those words hurt because I believed them.

In the end, I was grounded for two months, unless I had a babysitting job. Greta loved money, and she couldn't ever imagine giving up any opportunities where I could pay for things myself. The people I stole the steaks from never asked me to babysit again, but others who were unaware of the incident did.

The steak encounter made me more cautious. I stopped

drinking while babysitting and sometimes I didn't even fill my pint bottle while I was there, though I always took it with me just in case. On the way home from one of my babysitting jobs, the mother asked me to jump out of the car and post some letters. I happily agreed. I got out of the car but left my jacket on the seat. For some reason the woman picked it up and the pint bottle fell out of the pocket. It was empty but still smelled of alcohol. She didn't say anything to me, but later reported it to Greta. The pint bottle was the final evidence Greta needed as proof that I was an un-savable wretch.

She called my social worker and told her to come get me. It might have been devastating for me to know I was going to go to another foster home with strangers, but I was ready to leave. It also helped that over the final six months of my time with Greta I had been going to a therapist. She did both individual and family counseling, which meant Greta spent time talking to her too. At our last appointment just before I was shipped off, the therapist said something that made me feel better. She said, "Jean, I want you to know this isn't all your fault. Greta is a very difficult woman." Then she hugged me. It was the first sincere hug I had had in almost a year.

* * *

My social worker picked me up for the return to life in foster care with strangers. During the drive I repeated in my head the poem my mother had written for me as a birthday present when I turned 13.

There is a sentinel,
that lives within the sea.
He is the lovely dolphin,
friend to you and me.

He protects the harbor,
and guides ships into port.
Oh how gaily does he play,
when he and I cavort.

When I swim he glides by me,
alert for danger near.
He always keeps the sharks away,
I am so glad that he is here.

I know that when we play,
he wants to say to me,
Oh come, let's swim away,
and then we'll both be free.

But then I have to turn,
and head back toward the beach.
Oh my lovely dolphin,
your world's beyond my reach.

The words were soothing even if they made me a little sad.

* * *

In many ways, Greta's rejection was a blessing. In the time I lived with Greta, I had only visited my mother once and just for a day. Instead of visiting, Mom and I sometimes talked on the phone, but that was pretty expensive so we mostly wrote each other letters. The letters kept us connected and gave us something to look forward to in the terrible state of our new lives. After her last breakdown and suicide attempt, Mom was institutionalized and then later transferred to a halfway house. Jimmy joined the military as scheduled. I was sent to Greta's house, which was almost 150 miles from Mom. When Greta gave me up, I was moved back to the region of the Court that had jurisdiction over my case. The move put me much closer to Mom's board-and-care home.

Just like me, Mom was no longer able to make choices regarding her life. She was placed under conservatorship after the Court decided she was no longer capable of making her own decisions. A judge ordered her into long-term care because she didn't seem capable of caring for herself any longer. The mountain town my mother loved didn't have any facilities for people like her, so she was forced to move to a board-and-care home in the city below. The place provided Mom with meals, a bed, and medication three times a day. The rules were more relaxed than they had been at any of the psychiatric institutions she had previously been committed to. As long as she took her medications at the prescribed times, she was allowed to come and go as she pleased between the hours of 7 a.m. and 5 p.m. She was even allowed to have visitors. The place was really rundown, but it did put Mom into a more stable environment with fewer pressures.

After leaving Greta's house in early July 1981, I was placed into a foster home with a family that had emigrated from Poland in their teens. They were nice people, but they had a biological granddaughter whom they frequently cared for. She and I were forced to share a bed when she stayed over. The girl was way younger than me and very clingy. I couldn't stand her neediness and often fought with her over the space in the bed. The placement didn't last long and I was moved into short-term shelter care. That placement was almost like living in a hotel. The foster kids were only allowed to enter their rooms, the kitchen (but only at meal times), and the bathroom. I rarely saw the foster parents. All the kids they took in were teens, and along with the other foster kids there, I spent all my time working a concession stand at the recreational park nearby.

Once again my birthday passed unnoticed. I turned 14 years old renting out paddle boats and selling food to strangers. The experience of being forgotten on my birthday had become so normal that I might have forgotten completely if it hadn't been for a family celebrating a birthday for their young daughter. All the kids came to the concession stand to get cotton candy wearing birthday hats and giggling happily. While pouring the sugar into the barrel of the cotton candy machine and collecting the strings of sugar on a paper cone, I found it hard not to feel resentment at their happiness.

About two weeks before the start of the school year, my social worker placed me into a long-term home licensed to take up to four teenage foster girls at a time. The foster dad was an alcoholic who had been injured on the job years before. He was living off disability payments and stayed home all day drinking while the foster mother went to work in a factory sweatshop. They had three daughters and one grown son of their own in addition to the foster kids they took in. Two of their daughters lived at the house: a girl two years younger than me and a grown daughter in her late twenties or early thirties. The older of the two was married to a convict in prison and lived in a small studio unit behind the main house next to the pool.

The family was clearly dysfunctional, but my social worker Mrs. Hill kept telling me how important it was that I find a stable placement. She asked me to really give the place a try. I liked her so I agreed to stick it out. My motivation to stay primarily came from the fact that I was living close enough to the board-and-care home to visit my mom. I asked to visit as soon as I moved in with the family, but Mrs. Hill said I had to wait a couple of months to complete the required adjustment period. As always, that meant no calls or letters, either. Mrs. Hill said the adjustment period was needed to facilitate a smooth transition into my new family. However, it was really agonizing for me to know my mother was only a few miles away and I couldn't see her.

* * *

Mrs. Hill finally gave me permission to visit Mom. My new foster parents made it clear that finding a way to get there was my problem. I didn't have a ride, but it didn't matter. I was willing to walk the two miles even in the 110-degree heat that baked the region every summer. I got directions from my new foster mom Iris, a petite dark-haired chain-smoker with burdens of her own. Before leaving the house, I wondered what Mom would be like during our first visit. I hadn't seen her in over a year and I wasn't sure what to expect. After every hospitalization, she seemed to morph into a slightly different person from the one I had last known. Even though I left the house early, the summer sun had already made the day unbearable. As I walked the streets lined with rundown houses and low-income apartment buildings, sweat stained my tank-top and plastered my already too-tight jeans to my legs. The thick black eyeliner I had completely encircled my eyes with ran as sweat dripped into my eyes. Passing the tinted windows of the many liquor stores that served the drug addicts and prostitutes who frequented the neighborhood, I glanced at my reflection. In the smoky glass, I could see that I looked like a biker chick whose boyfriend had just beaten her up. I wiped the smeared eyeliner from underneath my eyes with my fingers.

The neighborhood grew rougher the closer I got to the industrial area where my mother lived in the board-and-care home. Interspersed between warehouses were motels and rundown homes. Graffiti covered the sides of buildings and walls. I walked with my shoulders back and jaw set firmly. I made direct eye contact with everyone I passed, giving them a slight upwards nod that said, *Hey, how ya doing*. By age 14, life had put me in enough bad situations to I know the key to my safety was to never appear vulnerable or scared. If you didn't look like you belonged in the neighborhood, you better look crazy enough to kill someone if you wanted to be left alone. I tried to look both crazy and tough.

When I finally arrived at Mom's board-and-care home, I was hot and sticky. I rubbed eyeliner off my cheeks one more time before I opened the gate of the facility inaptly named, *Spring Gardens*. There was nothing spring-like about the place. The courtyard was filled with gravel and was surrounded by a small collection of rundown buildings. The front structure closest to the street appeared to be the dining hall and the medication distribution area. Paint was peeling off all the buildings. The most positive thing about the place was there wasn't any trash lying around like there was in the rest of the area I had just passed through.

Mom had given me instructions to find the room she shared with another woman. Walking down the sidewalk that ran the length of the courtyard, I was repeatedly slowed down by Spring Gardens' various unique residents. "Who are you here to see?" they asked eagerly. Some wanted to touch me or shake my hand. A man who introduced himself as Charlie Chaplin shook my hand the most vigorously. Due to some sort of skin condition, his hands were extremely scaly and red. I tried to be polite and not jerk my hand away, but I was worried that he might have something contagious. While I was trying to extricate my hand from his grip, Mom came out of her room and rescued me. She was smiling broadly as she rushed up and snatched me from Charlie's vice-like fingers. In spite of everything she had been through, she still looked good. Her hair was done nicely and she had put on makeup. Talking loudly so that veryone around us could hear, she said, "This is my daughter. Isn't she beautiful?!" Then she guided me past the other residents sitting on door stoops and in the few chairs that sat in the courtyard. I doubted my beauty, but it was nice to hear Mom praise me. I had gotten no praise while I was living with Greta, and my new foster parents only seemed to notice my presence when there were chores to be done.

As we walked toward her room, I looked around. Lots of the residents greeted us as we went past, saying how lucky my mom was to get a visitor. I would later learn my mother was the only resident to ever get a visit from a family member, so it was understandable they were envious. Not all the residents greeted us; some sat rocking their bodies back and forth while muttering angrily at the demons that lived in their heads. Except for a few, the people I passed had a haunted, zoned-out, look on their face—the kind reserved for long-term psychiatric patients on serious meds. It was the look that antipsychotic medications gave someone, a human trapped inside a shell of their former self. I felt sorry for the people we passed. I couldn't image a worse fate than to be condemned to a life like theirs. It was a fear that consumed my thoughts throughout my teen years and into my early 20s, when there was still a high probability I might turn out like my mom.

When we reached the doorway of a small bungalow on the left side of the courtyard, Mom directed me through it. The room was stifling hot, even with the door open. Inside there were two small cots with a nightstand in the middle, a small wardrobe against the foot of each cot, and a tiny bathroom to the right of where we entered. Like the outside of the buildings, everything looked rundown and paint was peeling off the walls.

"Mabel, this is my daughter, Jean," Mom said, nodding toward a woman about 60 years old with a head of ratted gray hair and a ravaged face. Mable ignored me completely. She was busy sitting on the floor talking to herself in a range of strange voices. I said hello, but Mabel didn't respond. Mom leaned over and whispered in my ear, "Ignore her rudeness Baby, she's crazy." I turned and looked at Mom, unsure how to respond since everyone there was crazy, including her. She looked at me with her big blue eyes wide and at the same second we both burst out laughing. Then Mom dropped her voice to a whisper, "No really Baby, Mabel is super crazy. She came here from a criminal psychiatric institution. She had been there for 23 years for stabbing her husband 47 times while he slept." Then Mom opened her eyes very wide and nodded her head while mouthing, *"Crazy!"*

I looked at Mabel again; she was so old and frail-looking, it was hard to imagine her killing anyone. "Come on Sweetie, it's too hot to stay here. Let's walk to Jack-in-the-Box and get some food. I've been saving my allowance just for your visit," Mom said, as she slipped her arm in mine and guided me from the room.

As we walked away from the halfway house, Mom and I held hands. They quickly became sweaty but we didn't let go. We were so happy to be together again that the heat and the shitty neighborhood no longer seemed to matter. During our walk, I felt more comfortable than I had in a very long time. Curious, I asked Mom if she thought Mabel was dangerous. "No, no! She only killed her husband because the bastard almost beat her to death, and not just once. If you ask me, he deserved what he got. So it's nothing to worry about, Honey. She just seems weird because she's schizophrenic," Mom replied, as she gave my hand a squeeze. Since I had seen my father beat my mother on more than one occasion, Mabel's actions made sense to me too. I let go of my worries that Mom was not safe with her roommate and focused on the bliss of being with the one person I loved more than anyone in the world.

Mom asked about my new foster parents. I explained that Iris was nice. Not wanting to worry her, I avoided talking about the other members of my new family. Given Mom's new life, I did my best to make her believe I was happy in my new home. That's why I didn't want to tell her about the sheets and sheets of acid that belonged to my foster parents' oldest daughter that sat in the rear flat's refrigerator—acid that the daughter had offered me hits of just days after I moved in. Nor did I want to tell her about the blowjob I walked in on when I got home early from school one day, a blowjob that my new foster dad was getting in the living room from a previous foster daughter. Later, he had the girl come to my room to bring me beers, hoping to buy my silence. The girl explained she did sexual favors for the foster dad because he gave her money to buy drugs. She begged me not to tell anyone, and I didn't. She was 18 anyway, so it's not like the cops were going to do anything about it

The bad things in my life stayed hidden because I didn't want to worry my mother. During later visits, I would also avoid telling her about the two occasions the police stormed the house. The cops came to arrest the husband and the boyfriend of my foster parents' two oldest daughters, one for drug dealing and the other for armed robbery. Those arrests would later dictate the only family outing I ever went on with my foster family—a visit to Tehachapi State Prison to see the oldest daughter's husband. That ended with me getting letters in the mail from a prisoner I had never met; he had seen me during the visit and thought I was pretty. Cigarettes were all it took to get my home address from the oldest daughter's prisoner husband. If I hadn't lived in that foster home, and someone told me the things that were going on, I would have thought they were lying. But, I did live there, and it would have killed my mother to know the horrible truth.

Once we reached the fast-food place, Mom and I had run out of safe things to talk about. We stood inside, silently staring at the menu. Mom lit a cigarette, and then asked if I had ever had a Super Taco. I said that I hadn't. "You'll love them! Let's order four," she said, walking quickly up to the cashier. She placed the order, popped the cigarette between her lips, and reached into her purse to get her wallet. While she was extracting the money, I noticed her hands were shaking badly. I had never seen them shake that much before. It wasn't really a nervous kind of shaking, but more like an uncontrollable tremor. Watching her closely, I noticed her head seemed to have a similar tremor too. The movements worried me. I was terrified that she might have a serious disease.

When our order was ready, we found a table and sat. I looked again at her hands as she set her cigarette down in a tinfoil ashtray on the table. "Mom, are you okay? Your hands are shaking pretty bad. Is there something wrong? Are you nervous?" I asked, searching her face. I could tell by her answer that she was embarrassed.

"It's nothing, Honey. The drugs they give me make me move funny. I was hoping it wasn't noticeable," she said, crushing her cigarette out in the tinfoil ashtray. "Don't worry about it. Now go on and eat." Then she picked up a Super Taco from the tray and bit into it. I picked up one, too. Looking inside, I could see some sort of meat paste and a cheese that had the consistence and color of Cheese Wiz. It looked disgusting. I took a bite—it was revolting. It tasted nothing like the tacos Mom used to make for me at home. I loved those.

"You like it?" Mom asked, with bits of taco shell and lettuce moving around in her mouth as she spoke. Even while eating, she had a big smile on her face. She was happy—happy to be with me and feeding me tacos. I looked at her face—my mother's beautiful face—and I knew that the Super Taco in my hand was love.

The Court was never going to let us live together again. Mom had been given lots of chances, but each time, she got sick again. We were destined to experience only brief visits together—not life. Mom was trying to love me the best way she knew how, through food. She wanted to show me love with a Super Taco. The taco stopped being revolting, and for the rest of my life, I would eat them while remembering how much my mother loved me.

* * *

When 10th grade ended, I begged my social worker to find me a new placement. The dysfunction in the house had become too much for me to manage. I had put in two hard years with the family, trying to maintain myself in what my social worker thought was a "stable" placement. That effort, however, became a bitter pill to swallow because of the disgusting things that went on. It was so insane to me that I was being forced to live there because my mother was unfit. My foster father and his grown kids were just as unfit as my mother. Worse, they didn't even love me. I was simply a monthly paycheck that kept the foster dad in booze and the biological kids fed. At least my own dysfunctional mother loved me in spite of her problems. The unfairness of being kept in an ugly, unloving environment ate me up inside. The only person in the house I respected even a little bit was poor suffering Iris. She was not a bad person, and in her own way, she made a decent foster mother. Yet, she seemed as stuck as I was in a terrible situation.

The event that made me realize I could no longer stay in the placement was a drunken pool party hosted by the oldest daughter when her husband got out of the correctional facility. Behind the main house there was a small kidney-shaped underground pool. The pool and its small connected hot tub were rundown and stained. Regardless, the family loved having late-night parties there. It was early summer just after the school year ended. Everyone from the house, except Iris, was out in the warm summer night drinking and swimming. Officially, as a 15-year-old foster kid, I was not supposed to be drinking, but everyone still slipped me booze. At first the party was going fine. Then the daughter's husband started drunkenly throwing his 3-year-old stepdaughter into the pool. Having been raised around the pool from birth, the little girl knew how to swim. Like the rest of us she was having fun in the pool, but each time she climbed out the ex-convict husband threw her in again.

Even though I was drunk on whiskey myself, I could see that with every throw she was becoming more exhausted. Her fatigue had gotten to the point where she was starting to swallow water and sputter each time she went under. "Hey, she's getting tired," I yelled across the pool from my spot at the edge of the hot tub. The guy just laughed and threw the baby in again. It pissed me off. My heart raced and suddenly I felt uncontrolled rage. I leapt up and ran around the pool to where the dude was standing. He was a big guy with large muscles from doing "hard time" in prison but in my blinding anger I was unafraid.

When the little girl swam to the steps and cleared the pool, I shoved the guy from behind as hard as I could. Rather than just falling in, he decided to dive drunkenly as I shoved him. The strength of my push and his awkward dive caused him to enter the water with a lot of force. Before he could change course and surface, his head hit the other side of the pool. When he came out of the water, blood was pouring across his face from a gash on his scalp. The cut was deep and wouldn't stop bleeding. I stood stunned as I watched a cascade of blood run from his head and into the water. The party abruptly ended. When a rag and ice did not stop the bleeding, he was taken to the emergency room.

Everyone who stayed at the house disbanded to go sleep. A couple of hours later, I was lying wide awake in my bed when the guy came into my room to show me the 14 stiches he had been given. Looking at the bald spot where the doctors had shaved his head, I could clearly see how large and deep the cut was. I said, "I'm sorry," while trying to make tears well in my eyes—but I didn't really mean it. The fact that I wasn't sorry scared me.

* * *

Besides alcohol, drugs were also a problem for me in that placement. The exposure wasn't very surprising since the ex-convict husband was a drug dealer for a biker gang. Though I avoided the acid the oldest daughter had offered me when I first moved in (only because of fears about becoming psychotic like my mom), I did do the meth, coke, and various other pills I was offered. My drug problems weren't helped by the fact that my best friend in high school was dating a 35-year-old meth dealer. If drugs could not be had for free from someone in my foster home, I just went to visit my school friend and her boyfriend. Lots of 30–40-year-old men hung out at the boyfriend's house doing the drugs they had purchased. I was always welcome because they liked having a big-breasted 15-year-old girl around; likely because they thought I was going to have sex with them. I played along but never gave in. I just snorted their lines and drank their beer. But, the game could not go on forever and one of the guys became very aggressive in his attempts to get me into bed. Of all the older men hanging out offering me drugs, he was the most attractive.

Under the constant pressure by the better-looking methhead, and annoyed by the teasing I got back in the foster home for still being a virgin, I finally convinced myself it would be okay if I lost my virginity to a 35-year-old man. It was a horrible experience. Shortly after that, I stopped going to the drug house and even stopped hanging out with my girlfriend from school. But it was too late, the damage had been done. I felt disgusted with myself and with the horrible condition of my life. When in the weeks following that experience, I found myself sitting on various freeway overpasses contemplating jumping into the oncoming traffic—I knew I had to get out of that foster home.

* * *

By the time I entered my next foster home, I was just shy of 16 and had a boyfriend nine years older than me. The family who took me as their foster daughter were upper-middle class, lived in a nice neighborhood, and had two small kids, ages two and four. They had specifically requested a teen girl from Social

Services. The request was motivated by their desire to have a free babysitter. My new foster mother was in her 30s. She had been a cheerleader and beauty queen in high school. Being a stay-at-home mother was chafing at her desire to be popular and out in public. To facilitate her longing to be free of the drudgery of motherhood, I was brought in to cook, clean, and watch the kids whenever she didn't feel like it.

The family was not obviously dysfunctional, but I resented being a live-in babysitter with no pay. When I started to complain to them about the situation they made me a deal. "Tell you what Jean, you babysit and I'll let you leave the house unsupervised when I don't need you, even to your boyfriend's," my new foster mom told me in order to make sure I didn't complain to anyone else. I agreed. The ratio was not one-to-one: for several hours of babysitting I was given one hour to visit my mom or boyfriend. A month into the placement, I tried to swing a deal with them that would allow me to spend the whole weekend with my "Aunt Ginny," which was really my boyfriend. My request was denied, likely because they figured out I was lying about where I was really going. I had spent the last couple of months watching the kids all day so my foster mom could start her new "fun" job and go to jazzercise. It seemed so unfair that my request was denied.

It was the final straw. After years in foster care, I was tired of being neglected, taken advantage of, or abused. When my boyfriend suggested that I run away just two months after entering the placement, it was an easy decision to make.

Around midnight a few days later, I packed what little I owned. It fit into a single plastic rectangular laundry basket. When my boyfriend tapped quietly on my bedroom window to let me know he was there to pick me up, it was so easy to just walk out. I took the basket and quietly walked down the hall toward the garage. So that I wouldn't bump into anything, during the day I had practiced the walk from my room to the door that led from the kitchen into the garage. Once in the garage, I could exit the house quietly from the side door. My heart was beating a throbbing pulse into my head. *Please, don't get let me get caught, God*, I prayed to a savior I no longer believed in.

I knew nothing good was coming to me if I got caught. Once you were a runaway, decent foster placements were hard to find. If I didn't make it out safely, I knew my next stop would be a group home or perhaps even Juvy again.

My palms were sweating as I held the laundry basket under one arm and unlocked the side door in the garage that led outside. My boyfriend stood waiting for me in the shadows of a tree near the street. He led me to his truck, which was parked on the next block. I placed my laundry basket on the seat and climbed in. As we drove off into the night, I believed that my life was about to get much better—sadly, I was wrong.

* * *

It's really true what they say—"It only takes one time." Not long after running away I became pregnant following a single act of unprotected intercourse. It was a difficult situation to be in at 16 years old with no family to talk to regarding what to do. The news also came at the point when I realized what a terrible mistake I had made in running from one bad situation smack-dab into another, and the current one was worse than the previous. Prior to learning I was pregnant, I had been contemplating running away from my boyfriend to live on the streets of LA. Once I knew I was pregnant though, I didn't want to risk that kind of life. My boyfriend made it clear that he wanted the baby. To me, his intentions seemed tainted, as if it was more about keeping me trapped than wanting a child. I pondered sneaking off alone and getting an abortion. Feeling confused and lonely, I talked to single mom of two who lived in an apartment nearby. I told her I was about six weeks pregnant and considering an abortion. The woman tried to be very neutral regarding any recommendations she gave, but described the abortion she had at 19.

"My parents would have been very ashamed of me and against me having a child. I was still living at home while going to beauty school, I didn't feel I could disappoint them," she told me in her living room.

"Did you ever regret it?"

"Not exactly," she said. "I knew back then that I was not ready to raise a child, and my parents swore they would disown me if I had sex before I was married. That made me feel like adoption was not an option because then my parents would know I had been having sex. So I chose to have the abortion instead. The only hard thing is that even now, going on 15 years later, I still think about how old the baby would be now."

"Oh, that must make you feel a little sad," I said, immediately sure I would not want to experience that for the rest of my life.

"Yes it does, but I still believe it was the right choice at that time. Whatever you decide, just remember that no choice is going to be perfect."

Following our conversation, I decided I would keep the baby. It was a choice that would save my life.

* * *

As my pregnancy progressed, I became excited about becoming a mother. The situation with my boyfriend was very difficult, but by focusing on having the baby, I found moments of joy. My boyfriend decided we should move into a larger apartment when I was about six months pregnant. The place was nice, but my boyfriend got into an argument with the landlord upstairs over how loud they played their music. After they refused to turn it down, he shut off their apartment's breaker. That led to a fight and they called the cops. We were there only a month before we were forced to move again.

Because my boyfriend had to work, I ended up moving heavy boxes and furniture all day with the help of the woman who had told me about her abortion. By that afternoon, I felt a weird heaviness in my lower abdomen, and when I went to the bathroom I noticed a strange thick mucus in my panties. Since we were poor and I didn't have a doctor, I received free prenatal care from the nurses at Planned Parenthood. When I started having the weird symptoms I called there for advice. The nurse I spoke to told me that it was all completely normal and I didn't need to come in. At just 17, I was still too inexperienced to know that medical professionals were sometimes wrong.

By midnight I was in labor. At 6 a.m. my daughter was delivered exactly two months prematurely. She weighed 3 pounds 11 ounces. Instead of being able to hold her after the birth, they whisked her off to the Neonatal Intensive Care Unit, while I was unceremoniously dumped into the packed recovery ward of the county hospital. As I lay in a room surrounded by nine other women happily nursing their babies, I felt empty and sad. A short while later a photographer came in.

"Would you like me to take a picture of your baby?" she asked.

"Oh yes, please! I haven't even gotten to see her yet. I forgot my glasses when I went into labor and came to the hospital, so I didn't really even see her in the delivery room when they held her up," I said, truly excited for a picture of my new daughter.

"Okay, do you have her basinet number? I'll go to the nursery and take some photos now."

"I don't know that. She's in the NICU though. Maybe the nurses there can tell you."

"Oh, I'm sorry! I can't actually take pictures of the babies there."

I couldn't respond; I just began to sob uncontrollably. There was no one there to comfort me.

* * *

The day I was discharged from the hospital, I was pressured to give a name for my daughter's birth certificate. Since she had been two months premature I didn't yet have a name. When I finally got to see her in the NICU I was completely terrified—my daughter was so tiny and frail-looking with all those tubes and sensors attached to her body. I longed to pick her up, but I wasn't allowed to hold her. Naming her was something I'd always imagined I'd do while holding her in my arms. Being asked for a name again made me feel sad. In the end, with my boyfriend and me unable to agree on any other choice, we decided to name her after her grandmothers on both sides. I wrote *Joy Grace* down on the birth certificate paperwork with a sense of both love and dread. There was a small part of me that had a superstitious worry that by naming her after my mother, I might taint her with the possibility of our family sickness.

Joy Grace stayed in the hospital for 30 days. During that time she went through a number of very painful procedures and tests. She was fed through a tube, had blood drawn so many times from the same spots that her skin looked like meat-pulp, and she had burns from a monitor that was supposed to be moved frequently before it got too hot (which the nurses weren't doing). By the time I got her home from the hospital, she flinched and began to cry each time I touched her. It broke my heart because I loved her more deeply than I ever could have imagined. With time though, she calmed down and I could get her to sleep peacefully when I held her in my arms. For a little while, I believed that life was somehow going to be magically better, and that all the suffering I had been through was simply going to be forgotten—again I was wrong.

PART THREE

Chasing Success

Chapter 9: Tapestry

While I was bumping around various foster homes and then later bad situations, my mother was bumping around various hospitals, institutions, and board-and-care homes. She had done well while in Spring Gardens, staying stable, which persuaded a judge to give her permission to move into an independent-living low-income apartment building. That happened before my daughter was born, while I was still in foster care.

The place they put Mom in was terrible. Basically it was just a rundown motel room in an aging 10-story brownstone. Within the "apartment," if you could call it that, there was a king-size bed, a closet, a bath, as well as a counter with a mini-fridge and a hotplate. Cockroaches scurried along the floor, and the one window in the room had been permanently sealed shut. Mom was so excited to get the place because she thought maybe she could convince the Court to let me move back in with her. I was still living with Iris and her drunken husband the first time I visited Mom at her new apartment.

"See Baby, we could share the bed. It's big enough," Mom said, as she showed me the tiny room.

"Yeah, we could. I wouldn't mind that," I replied, with a sad feeling in my heart because I knew the Court was never going to let me come back to her again. I didn't say that, though, because she so desperately wanted us to be together. I did too, but I had finally faced the reality of the situation after so many failed tries at moving back in with Mom.

"Wouldn't it be so nice? We could buy a TV. Then we could snuggle in bed at night watching it like we used to. Would you like that?" Mom asked, patting the bed next to her as she sat down.

"It would be wonderful Mom," I said. I sat down next to her and put my arms around her shoulders. I felt so big by comparison. While I had grown to be almost 5'8" she actually seemed like she had shrunken smaller than her petite 5'2". The height change was like our emotional relationship. Somehow, we had managed to physically reverse our roles so that I became even more the mother and she the child. The fact that she was never going to really be the mother again made me want to cry.

"Come on, Mom, let's get out of here. I earned some money last week. Let's go eat," I said, pulling Mom up from the bed before I became depressed.

"Wait Baby, I need to fix my makeup."

She took her lipstick and a mirror from her purse. Her hands shook so badly that she could barely keep the deep red tint just on her lips. Normally, when she wanted to put on more makeup I felt angry at the extra time she wasted, but as she became more and more of a victim of her sickness and its treatment, I stopped letting my irritation slip out. I couldn't be mad at her while watching her struggle with such a simple task. Now, the only thing I felt was pity.

We left the building and walked a few blocks to a rundown diner. The place was filled with low-income elderly folks, homeless people who could afford only a single bottomless cup of coffee, and few others like my mom, struggling with their sickness. We used to go to a nicer diner a bit farther away until I told Mom I didn't want to go there anymore. I hated the way the "normal" patrons looked at my mother with distaste and whispered behind their hands. Their pompous disdain made me want to smash their heads onto the table and shove food down their throats until they choked. The experience was worsened by the fact that Mom wasn't able to recognize that they were ridiculing her. When they began to look in our direction and whisper, she would just stare at them in a very intent childlike way, as if they were some sort of fascinating bug on a stick. The longer she stared the more uncomfortable they would get.

"Mom, don't stare!" I would admonish.

"What, Baby?, I'm just looking at the people."

"Yeah, but you've been looking at them for a really long time. I think it makes them uncomfortable."

"No, they don't care. I just think they're interesting. I wonder how that woman gets her hair to stay that way?"

Nothing I said seemed to get Mom to understand that the people were making fun of her. The longer she stared the louder and ruder they typically became. "My god, that crazy homeless lady won't quit staring at us," was a common comment I would hear. That statement would make me seethe with anger. Though I said it sometimes too, I hated it when anyone referred to my mother as "crazy." Even worse, saying she was "homeless" was grossly insulting. Yes, Mom didn't have many clothes and the things she did have were old, but she took care of her hygiene. Most homeless people didn't do that.

Usually, I would excuse myself to go to the bathroom and make a detour past the table of people making rude comments. "Fuck you!" was the response I would hiss as I went by. Those types of incidents started happening too often at the nice diner, so we began to go to the rundown place where the people were more "like us." Since Mom had very little money, I paid when I could, but even then, we often had to order just one thing to share. Usually we got something sweet, like pie. Then we would sit for hours over our empty plate just killing time together. Likely the waitress hated us for taking up a booth or table, but rarely did we get kicked out.

The places Mom lived were always so awful that when I visited I tried hard to get us out somewhere so I wouldn't be compelled to cut the visit short. The hardest place to visit Mom at was the psychiatric hospital. There, Mom was locked in and couldn't leave. She was also usually not completely sane yet. At the height of one of her episodes, Mom required a lot of prescription drugs to get anywhere close to normal. The first few weeks in the hospital were spent getting the doses right. When I visited, she might be spewing delusions of grandeur or she would be so heavily medicated that I felt like I was trying to talk to a zombie. I hated those visits, especially when she would finally be sane enough to understand the things she had done when she was sick. It made me sad to see her helpless to control the things that happened to her.

* * *

Mom didn't make it long in her independent-living apartment. The pressure of cooking, managing bills, and loneliness—perhaps mostly the loneliness—brought on another breakdown. She did her psychiatric hospital stint, then was ordered back into the board-and-care home. Wherever she was, I visited her whenever I could. If for some reason I couldn't visit, she would become desperately anxious. When I did arrive again she would tell me, "Oh Jean, I'm so glad you're here. I thought you were dead. Please don't do that to me again," I would promise not to miss a visit in the future, but that was a promise impossible for me to keep. As the years wore on, I resented the fact that she never asked "why" I hadn't visited. It wasn't like I wanted to miss a visit; I usually didn't make it because something terrible had happened to me. Of course, as always, I never told her about those things because I didn't want her to worry about me and get sick again.

After Mom returned to Spring Gardens, she found companionship. The first relationship she had was with the live-in caretaker of the facility. He was a man with a haunted past who had overcome a 25-year heroin addiction. I think he had spent so much time in halfway houses himself that Spring Gardens was the only place he felt comfortable. It was clear he was a guy who was trying to make up for all the bad things he had done during his years of addiction. He wasn't much to look at, and I think he liked Mom a lot more than she liked him. But, he was really nice to Mom and helped her get the things she needed. At first his previous history as a violent gang member made me uncomfortable around him, but with time his kindness convinced me that his past was long behind him. Mom and he dated for about a year. They might have dated longer, but he died a painful death from pancreatic cancer.

Mom had another breakdown not long after her boyfriend's death, and ended up back in the psychiatric hospital. After she got out and returned to Spring Gardens, she was just a shell of the person she had once been. Whether it was the medication or a lifetime of battling mental illness, the vibrant woman who used to take me on adventures was completely gone. She became more and more zombie-like. When she wasn't zoned out, she was very anxious.

* * *

The next man Mom dated was Kyle. He also lived at Spring Gardens and was a diagnosed schizophrenic. Kyle loved my mother a lot, even from afar. It had taken him a long time to woo my mother into dating, because Mom didn't find him attractive. When I asked Mom why, she said, "I don't know. He just seems a little crazy. Plus, he has that limp arm he can't use."

Her response made me laugh. "You're crazy too, you know. He seems really nice. Plus, he really likes you. He's always bringing you chocolates and cigarettes. How can you not like a guy like that?"

I think the thing that finally won my mother over was the fact that Kyle was a really smart guy. He even had an MBA from University of California, Berkeley. His intelligence, along with little acts kindness, convinced Mom to date him not long after I had run away from foster care.

I'll admit—I loved Kyle. He was a nice man with a funny sense of humor. He was nicer to me than my own father had ever been. He was also good with money. If it weren't for the fact that Kyle's schizophrenia was difficult to treat, I think he would have been very successful in life, lame arm and all.

About a year into the relationship, Mom and Kyle snuck off to the courthouse and got married. That allowed them to move into the same room at the board-and-care. Then for a couple of years, Kyle carefully saved the small allowance he and Mom got from their disability checks. The board-and-care home kept most of the money they got from their Social Security disability payments, but gave them each 18 dollars a month to spend as they wished. After buying cigarettes for them, Kyle squirreled away the rest until he had enough for him and Mom to put a deposit on an apartment and pay the first month's rent. Joy Grace was about a year old when that happened.

The place they rented was in a very dangerous neighborhood, but it was cheap and it was theirs. Kyle used his financial skills to fill the place with furniture from a rent-to-own store down the street. Mom purchased necessities such as towels from Finger Hut. Mom had always been good at making a place look nice no matter how cheap the items she used—and it did look nice. For both of them it was a vast improvement over the rundown board-and-care.

I was really happy for Mom and Kyle. Things went well for a long while. Then one afternoon, I got a phone call from Mom.

"Jean, you have to come. Kyle has gone crazy. He was giving away all our money to people in line at the DMV. They asked him to leave, but he refused. They just called me and said I should come get him before he gets arrested," she said. Lately, he has also been calling the Russian Embassy because he thinks he's a spy. Oh Jean, what am I going to do? If he goes back to the hospital or to jail, I can't take care of myself alone."

I knew Mom was telling the truth about Kyle being sick. He had also been calling me and saying some very weird stuff. His last request was that I read his poems and help him get them published. I said I would try to help him, but when the poems arrived in the mail, they were just psychotic drawings with rambling disjointed words underneath. When he called me back to see if I thought they were good, I lied to spare his feelings.

"Mom, don't panic. We just need to convince him to go to the hospital. He will only need to go in for a week or two until his meds are sorted out and working again. After that, they'll let him come home. It would cost more to put him into care again. If the authorities know he has you to take care of him for less money, they're not going to do that. The rent's paid, so you'll be okay until he gets out. Don't worry, it's all going to be fine," I said.

It was hard to get Kyle to go to the hospital. He made a few more public disturbances before the police agreed to help us get him there. As I predicted, he only stayed until the doctors got him stable and then he came home. He apologized to everyone for his behavior and worked hard to resolve the financial problems he had caused by running up the phone bill and giving away their cash. In all of the mess, his devotion to my mother never wavered, but Mom took some time to get over all the insecurity he had caused her.

Mom and Kyle had their hardships for sure, but somehow they always managed. Their biggest challenges were related to either their mental illness or the side-effects of the medications they took. Both had periods when their uncontrolled symptoms made each other's lives more difficult, but at least they understood that beneath the mental illness there lived a good person. That was something others had a hard time seeing.

Having Kyle around relived some of the pressure I felt about always needing to be there for Mom. Without him, I'm not sure I would have been able to step back and evaluate whether or not it was healthy for me to be Mom's mother when I had my own daughter to care for. When he died, I felt like I had lost a friend and a savior.

Chapter 10: Ticket To Ride

I left my daughter's father *immediately* after my 18th birthday; a day I picked because I believed it was the only way I would not be forced to go back into foster care. What I didn't know at the time, was that the Court had actually emancipated me one month before my 17th birthday, which made staying with my daughter's father that extra year an unnecessary mistake. However, when I did leave and was on my own, I quickly figured out that being solely responsible for my daughter's well-being was very difficult. My self-confidence fell drastically as I realized how hard it was going to be to raise her alone. My sense of worth was not helped by a trip to the Social Services Department to apply for Aid to Families with Dependent Children or AFDC—better known to most as "welfare." Grandma Greta had always talked about people who took welfare as the lowest scum of the earth. Out of pride, I had not wanted to apply for government money, but I was close to destitute within a month of being totally on my own. There was no family to turn to; no sympathetic benefactor just waiting to rescue me; no job paying enough to an uneducated 18-year-old that would cover the cost of food and housing—let alone childcare—I was on my own and completely unprepared.

I did my best to stretch out what little we had, making do with less and less each day that passed. Three meals became two, and then one, just to make sure that what food there was went to Joy. I dropped pound after pound. My face became gaunt and my hips protruded sharply. Friends suggested I lay off the meth, but I had stopped doing drugs even before I got pregnant. Desperate, I knew I could only survive if I swallowed my pride and followed in my mother's footsteps, even though applying for AFDC was something I had always sworn I would never do.

The day I went downtown to the welfare office with Joy in tow felt like a trip to Hell. The worker assigned to process my application made me feel completely worthless. The woman basically spent the entire time implying that I was a "liar" and one of those "teen moms" who wanted to pop out a bunch of kids in order to live off the State forever. I left the welfare office feeling dirty. I should have felt relieved that I would soon be able to pay rent and feed my baby, but all I felt was an utter sense of failure.

In the weeks that followed, I received my first welfare check of a whopping 380 dollars. I desperately needed it to pay the rent on my tiny one-bedroom apartment located in one of the most dangerous parts of town. I had three pieces of furniture in my place: my daughter's crib, her highchair, and a stereo I had bought for two dollars at a garage sale. I slept on the floor with only a blanket, but I didn't mind. It was worth it to be free from an unhealthy and unhappy relationship. The apartment cost me 250 dollars a month, leaving me just over 130 dollars to cover food, clothing, transportation, diapers, and utilities. I had heard people complain about women who got rich off welfare. If they did, I had no idea how. For me, every day remained a tiring dance to make sure just our basic necessities were paid for.

Always fighting to survive drained me. Child support was awarded in the divorce, but because my ex did construction work that could be paid under the table, getting it was a problem. I wanted to work, but I knew that even if I found a job it would be as a clerk at a gas station paying the same (or less) as ADFC. It killed me to know that on the pay I would earn, I could not afford the childcare it would take to earn that paycheck. Mom was still in the board-and-care home and she was too unstable to care for herself, let alone my daughter. Leaving Joy home alone at night so that I could work while she slept was something I considered, but in the end, I could not do it. Leaving her by herself, even if she were asleep, would make me a worse person than someone living off welfare.

I agonized over all the possible options for survival. Endless thoughts floated through my mind. I began to contemplate suicide. I often wondered if my daughter might be better off if I put her up for adoption. I thought about dealing drugs like so many of the people I grew up with did. I thought about prostitution, but at the time I hated men so much that I knew I could never sell my body for cash. I envisioned myself being arrested for child-neglect while I left Joy home alone at night to work. It was agonizing because I wanted so badly to be a stable provider for my daughter. However, simply having a child made all the likely work options I had seem impossible.

In a strange twist of fortune, my future would be drastically altered by a suggestion from the wife of a drug dealer. Carly was married to the brother of my best friend from high school, and she was the first person I had ever really known who had attended college. She was a surgical nurse and worked in a hospital. She was more successful than anyone I had ever known, which is why I never understood how she managed to hook up with her husband Wayne. Carly and I saw each other rarely, usually when Wayne passed through town on his way to score drugs.

Wayne was a coke dealer in 1985—the heyday of cocaine use by professionals. He bought drugs on the coast to sell to river rats (AKA: rich boaters) who spent their recreational time playing on the Colorado River as it coursed through the Arizona desert. I had gone with Wayne once to purchase the large batches of coke he would then cut and bag into small amounts for resale. The house he scored from was not some seedy drug den. It was a multimillion-dollar house in an exclusive neighborhood. The only thing strange about the place was the people inside. Attractive young women agreed to be filmed having sex in exchange for drugs and a chance at life in the fast lane. Though I never saw anyone carrying a gun, intimidating-looking men hung out near doors and in the yard. It really was like a scene from a Hollywood movie. I never really had the desire to go back again after that first visit, so Carly and I sometimes hung out at my place and visited while Wayne did his thing.

It was during one of those visits that I told Carly about my demoralizing welfare experience. Carly never talked much about herself, but she was a great listener, perhaps because she had spent her childhood living overseas with her missionary parents. As I discussed my fears and frustrations, Carly tried very hard to be supportive.

"Jean, why don't you go to college? You don't have to be abused by bitter welfare workers the rest of your life. If you become a nurse like me, you can make a lot of money," Carly said, her tall frame propped up against the wall outside of my sparsely furnished one-bedroom apartment.

"I'm never going to get into college," I said. "I didn't even graduate. While I was in high school I took two periods of ceramics, auto shop, and joined the FFA so I could grow pot in the greenhouse. I'm not college material!"

"Look, you showed me your GED scores. You did pretty well on everything but math. Why don't you just take your scores to the college and see what they say? Come on, don't stay stuck like this!" my friend, said, shifting her body so she could look at me directly.

Looking away from Carly to hide my uncertainty, I replied, "I don't think I'm going to get in, but I guess I could go to the junior college and apply."

"No, Jean, just go to the state university first. You never know what will happen; maybe you'll get in. If you don't, no big deal; then you'll go apply at the junior college."

"Carly, even if I do get in, how am I gonna pay for it? I can barely pay my rent."

"You can get loans and grants. Just try, Jean. If you get in, the rest will get figured out, but you won't know till you try."

* * *

College was an option that never entered my mind as a means to make my life better. Why would it? I had dropped out of school before I had even started 11th grade. People from my family were not destined for college. No one in my family had graduated high school either; not my mother; not my father; not my aunt; not my uncle; not one of my four siblings. I knew that, like my mother before me, I would be hammered by poverty and hated by those who believed I wanted to live life sponging off their tax dollars.

During the weeks following Carly's visit, I talked myself into going to the university to apply. I was pretty sure I wouldn't get in, but I also knew that Carly was right, I would never know until I tried. Early one morning, I dressed in the nicest of my few changes of clothes—a black Crosby, Stills and Nash T-shirt and a pair of un-torn jeans. After packing a diaper bag for Joy and my purse with the documents I thought I might need, I loaded us into the 1961 Chrysler New Yorker that Wayne had helped me work a deal for with some guy down the street. It cost me the old broken down 1960 Dodge pickup in my yard and 150 dollars in cash, which Wayne fronted me until I could pay him back. The car was huge and I hadn't gotten my license very long before I got the car, which is why I was scared every time I drove it.

The university was located about 10 miles from my apartment at the base of the mountain range that had been my home as a child. As I navigated the New Yorker into a spot in the visitors' parking lot, I admired the layout of the campus. The buildings were spaced widely apart with large grassy areas between them. Trees planted strategically along the walkways provided shade from the brutal summer sun. Everything seemed well-kept and the ground was free of the garbage I had become accustomed to on the streets in my neighborhood. I felt a sense of awe as I carried my daughter toward the Administration Building. Like taking a breath after being underwater a long time, I realized that I desperately wanted to be accepted as a student there. It was a place so different from anything I had ever known. But, there was a problem—I was terrified. Having never known anyone in my entire childhood who went to college, I had no idea what to expect. I was 18 years old; a high school dropout with only a recently acquired GED; a person who had struggled with learning disabilities; and a new divorcé, as well as an overwhelmed and unprepared mother to my 1-year-old daughter. I was pretty certain I didn't have any of the things colleges wanted.

Entering the Administration Building, I followed the signs to the Office of Admissions. Since it was the summer quarter, there were few students milling around and the hallways had the peaceful hush of a church. My heart raced as I approached the Admissions window. I wanted to do everything just right so they would accept me. I readjusted my daughter on my hip when I got to the window. A petite graying woman in her 50s greeted me.

"Can I help you, Honey?" she asked, with a smile on her face.

"Yes, I would like to apply for admission," I said, nervously bouncing Joy up and down.

"Do you have your application filled out?"

"No, I don't have an application," I replied, pulling up the diaper bag strap that was about to slip off my shoulder.

"No problem. Here, let me give you one. You are also going to need your birth certificate and a copy of your high school transcripts. You can have the official ones sent later. If you have unofficial copies now, go ahead and attach them."

"I didn't graduate high school but I have my GED results," I responded, suddenly filled with panic that I wouldn't even be able to apply.

"That's fine, Honey. Here, I'll get you one. If you want, you can take it home to fill out and bring it back later," the woman said, handing me a thick application packet. Then she cooed at Joy and touched the tip of her nose. Joy laughed.

I knew I might not be brave enough to return. "I would prefer to fill it out now if that's okay," I replied. It was now or never.

"No problem, why don't you go over there to fill out your application?" The woman said, pointing to a series of tall metal tables across from us.

I moved toward the tables, awkwardly holding the application in one hand and Joy in the other. The diaper bag and my purse began inching their way off my shoulder as I walked. Just before the bags slipped, I managed to set Joy down on one of the tall tables. Frustrated, I roughly laid everything on the metal top and began digging into the diaper bag for a toy to keep Joy busy. While awkwardly wrapping my arm around my daughter to keep her from falling, I began to fill out the application.

I managed to fill in my personal information without much difficulty: name, address, last school attended, etc. I wrote "N/A" for all the requests for parental information, which also took very little time. At the final question I froze. It read, *Is there any additional information you think the university should know about you when considering your application for admission?* I wondered what I should say. *Should I tell them the truth—that I am an 18-year-old divorce, a high school dropout, and an ex-foster kid?* I asked myself. I didn't think they would like that, but what else could I put down? I had no scholastic achievements to talk about, no great GPA, no clubs I could claim to have been a member of. Added to my stress over what was the right answer was the fact that my learning disabilities made me a terrible speller. Worse, when I was nervous I stopped being able to be spell even the simplest words. I stared at the question for a very long time, knowing that even when I figured out what to say, I still wouldn't be able to write it down the way I wanted to.

Anger at my inabilities and feelings of worthlessness threatened to overwhelm me. I was tempted to throw the application in the trash and walk out. Sensing my agitation, Joy began to cry; her tears pulled me back to the reality of our situation. If I didn't try, I would never know if I could go to college; without college, our lives would be unlikely to improve. Without trying, I would give Joy nothing better than my mother had been able to give me. So I decided to tell the truth; there was really no other option. If I was going to be condemned for my past, so be it. I had nothing else to say.

Briefly, I described myself as a single teenage parent trying to improve my life. The words didn't flow easily, and I was forced to stop and rewrite sentences when I realized that I couldn't spell certain words I wanted to use. Afraid that I wouldn't be accepted because of poor spelling, I rewrote things using what I could spell. Once my application was complete, I re-read what I had written. The short paragraph sounded like a "Dick and Jane" 1st grade reading primer, but at least the words were spelled correctly. That seemed more important than sounding sophisticated.

I gave the application back to the woman at the Admissions counter without looking her in the face. I was convinced I was not going to get in and embarrassed by my limitation. I just wanted to leave, but she encouraged me to wait while she checked the application over carefully and took copies of my supporting documents. When she finished, I thanked her with my head down. Moving Joy to a more secure position on my hip, I turned to leave. As I walked down the hall, the woman called after me. Her voice sounded motherly, kind. I stopped, wondering what I had forgotten. I looked toward her. She was leaning her plump body over the counter in order to see me. There was a warm smile on her face. "Not too many young girls in your situation would do what you just did. I'm really proud of you. I think there is a good chance you're going to get in," she said, giving me a wink. I stared at her warm brown eyes, wondering if she really meant it, and I could see that she did. The hopelessness I was feeling lifted just a little.

On the walk back to my car, I stopped for a moment and let Joy down on the grass. Watching her uncertain steps, I thought about the woman's words and allowed myself to fantasize about what it would be like if I got in; what it would be like if I became the first person in my family to go to college. As Joy crawled in the grass, I stared at the buildings and imagined myself in them. Excitement welled inside me. Fear of failure battled it back down. I picked Joy up and continued to move toward the car. On the drive home, I was exhausted. The only thing I could do was wait to see if I was admitted.

When a letter finally arrived from the university, I stared at it for a long time before I got up the courage to open it. My hands shook as I tore the envelop open. I scanned the letter quickly, looking for the word "rejected." It wasn't there. Unbelievably, I had been accepted for the Fall Quarter. I was shocked. For more than a month, I had spent many hours convincing myself that I would never get in. There was something surreal about holding that acceptance letter in my hands. It took a few minutes for my shock to become elation. I wept and laughed. *Wow, I'm going to college—at 18—just like other people my age*, I thought.

I also wondered what the woman at the Admissions Office had done to help me get in. I thought about my response to the "what else should we know about you" section of my application. *Maybe people don't think I'm bad for being a foster kid or teen mom after all*, I pondered. Rather than feeling scorn because I was a teen parent or a previous foster kid, did the committee find some virtue in me that I had yet to see in myself? Whatever the reasons, I knew I was being given the chance to start over, a chance I wasn't going to waste. No matter how hard it would be, I was going to do everything in my power to succeed.

* * *

There is nothing like sleeping under a table with your baby in a house full of recovering drug addicts to make you wonder if you have made the right choice. I was 19 years old going on 20. Though I had just finished my first year and a-half of college successfully, I unexpectedly found myself homeless. It was a terrible blow because for the most part things had been going well—surprisingly well. My fears about being stupid had just started to diminish. It seemed that it was entirely within my power to get my degree. Things were not completely easy, but they weren't impossible either. I was feeling pretty good about the future when I came up against a series of unexpected events.

I had been living in my own little apartment since leaving Joy's dad, and that had gone really well for a long time. Then, returning from a trip out to the desert to visit Carly, I picked up a hitchhiker because I felt bad for him being stranded out in the middle of the desert. His work truck had broken down. He was only going about 20 miles to a nearby Indian reservation, but even that short ride gave us enough time to realize we liked each other. His name was Stanley and he was 15 years older than me. I dropped him at his tiny trailer out in the desert, promising to come visit him the very next weekend. That led to other weekends together and soon we decided we were in love. I began looking to see if I could transfer schools so that we could live together because driving 70 miles each way during the school week was just too hard. While my search for a new school continued, I picked up a weekend job in a deli/bar closer to Stanley's place. I still had my apartment for weekdays and school.

About five months after Stanley and I met, we went to a concert near the city where I lived. It was a weekend event, so we decided to camp out near the venue. During the day we went together with Joy to listen to the music, but I still had to work my evening shift out by Stanley's house. Stanley decided he didn't want to come back with me, so I left Joy with a sitter so he could continue enjoying the music festival while I worked. "I'll just hitchhike back to the campground and meet you there tonight," Stanley said, before I left with Joy.

With Joy asleep in her car seat, I drove past the concert venue around 11:00 p.m. on the way to the campground. On a backroad a few miles from the venue I passed a terrible accident. A Jeep Wrangler sat mangled and upside-down in the sand about 50 feet from a sharp curve in the road. It appeared as if it had rolled several times. There were several emergency vehicles with their lights flashing out into the pitch-black night, and a stretcher was being carefully loaded into the back of the ambulance. I felt bad for whoever was injured and sent a prayer their way, not once thinking it might be someone I knew.

When I arrived at the campground I didn't find Stanley, but I wasn't worried; I just thought he was off partying. The next day when he didn't show up, I became concerned. By late afternoon when he still hadn't arrived, I figured the best choice was to break camp and go back to Stanley's house to see if he was there. He wasn't. After pacing around for a couple hours wondering what to do, I called the police to file a Missing Person's Report. They told me I had to wait at least 48 hours, but recommended that I call the jails and the hospitals before I filed. I hung up and started dialing the numbers.

On about the fourth call, I got the terrible news: Stanley was in the hospital. He had caught a ride back to the campground as planned, but he never showed up because he had been riding in that flipped-over Jeep. According to the police report there were four men riding in the vehicle, all drunk except Stanley, but he was the only one who got hurt when the driver took the curve too fast and rolled the Jeep over. Stanley, having just hopped in as a hitchhiker, wasn't wearing a seatbelt. He was thrown from the SUV and broke his neck.

Stanley spent the next 30 days lying in a hospital bed, trying to adjust to the fact he was going to be a quadriplegic for the rest of his life. I visited him every day, but kept driving back to the desert every night so I could take care of his dog. With everything that was going on, I rarely went to my own apartment at all. My landlady, thinking I had abandoned the place, changed the locks and kept my stuff without even giving me any notice. When I finally did visit, I was told my stuff was gone and the place had been rented to someone else. I could have fought it, but I just had too much to deal with. I gave up the little stuff I had had there and just continued to travel between the hospital, the university, and Stanley's house.

Around day 14 of Stanley's hospital stay, I was standing by his bed when he asked, "Jean, will you marry me? We could have the minister come in and perform the ceremony here. What do you think?" I was shocked and overwhelmed by the proposal. It was asking a lot of a 19-year-old girl trying to take care of a 2-year-old baby. Marrying Stanley would mean also taking care of a quadriplegic, and I didn't think I was ready for that. Yet, I couldn't tell him no. I wanted to be a better person than that. I had seen my mom give away her last dollar to people in need even though she was likely no better off than them—watching her do that impacted me significantly. I didn't want to be the kind of woman who left a quadriplegic man while he was in the hospital. So I said yes.

"But Stanley, I don't want to marry you here. Let's wait until you're discharged. Is that okay?" I asked, hoping he would not be too disappointed.

After I agreed to marry Stanley, his mood improved and he seemed very committed to walking again. Staring at the metal halo that was screwed into his head that kept his neck from moving, it was hard for me to share his optimism. Still, I stayed positive and never discussed the hardships I was facing or my feelings of terror.

On the 29th day of Stanley's hospital stay, the doctor took me aside. "Jean, you need to take care of yourself too. Maybe tomorrow you should skip visiting and take a rest," he said in a caring tone. He was right; I was so tired and drained from trying to keep everything together. I told the doctor I would consider it. The next morning, I gave myself the luxury of sleeping in a bit and then sitting outside with Joy in the yard at Stanley's place, which by default had become mine. Instead of going to the hospital, I decided to follow the doctor's advice and give myself a rest.

The phone rang around 8:00 p.m. that night. "Is this the fiancé of Stanley Dower?" the person on the other end asked.

"Yes," I replied, as my heart began to beat wildly.

"I am so sorry ma'am, but Stanley passed away this evening. The doctors tried to resuscitate him but were unsuccessful."

I slid to the floor, clutching the phone to my ear. "I don't understand. He was just fine yesterday. I would have been there, but the doctor said he was doing well and that I should stay home."

"I'm sorry, but I don't know what happened. An autopsy will be performed. Hopefully that will explain his cause of death. Since you were not yet married, I'm afraid you're not considered his legal kin. His family has been contacted in New York. From this point forward, if you want further information you'll have to get it through them. They will be handling all the arrangements. I also want to let you know that we do have a social worker who does grief counseling in the hospital. You're welcome to stop in and see her if you wish."

Devastated, I cried long into the night. I felt so guilty that I hadn't been there with him when he passed away. Later, I would find myself feeling guilty for being relieved at the fact that Stanley's death meant I wouldn't have to care for a quadriplegic.

Stanley had been estranged from his family. They never even came to the hospital to visit while he was alive, and after his death, they had everything arranged by a lawyer. His body was flown back to his hometown for burial. I didn't have the money for a plane ticket to attend. I never even got to see his body at the hospital to say goodbye. It was as if he had never existed.

* * *

In a numb emotional haze, I moved back to the mountain town where I had grown up. My Aunt Ginny suggested I move into a tiny apartment right next her so I could help out her and my Uncle Eugene. Not so that she could help me, but so I could help her. Shortly afterward, my car broke down and I had no money to repair it. Winter was coming and I knew that I wouldn't be able to hitchhike with a baby 30 miles each way in the snow to get to school. So I abandoned my new place less than two months after I'd moved in. All my money had gone into getting that apartment, and because I had nowhere to move my things to, or help even if I had, I lost everything I owned once again. My choice seemed crazy to my aunt, but I was not going to give up going to school because of transportation issues. Though my aunt had a car, she decided to sell it to a stranger rather than let me use it. No car and no money meant my only option was to be homeless until I saved enough money to get another place closer to the college.

For several weeks, I pushed my daughter in a shopping cart from friend's house to friend's house, but I could only do that for so long. All the while, I managed to somehow keep going to class. The daycare at the university was the only stability Joy had. When it became clear that I had worn out my welcome on my friends' couches, I realized I would need to find another option. That's when an older guy in one of my classes told me I could stay at the house he shared with two other recovering drug addicts. What I didn't know at the time was the only space there for me and my baby to sleep was underneath the dining room table because the guy who had originally planned to move out and give me his room changed his mind. I tried to make it work, but it was just too much to cope with, so I moved into a Motel 6 until my money ran out. That's when I started taking enough student loans to do more than pay tuition.

As soon as I got my next financial aid check, I moved into an apartment. I lived there with no furniture, nor did I turn the utilities on. I did that so I could save enough money to get us out of Southern California where I was drowning in bad memories and demands from my family that I no longer felt capable of meeting. For the next six months, Joy and I ate cold food from cans and bathed in freezing water, all in hopes that life would be better once we got somewhere else.

* * *

My decision to leave Southern California was a difficult one. I loved my mom and Kyle, but I could barely care for myself and my baby. After school and caring for Joy, I didn't have anything left to give. I felt guilty about leaving, but needed to get away—far away. I applied to transfer to the farthest college north I could find that was still in California. Not long after applying, I received a letter saying that I had been accepted, but admissions for the upcoming year had been capped. That meant I would have to wait until the following year to transfer. The news was devastating. If I had to continue my life the way it was going, I knew I would not want to fight any longer to stay alive. For weeks, I went through the motions of living but felt lifeless inside. One day I missed my usual ride home from school and ended up hitchhiking to get home. I was standing by the sign for the University with Joy when a man in a nice car pulled over to pick us up. Normally, I tried to avoid taking rides with men, but it was getting dark, so I jumped in with my baby.

"Thanks!" I said, as I struggled to put Joy on my lap and my book bag between my feet.

"My pleasure! I'm Paul Sanders, the Dean of Admissions here at the University. I take it you're a student here?" he asked, extending his hand to shake mine. I nodded while taking his hand.

"Isn't it kind of dangerous for you to be hitchhiking? Wouldn't it be safer to take the bus?" he asked, as he pulled from the curb.

"I don't do it often. It's just that the bus doesn't run after 5 p.m. Normally, when I have a late class, I have a ride with another student who lives near me, but today she couldn't give me a ride."

"Oh, that sounds like a challenge. So, tell me, where can I drop you off?" he asked kindly.

There was something nice about the man, and he didn't seem to want sexual favors like so many of the men who offered to help me in some way. Before long, I was telling him my life story and how desperately I wanted to go to the university up north, but couldn't until the next year.

"Well, Jean, today is your lucky day! Turns out the Dean of Admissions at that school is my best friend from college. I'm going to call him first thing in the morning and see what he might be able to do to get you in this year."

I stared at him, dumbfounded. "Really?" I asked, tears coming to my eyes.

* * *

Less than two weeks later, I got a letter saying I had been admitted for the Fall Term. Since I had never been far outside of Southern California, I had to go on blind faith that the place I was going to would be better. I just had to make it a few more months and I would be on a plane. With a tremendous sense of purpose, I saved every extra cent I had to buy the tickets needed to get us out of an environment that seemed to rob me of hope at every turn.

The day arrived, and I stepped onto a plane for the first time in my life with my daughter. We had in our possession the clothes on our backs, a backpack with two changes of clothes each, a tent, two sleeping bags, and an envelope holding the few photos I had of my family. My mother was unable to come to the airport to say goodbye. I imagined her at home crying and suicidal, but even that image was not enough to make me change my mind.

When we stepped off the plane with our meager belongings, I was so hopeful that we had stepped into a better life...yet, things didn't really go as I planned.

* * *

Over the next 16 years, Joy and I would go through a lot together. For the first couple months in Northern California, we lived in a tent in the forest waiting for my financial aid check to arrive. It was beautiful, but very hard. We were several miles from town, and I would have to carry Joy there to get supplies or wash our clothes. Then we moved into a rundown house about seven miles from my school. We rode the bus, but again, I was on a route that had a limited schedule and sometimes I was forced to hitchhike to get back home. Even when we managed to catch the bus, we still had to walk almost a mile to get to our house. It was really hard to carry a heavy book bag and a child who had usually fallen asleep on my shoulder in the bus. Still, I didn't resent any of the hardships we went through. I knew we were doing it so that one day we would have something better.

However, *better* seemed as if it were perpetually sometime in the future, and with many years of struggle at every turn, I began to lose heart. After my 21st birthday, it seemed like life was destined to be hard forever. The house we lived in leaked terribly. My daughter was sick all the time, and needed surgery to remove her adenoids as well as have plastic tubes placed in her ears to restore her hearing long impaired by chronic congestion. Added to that stress, my landlord had trapped me against the house and tried to force himself on me. I fought him off, but then the house decayed unabated. Worst of all, I was having difficulty dealing with intrusive flashbacks from my childhood and frequently found myself curled up in a fetal position on the floor, unable to face the world. It seemed like a good time to check out. The family sickness reached out its long arm to claim another victim—but then I thought of my daughter—and I resisted. I called the ambulance for my one and *only* trip to the hospital. The next day, I was released, armed with a new antidepressant prescription and an appointment with a clinical psychologist. It was a trip my daughter would know nothing about, and one I swore never to repeat.

Chapter 11: Everything I Own

In 1989, five years after my daughter was born, I graduated with my Bachelors in Psychology. I didn't walk in the graduation ceremony because there wasn't going to be any family there to watch me cross the stage. Mom couldn't afford to come, and even if she had the money, her mental illness made her deathly afraid to fly. I like to think that she was proud of me, but by then she was no longer able to connect with the world the way she once had. Years of heavy-duty antipsychotics, lithium, and anti-anxiety medications had kept her Type I bipolar disorder, psychosis, and anxiety at bay; but the drugs had also robbed her of her personality.

After graduating with my undergraduate degree, I applied to graduate school. I got in. For the next two years, I worked on a Masters and then moved on to a PhD program when I was just shy of my 25th birthday. I completed my Doctorate in Neurobiology and Behavior six years later. The next step was a scientific post-doctorate, which I landed at a biomedical research center about 2,000 miles from the West Coast. Joy was growing up and entering her own difficult teen years. It was the start of her first steps toward finding her own way in the world. Life was growing ever better, but the road still had some very large and unexpected bumps ahead. Fortunately, since my only visit to the hospital years before, I had grown progressively better at dealing with life's troubling times.

* * *

I was busy packing the last of my stuff (books, mostly) into the ratty interior of my 1970 Suburban in preparation for the move to start my first post-doctorate position. I was just putting in the last items when my roommate Flynn yelled out the front door, "Hey, your sister's on the phone and she sounds upset."

"Fuck!" I swore under my breath. *What is it now?* I wondered. I shoved the box I was holding into the backseat and slammed the door angrily. Bits of rust fell from the aging metal body onto the cement driveway, reminding me just how old the truck was. Rust or not, I needed to get on the road. My new job was supposed to start in 10 days. The drive alone would take at least five days in my old truck, and then, I would have to find a place for Joy and me to live. I didn't have time to settle some petty fight or solve a family crisis. During the years I had lived away from Mom, I had developed some resentment over needing to be her parent so much of the time. That's why, in order to keep a healthy emotional distance between us, I visited no more than once a year for only two or three days. There had even been times when I didn't give her my phone number and instead called her just once a week. Otherwise, I felt compelled to rescue her from even minor problems that she was incapable of handling.

Wanting to get the phone call over with, I quickly moved up the beautiful stone steps of the four-bedroom house I so loved but would have to leave behind. Handing me the portable phone in the entryway, my roommate Flynn said quietly, "She sounds really upset."

Reaching for the phone I irritably thought, *Great! She and Mom had another fight and I have to deal with the fallout.* Five years prior, after being badly beaten by her boyfriend, Joanne had moved back to California to live with Mom and Kyle. Each year my sister lived there things seemed to become more and more explosive. Joanne had a drinking problem and struggled at times with her own mental health issues. After Kyle died of congestive heart failure, it seemed like their need for me to "settle" things got worse. Joanne had finally moved out to live with her boyfriend. Her departure left Mom alone for the first time in many years, but the drama still seemed to go on. I had to hear about it from both of them, often at all hours of the night. Eventually, I dreaded hearing from either of them, especially in my last, and most stressful, year of graduate school.

I moved back toward the truck, determined to get more packing done while I listened to what I thought would be yet another of Joanne's typical bitch-fests.

"Hey Jo, what's up?" I asked, pushing a box toward the truck with my foot.

"Jean, Mom's missing. She's fucking missing!" Joanne said, choking back tears.

"What? What do you mean missing?" I asked, wondering if my sister had been drinking and was maybe dramatizing things.

"She's gone, Jean! No one has seen her for almost a week and the police won't help find her!"

"Joanne, calm down, please. Are you sure she's gone? Did you try going to her apartment?" I asked, suddenly feeling very tired. I leaned against the side of the truck and stared up at the blue summer sky. At the periphery of my vision, the pine trees lining the driveway swayed in the breeze; I realized I was going to miss them.

"Of course, Jean! I went to her apartment, but it was locked up with all of her stuff inside, Joanne said. The landlord said she hadn't been at the apartment in a long time and wouldn't let me in because he was in the process of evicting her. He wants her stuff to cover the unpaid rent. I talked to the neighbors, but they haven't seen her either."

"Maybe she's staying with someone or is in the hospital. When I talked to her a couple of weeks ago she sounded pretty manic," I said, remembering our last phone conversation during which Mom told me she was going to China to marry Chairman Mao. She had also told me how much she loved me, but I was focused on how crazy she sounded. I had no way of knowing that it would be the last time I would ever speak to her.

"I called the hospital and the jail! She's not there! Something bad has happened, Jean! Maybe that drug dealer she let move in with her did something to her," Joanne said, as she began to cry.

I looked back into the garage at the boxes I still needed to load. I didn't want to have to deal with the crazy things my sister was saying. For years, I had been tired of dealing with all the insanity my family brought into my life.

"What did they cops say?" I asked, trying not to sound impatient.

"They told me to file a Missing Person's Report, but Jean, they don't care. They're not going to look for her. The cop I talked to told me they suspect foul play. He said he had been out to Mom's apartment several times because she kicked the drug dealer out and he came back threatening her."

I could hear the anger in my sister's voice, the fear. I knew just a little about the drug dealer from what my aunt and Joanne had told me. He was some HIV-infected drug addict at least 25 years younger than my mom. He needed a place to live and Mom had let him move in because she was suffering from another episode of bipolar disorder. According to Aunt Ginny, my mother and the HIV-infected addict were having sex—unprotected sex. The whole thing was so terrible, so upsetting…even unbelievable, if only it weren't my mother. I had seen her sickness over a long period of years, and I knew the story was entirely possible. It was also so upsetting that I had stopped thinking about it over the previous months. Instead, I threw myself into completing my PhD dissertation. I just didn't have it in me to complete my PhD and rescue my mother at the same time.

"Fucking cops, even if they suspect foul play, they aren't doing anything. What should we do, Jean?" Joanne asked in a quivering voice.

It was easy to understand my sister's frustration with the police. About a month before, when I first knew that Mom was starting to get sick again—her increasingly bizarre phone calls to me the obvious sign—I called the police every day asking them to take her to a mental hospital and have her admitted. It was clear to me that she was becoming a danger to herself. It took about two weeks before they got tired enough of my calls before they were willing to go out to her apartment for a Welfare Check. When I spoke to them after the visit, they told me she did seem mentally ill, so they took her to the psychiatric hospital. I called there the next day, but she had already been released because the doctors did not feel she was enough of a danger to herself or others to warrant being kept against her will. Now Joanne was telling me she was missing.

I opened the door to my truck and slipped into the front seat. The inside was hot and smelled of dusty old books. I leaned my head on the steering wheel and thought about all I had left to do in preparation for my move. For a few minutes, I stopped hearing what my sister was telling me. She was clearly upset. I knew I should be upset too, but I wasn't; I just felt tired. Returning my attention to Joanne, I tried to sound supportive.

"Joanne, try not to worry. I'm sure they'll find her. Here, give me the number of the police and the name of the person who handled the Missing Person's Report. I will call them and make sure they're doing everything they can," I offered, feeling annoyed that I would have to do this—all I needed was one more thing on my long list of things to do. Once Joanne seemed sufficiently calm, I hung up and got out of the truck, grateful that the conversation was over. I wondered if I had seemed uncaring when I ended the conversation—it was something I suspected might be true about me.

Back in the house, I told my roommate what my sister had said. "Wow, Jean! I'm so sorry. That's really weird. Are you all right?" he asked. I considered his question. *Am I all right?* I wondered. I ran through a mental checklist of emotions I felt at that moment. I realized that I actually felt a sense of relief. Then I felt guilty for feeling relieved. I tried to process how learning that my mother was missing could ease my feelings of stress. I thought again about the last time I talked to my mother. She had said so many crazy things—I just needed a little bit of time away from all that and being responsible for her illness. Just enough time for me to get my life resettled again, that's where the relief was coming from. What I didn't know as I stood there thinking about how I felt, was that my mother would not be found again. It would not turn out to be what I suspected—just a short disappearance before she ended up back in a psychiatric hospital again—she had disappeared forever.

*　*　*

In the days following my mother's disappearance, I was dealing with my own crisis. Packed full of stuff, my 1970 Suburban blew out a couple of cylinders on the Grapevine, a steep grade that crosses the Tejon Pass that separates California's Central Valley from the palm trees of Southern California. I had promised Aunt Ginny that I would visit the region where I grew up and try to get the police to do more about Mom's disappearance. Joanne had already started off on her own move to begin a new life with her boyfriend in another state, which left no relative in the city where my mom went missing to follow up in person with the police. I was supposed to do that during my short visit before starting my new job.

Joy and I had just hit the steepest part of the mountain pass when the cab was filled completely with smoke. Jerking the Suburban over to the side of the road I yelled, "Get out Joy, quick!" The smoke was so thick, I was sure the truck was on fire. When the smoke cleared a bit, I put my hands on the hood. It was no hotter than you would expect it to be in 90-degree weather. Cautiously, I opened the hood, still expecting to see flames. No fire, but smoke was pouring out of the manifold exhaust vent. "Fuck! Fuck! Fuck! I can't believe this, fuck!" I ranted, while Joy looked on fearfully. Assessing the situation, I knew I was too broke to call a tow truck. I had spent a lot of time working on the Suburban, and I knew I was going to need a new engine. If I didn't want to abandon the truck altogether on the Grapevine as so many had done before me, I knew I would have to limp it at least as far as my aunt's house about 150 miles away.

Once the smoke cleared completely, I checked the oil, which the engine had been burning at a fairly rapid rate. I had bought a case of oil, expecting the worst, and had been stopping about every 100 miles to check the level and add more. This time the oil was low and thick like tar. I added fresh oil and told Joy to get back in. I turned the key in the ignition, praying that the engine would start. It did, but with a loping misfire. "It runs, that's all I need," I said, before putting the truck into gear. I started going very slowly along the edge of the road while thanking Chevy for making the straight-six cylinder engine—a hunk of metal that seemed capable of running on just one cylinder.

The truck moved steadily along, but within a couple of minutes the cab was again so full of smoke that Joy and I couldn't breathe, let alone see where we were going. I stopped and shut the engine down again. "Mom, are we gonna be okay?" Joy asked.

Even though I wasn't sure myself, I told her, "Sure, we're gonna be just fine, Honey. Don't worry." Getting out one more time, I opened up the back of the Suburban and dug through my collection of tools and spare parts to see if there was any way to plug the exhaust manifold to keep the smoke from blowing back into the cab. In my pile of "just in case" junk I found about a five-foot length of radiator hose and some wire. Under the hood, I was able to wire the radiator hose onto the exhaust vent on the manifold. Then I ran the hose out of the engine compartment and wired it up underneath the Suburban as far as it would go. When I started the truck again, thick white smoke billowed out from underneath near the already-smoking tailpipe. My fix kept the smoke from immediately blowing back into the cab. Once more, we had a chance to make it to Aunt Ginny's house.

"Joy, climb over the seat and close those back windows to keep the smoke out," I said, as I slowly put the truck into gear one more time. Staying on the edge of the road in the emergency lane, we limped up the rest of Grapevine stopping, about every 10 to 15 miles to put more oil in the truck. I felt a palpable sense of relief when the grade began to slope downward. If we could just make it to Aunt Ginny's house, I knew I could leave the truck in her yard and buy a Greyhound bus ticket to get us the rest of the way across the country. It took us about eight hours to travel the 150 miles to Ginny's place. I bought more oil at an auto parts store at the base of the mountain, and an additive called "No Smoke." With the truck as well prepared as I could get it, we started up the mountain. "Come on Beast, you can make this," I said, patting the dashboard in the gathering darkness.

By the time we reached Aunt Ginny's house, both Joy and I were worn out by the stressful day. She was nice about our late arrival. As I explained what had happened, she assured me that leaving the truck was not a problem. Joy and I fell asleep early on the pull-out couch in her tiny living room.

Lying there stressed and restless, I realized that with limited money and no car I would not be able to visit the police department in the city below to find out more about my mother's disappearance. I knew Aunt Ginny would be upset about that, but there was only so much I could do. Ginny and Mom had talked almost every day on the phone since Mom and Kyle had gotten their own place. I knew Auntie missed Mom more than anyone. Still, I was stressed and needed to get to my new job; figuring out where Mom had wandered off to would have to wait.

Two days later, I asked my aunt's neighbor if he would give Joy and me a ride to the Greyhound bus depot. Not only did I need to get started at my new job and Joy started at her new school, talking to Aunt Ginny about Mom depressed me. She had so many more details than I did about Mom's last weeks before her disappearance. I knew, of course, that Mom had gone crazy again because her medications (some were toxic at high doses) were not being properly monitored, which is why she ended up in an ER with failing kidneys. Doctors had to take her off all medications to prevent further damage to her organs and get her system working right again. It was from that point that she transcended into another extreme manic phase with psychotic delusions. I had heard through phone calls with her the transition from sane to insane.

At first, the transition had been pleasant as Mom came out of her drug-induced zombie-like state. We had a few weeks of normal conversations on different topics, the first conversations we had had beyond, "How are you?" in years. But then, Mom began to descend into madness. Her speech became faster and it stopped being a conversation because she did all the talking. Then the content changed and her delusions of grandeur about being involved with important people took over.

I knew about Mom's transition into mental illness. What I didn't know, but learned from Auntie during my visit, was that Mom had been taken advantage of by her sleazy apartment building neighbors. Prone to spending sprees and a sense of immeasurable wealth when sick, Mom gave people anything—all they had to do was ask for it. They cleaned out her bank account and her furniture. The worst of the bunch was the HIV-infected drug dealer who Joanne had said moved into Mom's apartment. After she tried to kick him out, he had made threats that he would kill her. The police were called to the apartment several times due to violent disturbances. That's why when Mom went missing the police suspected foul play. Knowing what had really gone on made me sick to my stomach.

I left my aunt's house on the mountain feeling sad about Mom, and overwhelmed that I was now going to have to manage my new life without a car in a city I didn't know. Over the next few months, I did the best I could to manage my new life and not be paralyzed by unexpected moments of sadness.

With no news from the police or my mother, I began to feel certain that she was dead. It did not seem possible that months could go by without any contact—unless something horrible had happened. My move meant that Mom couldn't get ahold of me, but Aunt Ginny had had the same phone number for more than 30 years. Everyone knew Auntie's number by heart, my mother included. Even if she had been institutionalized somewhere, eventually she would have given hospital staff Aunt Ginny's number. The more time that passed, the stronger I felt that she would not be found.

* * *

After Mom went missing, I focused on my new job at a large primate center doing biomedical research. Joy started 8th grade at a school filled with skinny blonde girls who came from money. I had lied about my address to get her in there because I was worried about her going to the gang-filled school in our actual zip code. Turns out, I made the wrong choice. Joy was miserable among all the snotty girls. Eventually, I got caught in my lie when someone from the school needed to drop Joy at home after a late group activity.

They told me Joy would have to leave the school, or I would have to pay the cost of her attendance. I felt it was better to keep Joy there until the end of the school year. That meant I had to pay the school thousands of dollars. I borrowed money from several friends and Joy rode it out until the end of the year, rather than facing a mid-year disruption. It was a commitment to quality education and to the kind of stability my childhood had not afforded me.

Knowing high school was coming, I moved us into a better neighborhood. The house I rented cost me more than half my tiny postdoc salary and it was sparsely furnished, but Joy really liked it. I continued trying to publish scientific research that might one day lead to a decent job with decent pay. In the meantime, Joy did her best to navigate growing up. But we were facing some new challenges. Joy and I were at odds all the time. She was frequently angry and ashamed of our poverty compared to the other kids she knew. After I had repaired my old Suburban and brought it back, Joy refused to be seen in it at school. This was difficult for me to understand because I thought that any car was better than no car at all. Little fights started happening all the time. I didn't know what to do with a teenager, and I just became stricter and stricter. Joy responded by withdrawing from me and lost herself in the fantasy world of multi-user computer games.

As Joy and I drifted further apart, I felt lost and like a failure at the one thing I cared about the most. I thought perhaps the answer was to get married again. After a whirlwind romance with a British rockabilly musician, I ran off to Vegas and got married—it was a hasty choice. Understandably, Joy responded by acting out even more. As in many times in my life, I had hit yet another painful bump in the road. My daughter hated me. With my mother still missing and my marriage showing cracks, I decided I needed to get back to California.

I took another postdoc assignment doing AIDS research at a prestigious biomedical facility in Southern California. Worried that the move would be as stressful as the last, I sent Joy to stay with a friend in New York for the summer. Thanks to 4-dollar-a-gallon gas and the Suburban's terrible fuel efficiency, there was no money left by the time my new husband and I reached SoCal. We lived in my truck for several weeks with two dogs until I got my first paycheck. Then we rented a tiny, excessively expensive house. Joy joined us from the East Coast, but it was a rocky reunion. I felt sad that things weren't magically improved by the months we had spent apart.

My new job didn't pay enough for the high cost of living in Southern California, so I secured a second job to keep us afloat financially. The long hours I worked made the distance between Joy and me grow wider. We fought more frequently. My marriage was also reaching its final conclusion. Not long after the move, I asked for a divorce. In the chaos, Joy decided she didn't want to go to high school any longer and took her high school proficiency exam. She passed with exceptionally high scores and started working fulltime to pay for her own phone and extras I never had money for. That took some of the pressure off me financially, but things were far from okay.

About six months after her 17th birthday, Joy moved in with her boyfriend who lived in Arizona. I could have forced her to stay with me, but I knew that would just cause her to run away. It was a sad period for me. I had always imagined Joy would graduate high school and go happily off to college. It worried me that she didn't want more from life than to be in a relationship and be taken care of.

I also worried she was giving up her power for false security; that she would be trapped in something that didn't make her truly happy, just as her grandmother had been. In the end, I was helpless to change her direction. I felt the wisest choice was to accept what she wanted to do if I hoped to have any relationship with her at all. However, it was hard for me not to feel like I had failed as a mother, even though I had tried so hard.

* * *

Trying to find resolution when someone you love is missing—literally missing—is very difficult. With Joy gone and my marriage over, I struggled to deal with the loss of all my loved ones—particularly my mother. I didn't know what happened to Mom, but I was gradually coming to terms with the fact that she was likely no longer alive. Aunt Ginny, however, refused to believe she was dead and took all kinds of things as signs that she was still with us.

"Your mother called me last night. It was just someone breathing on the other end, but I know it was her. I think she didn't want to talk so she hung up without saying anything," Ginny would tell me over the phone.

Then I would have to shift from my melancholy acceptance of my mother's death to a glimmer of hope that she was alive. Dark images would be replaced with cautiously optimistic ones. I would imagine Mom alive somewhere. I would call the police to see if they had any new information on the case. Unfortunately, they didn't. With time, hope would bleed away again and I would go back to believing Mom was dead. It was an awful cycle with no ending. It exhausted me.

After Mom had been missing for about five years, Aunt Ginny called to tell me that Mom had called her in the middle of the night and said just one phrase, *"oat fart."* Since this was the same phrase my maternal grandmother had used when suddenly coming out of a catatonic state, in my mind, those words made it very plausible that Mom had actually called. *Who else would know that phrase?* I thought. My cycle of hope began again.

I called the police one more time to see if they knew anything more—they didn't. They recommended that I come in and give DNA to try and match it with any Jane Does fitting my mother's description. That was just too gruesome for me to think about. I tried to hold onto my aunt's belief that my mother was alive, but images of her having been brutally murdered in some ditch popped into my head and stayed there. I decided that if she was dead I did not want to know, because then, I would have the ugly truth forever inside me—the truth that a woman with a good soul had endured a terrible death. What daughter would want to know that?

Not long after the "oat fart" incident, I received a call that Aunt Ginny was in the emergency room. I rushed to reach her. When I first arrived, she didn't know who I was, but 30 minutes later she did. Over the next four months, she would slip in and out of delirium, knowing and then not knowing. Sometimes she was in the past, sometimes the present. One minute she was there with you laughing about some joke she just told; the next, she was staring at you with a haunted look in her eyes as if you were an ax murderer. As the months moved on, she spent more and more time with the haunted look and not knowing who I was.

Stepping in to manage things at her small cabin, I asked her neighbors if she had been behaving oddly. "Yes, for some months," the woman right next door told me. That was when I knew Auntie had not actually heard my mother's voice on the phone. Whatever was happening in her brain had caused her to believe Mom had called. The phrase "oat fart" was only a phantom memory confused with the present. Mom had not called. Instead, my aunt had a disease that was affecting her mind. Once again I was forced to face the fact that my mother was most likely dead. Eventually, my aunt was placed into hospice care to wait for her final curtain call. There was confusion about my aunt's sickness and cause of death until the autopsy. The report said it was metastasized lung cancer.

Aunt Ginny died six years after my mother went missing. She and my mother had been very close. I tried to imagine that they were together in another place—happy. That was hard to do, however, because I still wasn't 100 percent sure my mother was dead. With Ginny's death, the only relative I still had any contact with was gone, and with her, any connection I had to my childhood. Like so many painful times in my life, I was alone when I buried my aunt next to her husband Eugene. As I watched them shovel the dirt into the grave, I realized that my mother had also lost the only phone number she would know to call if she was still out there alive. After that, it seemed silly to hope anymore that I would find her again.

* * *

In 2009, 11 years after my mother went missing, I had a service for her in the last place I remember her being happy. It was a place I had taken my mother to about two years after Joy Grace was born. During that period, I frequently picked Mom up from her board-and-care home and took her out somewhere. The visits were difficult. Though she loved being with me and the baby, if we were out in public, she would often have panic attacks and be unable to move. This would hold up lines of people behind us, and even if that didn't happen, it caused a scene while I tried to calm her down.

After several stressful visits in a row, I decided our next one would be someplace out in nature because my mother had always loved being there when I was a kid. I drove Mom out to a local stream where I often hiked. When we first got there, Mom didn't want to get out of the car. Slowly, I coaxed her out and down to the stream. She stood nervously for a long time watching Joy and me wade with our shoes off. Then she took off her shoes too and waded into the water. "Oh, this is nice!" she said with a big smile. It was the last time I saw her truly happy and relaxed.

By the time I buried my mother in spirit, I had figured out I didn't want to be a scientist after all. I had also been through several jobs, several boyfriends, and a very short marriage to a second husband—and so, as in so many other times in my life, I faced the painful experience of laying my mother to rest alone. It was the first time I allowed myself to really grieve for her. The pain was so terrible and intense. All the years of not knowing had built up sorrow like a lake growing larger and larger behind a dam. Standing in a copse of trees by the stream Mom had once happily waded in, I let go of a feather. It was a blue jay's feather. I had picked it up on a solo motorcycle trip to the city where my mother and father had met. It floated high into the air after being caught by a strong gust. Watching it swirl into the sky, I thanked my mother for the gift of life and the love she had shown me. Then, opening a Bible randomly and serendipitously given to me by a Biker for Christ near where my parents fell in love, I read Psalm 23:4, "Yea, though I walk through the valley of the shadow of death, I will fear no evil: for thou art with me; thy rod and thy staff they comfort me." I placed the book of scripture into an opening in the largest tree. I wanted my mother's spirit to find comfort there should she ever need it. Then I sat on a rock and sobbed.

* * *

The faucet of sorrow I had opened didn't end on that rock by the stream. My tears had washed away some of the pain I carried, but for many months afterwards I was not myself. I had buried my aunt and I had buried my mother, at least symbolically. Joy was off building her own life in another state. I felt detached from my life and disconnected from the things I once believed I wanted. Then a raccoon ate all the goldfish in my pond; after that I saw no reason to stay in Southern California.

I decided it was a good time to follow my dream of living overseas. I secured a job and an apartment in the tropics. By that time, Joy had moved to Michigan (my mother's home state) to go to college. I sold almost everything I owned in preparation for my new ex-patriot life and made a visit to Joy before flying out. We decided to take a trip together to see the town where my mother was born. While I was there, I mailed a postcard to myself at my new address overseas. It read, *Hey Mom and Auntie! I finally made it to your hometown. Miss you!!! Love, Me.*

* * *

I will admit that since saying goodbye to my mother formally, my grief sits silently waiting for something to crack open my armor wide enough so it can escape. Small reminders pop up and chip away my resolve to accept her death. This past Christmas time, NPR did a story on a mass paupers' grave for the Jane and John Does never picked up from the LA County morgue. I was stringing lights on my tree when the story came on. Minutes later, I was lying on the floor weeping uncontrollably. When I finally stopped crying, I was angry with NPR for doing such a depressing story at Christmas time. *Isn't this supposed to be a period when life is filled with cheer?* I thought plaintively. Thinking of my mother buried in an unmarked pauper's grave, as her mother had been before her, was terrible to imagine. Even today, as much as I try, I can't get rid of that image in my head—the bodies of forgotten people with my mother lost among them. It sits along with the images of her body in a shallow grave in the desert; her body rotting in a California aqueduct; her beaten and bound body being thrown out with the trash. Those are the images I have on bad days. Once in a while, they are mixed in with images of her living happily in a retirement home or a really nice psych ward. On a really positive day, I see her sitting on the porch of some nice family that takes care of her. Sometimes, I imagine her up in Heaven laughing at naughty jokes told by my aunt. But, I may never know what happened to my mother, so I try my best not to have any images at all.

* * *

The first dream I remember having occurred when I was around four or five years old. In my dream, I was riding upon the back of a huge white Pegasus. Looking down from my perch, I could see the entire town where I spent my early years engulfed in flames. I felt a sense of panic that my family was trapped and going to die. I urged Pegasus to fly lower. We dropped closer and closer to the fire, and then out of the smoke and flames, appeared my mother and my siblings standing on the porch of our burning house. They were screaming. I swooped in and pulled my family onto the back of the winged horse. I woke up just after we rose above the flames and headed into the clear blue sky.

That sense of wanting to save my family has stayed with me until this day. But I couldn't save them. I could only save myself, and in doing that, I was able to save my daughter. Through my work, I am also able to help other foster youth save themselves. Sometimes that is all we can do. I live with a bit of regret that I could not do more, but I have reached a place of acceptance and understanding of the limitations we all face when trying to rescue someone else. There are times when rescue just isn't going to be possible. Coming to terms with that when it's someone you really love is incredibly difficult.

Over the almost 20 years since my mother went missing, I've often thought about her last words to me. They were, "Remember Jean, I love you." The words may have been tainted by her insanity at the time, by the terrible unraveling of her mind, but I know they were true. My mother did love me—just as I love my own daughter with unending intensity; and, in spite of everything, I continue to love my mother with all my heart. I couldn't save her, but I hope wherever she is, she can feel my love.

Epilogue

Life as a *Dependent of the Court* had lots of difficulties, but for me the waiting was the worst part. Waiting for the social worker to arrive; waiting for the hearing to start; waiting for the judge to take the facts under consideration; just plain waiting for someone else to strip me of what I knew and loved. The wait slowly killed my mother's spirit because she had no way to change what was going to happen. Seated on wooden benches reminiscent of church pews, my mother would agonize away the minutes before the judge entered his/her decision into court records. Once the decision was announced, one of two things would happen: 1) If the decision was favorable, my mother would hug me in joyous celebration and tell me how everything was going to be better; 2) If the decision was unfavorable, she would desperately cling to me before I was taken away. In those last fleeting moments, so precious to us both, we would try to store up the affection we would no longer be able to give or receive. You never knew until the wait was over which it would be.

In the end, minutes, hours, days, and if we were lucky, sometimes years, were shared according to the decree of some judge. After all the waiting—all the soul-sucking waiting—I took what I could get and savored every moment. No matter our problems, my mother's love—and even sometimes her insanity—was far better than the negligence and abuse of strangers. Never once as a child did I doubt that I was loved. In spite of my mother's terrible mental illness she loved me, and I loved her. When I think about many of the other foster kids I grew up with, I feel such sadness for them because they had no one to love them. Many didn't have anyone to call them, to write them, to visit them. I did. Having someone to love me, someone I could love back, was a buffer in a world where people kept me for money, for labor, to abuse, but never really gave a shit about me.

Like many manic-depressives, my mother had periods in which she was relatively sane. The worst of her bipolar episodes tended to occur in the summer near her June birthday. Her extreme fear of growing old and unattractive may have had a lot to do with the flavor of her bipolar summers. When Mom returned to normal, usually sometime in the fall, that's when she felt enormous guilt over her periods of insanity and did her best to make up for it. She helped out at school events, told us constantly how much she loved us, and went around in threadbare clothes to make sure every extra cent of money from her meager welfare checks was spent on us kids. When the holidays came around she would go all out. Unless a period of depression snuck up on her and she became suicidal, the holidays were times of great joy. In those periods in between, her love for us kids was very clear. My mother behaved in some horrible ways, but she was not a terrible human being. She was person with a disease she could not control. Wherever my mother is at this moment, I hope she can see that she planted the seed of love that allowed me to care enough for my own child to overcome many obstacles. That love, combined with hard work, broke through a cycle of instability that was generations old.

In the "Acknowledgments" section of my completed doctoral dissertation I thanked all the people who helped me over the years to follow my dreams. Sadly, I don't think the list included my mother. It included therapists, friends, lovers, teachers, college administrators, and most importantly my daughter—but not my mother. I regret that now. Though my daughter was, and continues to be, the single most motivating force in my life, it was my mother who gave me the seed of love that kept me from being damaged beyond repair. With that seed, I became more than the expected "negative statistic" kids from the foster care system seem destined to become.

* * *

It's not to say that my mother's love completely saved me. My sense is that when my odyssey in Juvy came to an end, I was different—distinctly different. A part of me had died an early death and I lost my innocence. A crack inside that was once hairline, widened like a sinkhole under a parking lot. Bits of me shattered until a kind of blackness filled in and took the place of who I once was.

During those first two foster care placements away from my mother, I decided I had to be tough and never let anything hurt me. I knew that to survive I would have to become indifferent to the people around me. I had learned to be tough in response to physical pain because of my dad, but with my mom I had been allowed to be emotionally sensitive. When I cried during animal shows because something got killed, my mom held me and said it was okay. To my siblings, I was a big baby, but to my mother, at least in her good moments, I was a sweet, sensitive little girl. Inside I cared so deeply that no person, animal, or insect be harmed. The day the cop knocked on our door to take me away changed all that.

Over time I learned to bury soft emotions deep. On the surface, I replaced those with indifference. Something just clicked off, like automatic lights shutting down in a long tunnel; but once clicked, I couldn't automatically turn those lights back on again. It was like there was some sort of power outage making the grid fluctuate and my emotions became unreliable.

It is strange to be able to pick a single day that changed me forever. It didn't happen overnight, but it started with Juvy. Soft emotions were replaced with hard ones and I learned how not to feel the hurts so much. It was an imperfect system. Emotions had to go somewhere and become something, even if I stopped understanding what they were or where they came from. Gentle parts of me became filled with anger and resentment. Inside, I grew bitter toward the well-meaning police officer who had taken me from my home; angry toward those then charged with my care; bitter toward my father and siblings for leaving me; but mostly, I developed a deep and heated resentment toward my mother, intermixed with an agonizing and enduring love.

I resented Mom mostly for having children by three different husbands. Over her lifetime, my mother would have six husbands, nine pregnancies (four of which ended in miscarriage or stillbirth), and five kids. I was live birth number five from husband number three, making me the only child to come out of my parents' union. Once I entered foster care, her promiscuity meant more to me than just waking up to strange men in our house, it had made me an only child for all practical purposes. That sense of being totally alone came partially because I was the only kid in our family who ended up in foster care. My journey was unique, and I never really connected again in the same way with my siblings. The greatest connection I was able to maintain was with my mother, but even that connection was complicated.

I loved my mother deeply, and my real father too, but living in their world meant accepting hurt with as much certainty as knowing that the sun is going to rise. So, unlike the baby goat that I desperately wanted to come back, when my parents were gone completely from my life, I will admit there were times when I didn't want them back. I wanted love. I wanted caring. I wanted attention. I wanted to not be invisible. I wanted all the stuff parents are supposed to give, but when you can't get those things from the people who are supposed to give them to you, you learn not to want those things anymore. You get numb; at least that's what happened to me. Once I became numb, the hurts didn't wound me as much, but pleasures didn't feel as good either.

I never had contact again with my father after his final phone call about taking my things to the dump. I think about him from time to time, sort of hoping he's dead. My brothers Jerry and Jimmy lived relatively short lives; Jerry died in his 40s and Jimmy in his 30s. I didn't know that, however, until many years later. I found Jimmy's gravestone long after he died. I don't know who chose the epitaph, but it could not have been more perfect. It read, "Finally at peace." It makes me sad to think I know so little about by siblings' adult lives, but they remained strangers to me because it just felt safer that way. I had learned the art of emotional and physical distance to survive. My sisters had their own children, but again, we didn't remain close, as we each struggled to make something more of our lives. No one stayed in my life except my daughter because I wanted it that way. Men came and went, but most I never loved too deeply or cared much when they were gone.

Before my daughter was born, the little bit of love I had, was saved was for my mother. After my daughter's birth, most of my love, and especially my energy, went into giving her the emotional stability I never had. I let myself love my daughter in ways I had not thought possible, even if I had difficulty showing it. She was the spark that kept a flame going in my numb heart. My daughter has always remained the most important thing in my life, though I know that much of the time she was growing up she doubted that fact. I can't blame her. Over the years, we had to grow up together. Our growing was full of all kinds of mistakes and regrets.

Along the path to a better life, I have failed miserably at many things. Besides failing at being the ideal mother, I have failed at: relationships, selecting good jobs, more relationships, and being stable in the way American culture tells me I should be. But, I wouldn't trade any of it. I am, if nothing else, an amazingly resilient human being always ready for life's next challenge. If my daughter, or any other person for that matter, asked me today for advice about life, this is what I would tell them: "Do not to give up! No matter how bleak it seems right now, there is something better waiting for you." I know what it's like to want to give up, and to even take action toward that end, but you won't get a chance to see how life can turn out if you just give up. The only way to overcome obstacles is to face them with hope, hard work, and flexibility. Doing that leads to amazing things.

I won't pretend that my life now is perfect, but I will say that it's better than I ever hoped it would be. It got that way because I waited for my darkest moments to pass and light to re-enter my life—and, it always did. I have come back from a past of physical and sexual abuse, neglect, incredible loss, homelessness, drug and alcohol-based coping, uncontrollable anger, and attempted suicide.

By not giving up and sticking it out, I have found joy in the smallest things, pleasure in my gifts, and meaning for my existence. I am far from perfect, but I remain proud of who I am. There is no doubt that I have beaten the odds laid out against so many foster youth. Unlike them, I never ended up in prison; I didn't stay in abusive relationships; I am not addicted to drugs or alcohol; nor did I die before my 21st birthday as I once believed I would; and most importantly, I did not live a life like that of my mother, which was one of my greatest fears. Instead, I got a college education; I became a scientist and studied things that fascinated me; I became a university professor; I traveled the world even though I had never been on a plane until I was 20 years old. I became an artist and created paintings of beauty that released my pain and brought me pleasure; I became a musician, though I only ever played for myself because it was just something that made me feel good. I did all of this because I decided not to be a victim of my past.

* * *

Incredibly, more than 30 years have gone by since my daughter came into the world, a tiny premature baby weighing only 3 pounds 11 ounces. I remember looking at her in the incubator and feeling so scared that she would be taken from me before I ever got to know her—but she made it! That meant I had an obligation to be the best mother I could be. The choices I made to try and improve our lives required of me (and my daughter) a lot of sacrifice.

Education alone required a commitment that led to the exclusion of many other things. I didn't mind that commitment myself, because I knew the end goal was worth it; but for my daughter, such intense focus on my part was difficult in many ways. There was a time when my daughter hated me for spending so much time studying and working in a lab. Not only did she resent the time my education required, she also hated the fact education cost so much, because in her eyes, those costs kept us constantly poor. When she was age 15, during one of our all-too frequent bitter arguments, she screamed at me with intense hate, "I will never go to college! That's the stupidest thing anyone can do." Her words broke my heart.

Education was not something anyone in my family had. Both my parents had only junior high educations, and like them, all us kids were high-school dropouts. I never thought I would go to college, but once I got there, I realized that education was the best ticket one could hope for to obtain a better life. For a long time, my daughter didn't seem to agree.

After she moved out and transitioned into adulthood I felt a slight pain, like the constant prick of a needle in my heart that her life would turn out badly. If that happened, it would mean that all the sacrifices I had made along the way meant nothing. My focus on education had been for her. She was the single most motivating factor in my life to make it better for *us*. I didn't know any other way to get us out of the environment I had come from, except to get a college degree.

My mother could not be there for me when I walked across the stage to receive my Bachelors or PhD. It was lonely to grow up without a mother who could be there for me in the way that daughters need mothers to be. Yes, my mother loved me, but she missed the biggest accomplishments and challenges of my life because she needed me to be her parent. That was not something I wanted for my daughter and being a strong, dedicated parent drove how I behaved in the world.

For her sake and privacy, I decided not to tell too many stories in this book about my daughter and our lives together. Let it suffice to say that like many women, I still feel a twinge of guilt that I wasn't a better parent. I have lots of good excuses to justify why I wasn't: I was a teenage mom just barely 17 years old when my daughter was born—a baby trying to raise a baby; I was single—no husband to help carry the stresses of life and parenthood; I was poor—desperately so; I had no family to help me—even those still around had nothing to offer…no money…no ability to help out with childcare…no practical parenting advice… nothing… nada… zip!

In moments of self-forgiveness, I can find lots of justification for my failings as a mother, but in the end, it doesn't change a damn thing. Perhaps I was best mother I could be, but I know there were times when it wasn't enough. My daughter suffered and I can't take any of it back. Regardless, I am grateful to her for making my life worth living, and at several dark moments in my past, she was the only reason I didn't take my own life. I am so thankful to the Universe for bringing her to me.

* * *

Being there for my daughter at her graduation was one of the greatest accomplishments of my life. It proved to me that I had achieved my most important goal—to be my daughter's parent in the way my mother could never be mine. As Joy walked across the stage to receive her diploma, I wept. I did the same when she got her Master's degree. The intense welling up of emotion surprised me. I knew I felt great joy, yet I couldn't stop sobbing. The sobs came from a place of profound relief. Our lives had been so hard when she was growing up and there were so many obstacles to overcome. To see her walk across that stage, smiling and proud, brought forth the rawest and most true emotions I have ever experienced. It was a moment when I felt the weight of all that we had been through leave my shoulders. I thought, *what a gift—we both beat the odds*. It was the best possible alternate ending to a life that turned out as no one would have expected.

∞

Acknowledgments

Daughter of mine, without you, this book would have never been written. Thank you for all you have brought into my life!

Mom, wherever you are, I love you from the bottom of my heart. I remember your love more than anything else no matter how dark the past. Thank you for that gift.

Jamie Bennette, Maddy Day, Anne Dohrenwend, Jeff Hobbs, Raven Jones, Melissa Raap, Mary Jo Sekelsky, and Shannon Turner, thank you for being considerate enough to read my work even before it was copyedited. Your thoughtful comments and touching testimonials wiped away any doubts I had about my skills as a writer. Shannon, Raven, and Jamie, your support was particularly special because it reminds me I'm not alone.

To my friend and girl Friday, Tynesia, your cheerleading at the book's final stage of development was so encouraging. Thanks for seeing the potential in me to be a good college coach to former foster youth, and for dragging me to the meeting that landed me the job. Without my other girl Friday (and Monday, Tuesday, Wednesday, Thursday, and the occasional girl weekend), aka Katie T. Sunshine, this book would have been *full* of errors. Thank you so much for your expert-eye at zero cost. All I can say is, "You Rock!"

Thank you also to Curtis Phillipson for his unflagging friendship over the years. Curtis was my colleague when I first became inspired to write this book in 2001. His kind acts and ongoing support have meant a lot to me. I am mindful that sometimes when I need it most, there are really good people in the world. And Curtis, thanks for rescuing me and the dogs at LAX when we got stranded after returning to the United States. That day just sucked. Without you, it would have been even worse than the hair-pulling terrible it was.

Vanessa, Leah, and Mimi, thank you for being the first to buy, or at least attempt to buy, my book. Your early purchase efforts made me feel like I have real friends out there. Vanessa, it particularly warmed my heart that you were willing to pay more than the purchase price to get the dang thing shipped Down Under.

To all my other friends—near and far—each of you helped in one way or another to keep me sane enough to reach this place in life. Even if we almost never see each other, your ongoing presence is a reminder I'm not alone. Gratitude!

Endnote: The chapter titles in this book were selected because the songs create an emotional journey reflecting my feelings at different times in my life. It is the emotions the songs create, more than the words themselves, which express the complex feelings I had/have regarding my life. If you would like to explore that journey yourself, here are the artists the chapter titles are taken from: *Behind Blues Eyes-* The Who; *Strange Magic-* ELO; *Delta Dawn-* Helen Reddy; *Smiling Faces Sometimes-* The Undisputed Truth; *Another Brick in The Wall-* Pink Floyd; *Take Me Home Country Roads-* John Denver; *You and Me Against the World-* Helen Reddy; *A Horse With No Name-* America; *Tapestry-* Carol King; *Ticket to Ride-* The Beatles; *Everything I Own-* Bread. For the epilogue, I didn't use a song for the chapter title, but the song that feels right to end the book with is *The Way We Were-* by Barbra Streisand. I recommend listening to the songs in the same order as they appear in the book.

Made in the USA
San Bernardino, CA
01 May 2016